M. D.

David Smyth

You Can Survive Any Financial Disaster

Strategies to Beat Triple-Digit Inflation, Severe Depression, Even Wartime Catastrophes

Henry Regnery Company•Chicago

Library of Congress Cataloging in Publication Data

Smyth, David, 1929-
    You can survive any financial disaster.

    Includes index.
    1. Investments.   2. Inflation (Finance)   I. Title.
HG4521.S7113   1976   332.6'78   76-6287
ISBN 0-8092-8131-7

Published by Henry Regnery Company
180 North Michigan Avenue, Chicago, Illinois 60601
Manufactured in the United States of America
Library of Congress Catalog Card Number: 76-6287
International Standard Book Number: 0-8092-8131-7

Published simultaneously in Canada by
Beaverbooks
953 Dillingham Road
Pickering, Ontario, L1W 1Z7
Canada

For Helene and Clifford
Salud, pesetas, amor y tiempo . . .

Contents

Warning

The author and the publisher of this book cannot give any guarantee of the competence, honesty, or reliability of the many businesses in such a variety of fields as are dealt with in this book. We do not endorse any organization, firm, or government mentioned in these pages. Even if we could thoroughly investigate the organizations, any of them might be taken over by a different management between the time this is written and the time you read this book. Consequently, before dealing with any of the firms or other organizations mentioned in the following chapters, you must make your own judgments of their integrity, competence, and reliability.

We do not exempt from this disclaimer of responsibility even such well-reputed entities as the United States Federal Government, the British Government, and their various subordinate local governments, such as the City of New York.

Foreword to doomsday

People tend to talk of 1929 as though it were the ultimate experience in financial disaster, the crash of all crashes beside which everything else pales into insignificance. Perhaps the time scale of human existence has something to do with this: one has personal memories of one's father and grandfather, but Great-grandpapa is usually just a name on a tombstone somewhere. And besides, there were eight great-grandparents, which depreciates their value.

For the vast majority of people now living 1929 was Grandpa's era. As Nietzsche said, with the grandfather all time ceases for the ignorant. The family memory goes back no further, unless one makes a deliberate effort at historical research.

If you look back further than the memories of today's old-timers, 1929 was only one of many panics, crashes, depressions, and financial disasters in the history of the United States. It may perhaps have been the worst, but it is unlikely to be the last. Inflation is no new experience in this country either.

The American republic started out in life with a brand-new Continental currency, an unbacked paper issue which soon became so debased—down to one cent on the dollar—that "not worth a Continental" became a byword. After the panic of 1819 there was a financial crash in 1837 in which most businesses in the South went bankrupt. In the depression of the late 1850s and early 1860s there were bank failures across the nation, with eight out of every ten banks in Illinois alone going under.

This was followed by the inflation of the Civil War. In the North the government spent more money in four years than in the entire previous history of the United States. Washington issued $450 million in unbacked paper greenbacks. Prices soared and the greenbacks sank to one-seventieth of their original value. In the South, Confederate bonds and money became totally worthless.

The depression that started in 1873 could be compared with that of the 1930s. Wild speculation in railroads ended up with scores of railway companies defaulting on their bonds and going into bankruptcy. Businesses failed by the thousands over a four-year period throughout the country. There was no work, and breadlines multiplied endlessly.

In 1893 over-extension of credit, speculation in Florida real estate, and manipulation of the monetary system plunged the country into a crash that wiped out 15,000 business firms and carried nearly 200 railroads into bankruptcy.

There were other financial calamities: in 1907; just before World War I, in 1913; and just after it, in 1921. But we might as well stop with the 1893 affair, because it makes a point.

Barely five years after this financial prostration the United States was decisively defeating a major European country in the Spanish-American war of 1898, extending its global reach as far as the Philippines, and laying the foundations of a worldwide power amid a tide of growing national pride and prosperity.

The writers of economic doomsday books who predict the imminent collapse of the entire American economy tend to talk as though 1929 were the prelude to the end of the world. The next time around, they imply, it will be the real Armageddon.

It is probably unnecessary to be alarmed by these prophecies as far as the United States is concerned. The nation has survived many times before. No doubt it will survive again.

The point is to survive oneself. The people who did not make it in the past were those who held their savings in Continental currency; those who had their money in failed banks in 1837, 1861, and 1933; those who invested in Civil War bonds, hoarded greenbacks, or put their money into railroads that went bankrupt. For these people the breadlines were waiting.

And that is what this book is all about: not to predict some vast, nameless horror of a financial holocaust for the nation, but to make a down-to-earth appraisal of what measures you should take to ensure your own personal survival and the safety of your family the next time around.

There will be a next time sooner or later. Inflation is already with us. So was the worst recession of the last 40 years. The War to End All Wars is now known as World War I. And as far as the monetary experts are concerned, neither the hard-money gold standard enthusiasts nor the Keynesian inflationists have had much success in controlling the ups and downs of the business cycle, which will certainly touch bottom again as it has several times in the past 200 years.

1

Inflation and depression:
Two sides of the same bad coin

> If long continued, inflation at anything like the present rate
> would threaten the very foundations of our society.
>
> —Arthur F. Burns, Federal Reserve Board Chairman,
> on the double-digit inflation of 1974

"Many Americans believe something is wrong with the United
States economy, and nobody knows how to fix it. The economic
ideas and policies employed during the Great Depression and
through a long era of post-World War II prosperity seem to have
worn out, in the view of many analysts."

So said the *Wall Street Journal* on May 9, 1975. The financial
daily went on to cite a growing realization among business
economists that there is something wrong with the long-
dominant economic theories of John Maynard Keynes, which
stress manipulation of government spending and taxation to
manage total demand in the economy. Instead of evening out
the economic ups and downs, these policies are reinforcing the
tendencies to boom and bust.

1

Meanwhile, under a Keynesian system, inflation races on regardless of the business cycle. Which is not surprising really, considering that the politicians running the government—whichever party is in power—love the first part of Keynesian theory about pumping money into the economy to get it going. They do not like the second part, where the government is supposed to take money out of the economy to cool it down when it gets overheated. Who ever heard of a politician insisting that all pork barrels should be empty?

Will a new economic genius be able to come up with some economic system to replace the now rapidly failing half-Keynesian political economy? Who knows? One possibility, of course, is that a total collapse of Keynesian economics in what remains of the capitalist world will lead to a Marxist world order as the Communists move in to pick up the pieces. (What you should do in such an eventuality is considered further on in this book.)

However, rather than any new economic theory gaining worldwide acceptance it seems more likely that life will take its usual course: things will just sort of muddle through from one crisis to another and some new economic order will arise piecemeal from a series of patchwork repairs.

For the present, one certainty is that prices have continued rising in the midst of the worst American recession of the last 40 years. According to classical economic texts, things are not supposed to happen that way.

The anomaly has confounded not only the economists but also the ordinary people who survived the depression of the 1930s. Many of these older citizens thought they had learned how to stretch a dollar to make ends meet in hard times, but their economic world has been stood on its head. According to their folk wisdom, prices went down in a depression. Not any longer. The frugality, the thrift, the ingrained habits of saving they learned 40 years ago are useless now.

The carefully planned $200-a-month retirement income that promised such comfort for old age years ago won't even cover the rent now that the Golden Years are here. The painfully collected savings account earning 4% will melt away entirely in just a few years under the steady erosion of an inflation running at times to 12% or more.

Every so often one of these elderly men or women is found dead in a cheap rented room, a few food stamps by the hot plate, a couple of packets of the cheapest brand of oatmeal attesting to the last inflation-pinched diet. How much is left out of a $250 monthly Social Security check for eating when the monthly rent goes from $100 to $150 a month? When other increases are sure to come as the price of heating oil is quadrupled for the landlord? When supermarket prices are marked higher and higher month by month?

These elderly people worked hard all their lives, and they feel betrayed by a system that robs them of the little they managed to save. We live in a humanitarian society in which a very small percentage of convicted criminals ever go to prison, in which about one out of every seven persons in New York City lives on welfare payments. Nobody wants these senior citizens to starve in their last years. How can they be rescued from the ravages of inflation?

The remedies are likely to cause as much social and political disruption as the disease. One new idea that might well catch on is indexation. Bank savings accounts, Social Security benefits, insurance annuities, wages, salaries, and many other things would be "indexed" to the rate of inflation. If the cost of living went up 20%, then pensioners and wage-earners would automatically get 20% increases. Their lives would be inflation proof—and once again the politicians would evade the unpleasant consequences of stamping out inflation itself.

Inflation has become a worldwide phenomenon, and in foreign countries indexing has made giant strides in recent years. In Brazil, for instance, long a world leader in inflationary economics, almost the entire economy is now indexed to the cost of living, right down to home mortgages and installment payments on new cars.

In the United States, where inflation so far has been relatively mild compared with the triple-digit variety in countries such as Argentina, Chile, and Uruguay, indexing is already giving some protection to about 7.5 million unionized workers, including 600,000 post office employees, as well as 31 million Social Security recipients, 2 million retired military and federal employees, and 19.6 million users of government food stamps.

It could be that indexing will spread, simply as a stopgap measure to plug more and more holes in the inflationary economy, until it becomes a pervasive way of life. Inflation would then be plugged into the economy permanently, one price rise triggering the automatic indexation of another price, and so on and so on interminably.

The next big step could well be indexed mortgage loans. Indeed we are already halfway there with the variable interest rate mortgages now allowed by law in some states. If inflation continues running into double digits over the years, some such measures will come up simply as a matter of necessity. Otherwise mortgage money will not be available at all. Who on earth is going to lend money out at 9% (the maximum mortgage interest allowed by law in some states) for 20 to 25 years when the inflation rate is clipping 12% off his money every year?

We have already seen what the inflationary way of life means to the survivors of the Depression. What will it mean to you in the years ahead? Will you be able to pay all cash for a house if no home financing is available? Will you be able to meet variable interest mortgage payments when interest rates climb to 12, 15 or 20%? Will you be able to pay off an indexed mortgage when the original $30,000 debt is indexed up to $100,000 or more in addition to the double-digit interest rates?

What about your present salary and your company pension? Will they keep up with soaring double-digit inflation? Where are they going to be 20 or 30 years ahead if they do not contain some kind of indexing protection for you? What about your investments? How would indexing affect the prices of stocks? Is anybody going to say "the cost of living is up 30%; therefore IBM should be up 30%?" Not under our present economic system, at least for common stocks. But indexed bonds have already come in Brazil, Britain, Israel, and other countries.

When such bonds are introduced in the United States, any traditional-type bonds you own will suffer huge declines in value. A bond with an immutably fixed 5% or 8% interest rate will just not be able to compete with an indexed bond that pays the same interest rate plus whatever percentage the cost of living goes up each year and is redeemed at maturity for, say, 8,000 inflated dollars instead of $1,000 face value.

Unwary owners of traditional-type fixed-interest-rate bonds would then be wiped out. But this would not be the only consequence. One enormous buttress of government financing, corporate borrowing, and municipal and state loans would collapse, leaving a gaping hole in the American economy, as well as a horde of ruined bondholders lying dazed in the dust and rubble. Perhaps it was this sort of picture that Federal Reserve Chairman Burns had in mind when he warned that double-digit inflation would threaten the very foundations of society.

Make no mistake. Your financial survival is at stake. If you fail to see what is going on around you in the economic world and don't adapt to the changes that are coming, all your hard work will be in vain and everything you own will be swallowed up in the inflationary vortex.

But there is no reason to despair. There are measures you can take to protect yourself, against anything a mismanaged economy can throw at you, from runaway triple-digit inflation to a 1930s-style depression, plus all the social turmoil and political upheaval these economic events would cause—even revolution or war.

You just have to see the dangers as they loom ahead and make your plans in good time. This book will examine the specific things you can do to make yourself safe against almost any eventuality. Let others stand in breadlines when depression comes, their wealth having been consumed by inflationary fires. You and your family may be as safe as one can be in this uncertain world.

This is a world in which ignorance and bad faith compete for preeminence in human affairs, particularly in the actions of governments. Wherever you may live in the world it is a good rule of thumb to distrust anything the local government tells you about the economy.

Indeed one can only wonder whether economic ignorance or bad faith is at work when the government urges the citizenry to Whip Inflation Now. The individual citizen is the victim of inflation, not its cause, and he can do nothing to defeat it. The government causes inflation quite simply by printing too much paper money or expanding credit unreasonably, and it could stop inflation cold turkey tomorrow morning by stopping the printing presses and reversing its easy credit policy. It does not do so for political reasons, because the neo-Keynesian economy depends like a drug addict on greater and greater injections of paper money. As soon as the supply stops, the economy falters, slides back into recession and may plunge uncontrollably into a depression. What politician of any party wants that? Who wants to be the Herbert Hoover of the 1970s?

So as soon as the money spigot is turned off and unemployment rears its ugly head, all the politicians take fright, the WIN buttons are hurriedly put away, and stagnation, recession, and depression rapidly replace inflation as the "great scourge" of the American people.

When you see politicians talking that way on your nightly television news program, hold on to your hat for the next roller coaster ride on the inflationary switchback—more inflationary money is on the way.

The reasoning in this book, as you may have noted by now, is based on a cautiously low appraisal of human competence and reliability, especially where politicians are involved. When you have a legislator with a reputation for fiscal conservatism talking calmly of $60 billion budget deficits on becoming President, it is time to doubt that any politician will ever do anything to contain inflation if not forced to act by events. And when you have another President preaching friendship with Red China and detente with the Soviet Union after a lifetime of hardline antiCommunism, it is time to conclude that things are not always what they seem.

Then you have another candidate for the White House who preaches friendly coexistence and unilateral disarmament as the road to universal peace. It is not improbable that despite all his good intentions the first years of such a chief executive will be marked by Cuban missile crises, Berlin wall confrontations, military campaigns in Korea or other such unpleasantnesses as he desperately tries to persuade Moscow and Peking by force of arms that peaceful coexistence is not the same thing as piecemeal surrender.

These political comments are made in a nonpartisan spirit. However, it does appear to be a vague general rule that Republican administrations tend to get the country into depressions while Democratic administrations tend to get it into wars.

Since this world is an unpredictable place, the suggestions in this book on how you should ensure your own financial safety take the uncertainties and the unexpected into account. If there is one basic thought running through each chapter it is this: What is the worst that could possibly happen? And what can one do to meet the worst if it comes?

You might suppose this way of thinking leads to an unduly gloomy outlook on the future. It would be gloomy only if there were nothing to be done about it. But there are plenty of things you can do, and this intensely *practical* book will supply you with facts, figures, names and addresses of banks, brokers and other organizations that can help you with their services.

But here, too, you are urged to make your own realistic appraisals of integrity, competence, and reliability before dealing with any of the firms or other organizations mentioned in these pages.

In days long gone, British gilt-edged securities were "as safe as the Bank of England." But as this is written, the *London Financial Times* index of British Government Bonds has hit an all-time low of 49.19—less than two-fifths of its 127.4 high reached January 9, 1936.

In other words, investors who put their financial trust in the British government lost three-fifths of their nominal capital, and with all the inflation between 1936 and 1976 they lost more than four-fifths. Small wonder that a financial critic described British Government Bonds as "certificates of confiscation."

The investors who lost money in them were living mentally in the age of Queen Victoria. And investors who have bought long-term United States bonds backed by the faith and credit of the Federal Government have been living in the age before 1933, when President Roosevelt banned gold ownership, cancelled obligations to pay debts in gold, and launched the country on a sea of unbacked paper money.

American bondholders will not want the mental pain of calculating here how much they have lost in purchasing power to inflation from 1933 to the present time. If we want to avoid such pain in the future let's live mentally at least in the inflationary present, and if possible anticipate all the nasty surprises that a brave new post-Keynesian world may bring.

2

Inflation:
The insidious danger

The reason most Americans are not as aware as other peoples of the danger of holding unbacked paper currency, such as the present-day United States dollar, is that for most of the last 200 years the United States has enjoyed comparative monetary stability. Despite passing aberrations, such as the Civil War inflation, the dollar has held up much better for far longer than most other currencies in the world. And this could be a nasty psychological trap for Americans who still put their faith in a currency that no longer deserves any more trust than a politician's promise.

After the Continental currency debacle, the United States government in 1792 fixed the value of the dollar at $19.75 per ounce of gold. This held until 1834, when the gold price was raised to $20.67. For the next hundred years—spanning the entire growth of the United States from a poor, struggling backwoods economy to the world's major industrial power—the official valuation of the dollar remained rock-steady at $20.67 per ounce of gold. Then in 1934 President Roosevelt abruptly hiked the gold price, or rather he devalued the dollar, to $35 an ounce.

Even more significant, however, was his ban on gold owner-ship by private American citizens, who were thus legally pre-vented from buying the precious metal to protect themselves against paper currency depreciation.

This perhaps marks the decisive step in converting the dollar from a hard currency backed by real value into a fiat paper money that is depreciable to almost any imaginable extent by a government decision to print more dollar bills. It was preceded by an earlier weakening, the Federal Reserve Act of 1913, which provided for gold backing of only 40% of the notes in cir-culation. After World War II the gold backing required for Federal Reserve banknotes was cut down to only 25%.

In 1968 the gold backing required was reduced to zero, which meant that from this time forward the United States govern-ment could issue unlimited currency without any gold backing whatever. The next steps were formalities: in 1971 President Nixon marked the dollar down, and the gold price up, to $38 an ounce. In 1973 he devalued the dollar again, to $42.22 an ounce. And, reaching the logical end of this process of debasement, he declared the dollar totally inconvertible into gold for anyone, including foreign central banks.

The official United States gold price by this time was totally meaningless. Buyers and sellers on the world's free markets were soon valuing gold as high as $195 an ounce. To put it another way, the worldwide free market was saying that the American dollar was worth less than a quarter of what the American government claimed it was worth.

Once you realize that the dollar is now an unbacked paper currency without anything of value behind it, you have only to look at other currencies of this type to realize what is likely to happen to the dollar within your lifetime. Experience in every other part of the world shows that in a relatively short time its value will decline progressively towards zero.

The classic case of paper currency debasement is the great German inflation of the 1920s, in which prices rose by 14,000% in a single year. The German mark, which was valued at 4.2 to the dollar in 1921, sank to 11 trillion marks to the dollar in 1924. By this time, of course, it was worth even less than the paper it was printed on, and a new Rentenmark was issued, worth one trillion old marks.

While the great German inflation is usually cited as the classic horror story of monetary affairs, it is really a special case. This was a nation defeated in war, stripped of its productive capacity and saddled with a ruinous load of war reparations. In the circumstances the results were to be expected. It is only the magnitude of the figures and the absurd extremity of the process that is staggering. It left a scar on the German mind much akin to the Great Depression's psychological impact on Americans.

After World War II the German currency collapsed once again. But this time the government moved quickly to nip the problem in the bud. The old currency was simply abandoned and on June 20, 1948 everyone in the country was issued 40 new marks. The slate was wiped clean and every German made a new start in life with the equivalent of about $10. Since that time the German currency has been kept one of the strongest and most stable in the world. This is only to say, however, that German politicians and government officials are more cautious than those of other countries because they face an electorate that has a special horror of inflation. The mark is not convertible into any specified quantity of gold. It is a paper currency like any other, and it has lost nearly 50% of its purchasing power in the last quarter century. It only looks good in comparison with other currencies, such as French franc or Italian lira.

Other extreme inflations were also set off like powder trains by wartime conditions. The Czarist rouble's decline was in the order of 500 million to one, the Polish zloty nearly two million to one. In 1946 Hungary created a new currency unit, the forint, to replace the pengoe. The official conversion rate was one forint for 400,000 quadrillion pengoe. Also after World War II, a month's wages in China was a large wheelbarrow of paper money. The new Communist regime swept this away with its own money, the jen min piao, which sank in turn and was replaced in 1955 by the yuan, at the rate of 10,000 jen min piao for one yuan.

While these examples make good scare stories, they are not

really comparable to any probable situation in the United States in present circumstances. They were born of war, and generally of defeat as well. It seems excessively gloomy at this time to anticipate a situation in which Americans would have to start out all over again to remake their lives with ten New Dollars, as people did in post-World War II Germany. If you do want to visualize it, however, that is the time to avoid paper money like the plague and to hold gold coins, silver coins, land, buildings, anything with a real value of its own rather than dollar bills or a savings account. The aristocratic von Thurn und Taxis family had to take their 40 marks like everybody else, but they still held the thousands of acres of forest land their clan had owned for centuries in Bavaria.

There are other countries whose monetary circumstances are more directly comparable to those present in the United States. These are countries that have enjoyed long periods of peace, have a wealth of natural resources and an active, capable population. Their only major problem has been political and fiscal mismanagement.

One of these is Brazil, a nation comparable in territory and natural wealth to the United States. In the nineteenth century the Brazilians had a monetary unit named the real. Having no backing in gold or anything else, reals were fatally easy to print, and so many were issued that prices rose to the point where the number of zeroes involved made business transactions unwieldy. The solution was to issue milreis, the equivalent of one thousand reals. The government once again overworked the monetary printing presses, and over a period of decades the milrei sank to such low estate that it in turn was scrapped in favor of a new paper currency unit, the cruzeiro, worth one thousand milreis.

The cruzeiro came into existence around the time of World War II, but after another quarter century it became necessary once again to lop three zeroes off, and the cruzeiro gave way in 1967 to the New Cruzeiro, worth one thousand old ones.

So you have this progression over a period of a century or so: the real becomes one thousand milreis, which becomes one million cruzeiros, which becomes one billion New Cruzeiros. Your currency unit today is worth only *one billionth* part of what it was a hundred years ago. And it is still depreciating at a rate that suggests the probable creation of a New New Cruzeiro in a few years' time.

This is the sort of result that can be expected over an extended period of time in a country where the currency has no backing in precious metals, but is simply a fiat money created at will by the politicians running the government and the currency. Which, as we have just noted, is now the lowly status of the United States dollar.

Institutionalized inflation has been a way of life in Brazil for many decades. In the United States we are just seeing the beginnings of a way of life shaped by a totally unbacked paper currency. The decline in value of the paper dollar may not be as precipitous as that of the Brazilian currency, but over the years the process will certainly be similar, as long as the nature of political leaders remains constant and as long as there is no gold or silver backing.

The overall economic results of an inflationary monetary system are debatable, as nearly everything is in economic theory. Brazil is said to be booming, with a growth rate of 10% a year, despite the inflation—or perhaps because of it, depending on the economist you are talking to. The inflation itself continues at 35% a year in 1976. But this is a nation that started out with the same vast potential as the United States, and yet it has a gross national product that is one-twentieth the size of the American economy. The increase in the United States economy in one year alone at times exceeds the entire production of Brazil.

A large part of United States economic growth was achieved in a period of about 100 years in which its currency was backed by gold. It is tempting to say this growth was achieved because there was no inflation. One ounce of gold was worth $20.67 in January 1934, exactly the same value as in 1834. In those conditions saving was worthwhile and the capital formation needed for growth could take place. Perhaps one can infer a direct cause-and-effect relationship as the main factor. But no doubt other factors were involved, too, such as immigration patterns and the system of business organization in both countries. Conclusions are seldom clear-cut in economic studies.

It may well be that under the present system of fiat monetary inflation, United States economic growth will go to pot, but in any event we are concerned here with results on the personal level rather than with big predictions about the national economy.

It is only common sense that in a prolonged inflation of the Brazilian type, one uses cash to buy something of solid value as quickly as possible before the money becomes worthless. It does not matter whether the purchase is a car, furniture, housing, land or works of art. Anything is better than holding money in a checking account or a savings account, where, over a normal 70-year life-span, it will be well on its way to a one-billionth part shrinkage.

Americans have obviously not yet made the mental adjustment required to grasp inflations of this magnitude. A Wall Street economist, Sam I. Nakagama of Kidder, Peabody & Co., noted in one of his fortnightly surveys of the United States economy that as the inflation rate moved up from 1 to 2% in the 1960s to 12% and higher in 1974, the figures showed this trend: "When prices are rising rapidly, consumers tend to spend less and save more." In Brazil and other countries where people have had longer experience of entrenched inflation, they do the exact opposite.

Perhaps personal experiences are the clearest way of illustrating inflationary monetary losses on a scale that most Americans still find hard to relate to their own lives. If the paper dollar follows the same path as all other paper currencies so far, they will in a few years have similar unpleasant recollections of their own.

The author of this book first saw a dollar bill in 1946, when he was 17 years old. He bought it from an exchange dealer in Buenos Aires, his home city then, to make a small mail order purchase in the United States. That dollar cost four Argentine pesos. The same dollar today, despite all its depreciation in 30 years, would cost 24,000 pesos—if pesos existed, which they no longer do. They were withdrawn from circulation and replaced by New Pesos worth 100 old pesos.

In 1923 my father took out a life insurance policy in Buenos Aires with the Norwich Union Life Insurance Society, which was and is one of the most reputable British insurance companies. The policy had a face value of 12,000 Argentine pesos, worth at that time about $4,000. My father died in 1972, but I have never bothered to collect on the policy, although I am the sole beneficiary. I keep it at home as a curiosity and a reminder of what inflation can do to one's best-laid plans over a period of 50 years. If I turned it in I would get about 50¢ for it.

And yet Argentine inflation has had nowhere near the virulence and persistence of the Brazilian experience. There were lengthy periods of relative monetary stability, just long enough to lull people like my father into a false sense of security. When Argentine inflation really got going after World War II, he was mentally conditioned to a reasonably sound money system and never made the psychological adaptation to the new era. He was always buying the most conservative bonds and preferred stocks on the Buenos Aires stock exchange. Every single investment was practically wiped out in about ten years.

I always think of my father when I read about retirees eking out money-pinching existences in Florida rooming houses, worrying about their dwindling savings accounts, their New York City bonds and Con Edison preferred stock. Like him, they never made the mental adjustment to the brave new world of monetary debasement. The most sensible thing my father did about inflation was to buy his own apartment for retirement in the best residential area of Buenos Aires. The property is still worth what he paid for it 20 years ago, in any country's inflated currency.

All this happened in a country untouched by war in the last 100 years, a neutral nation that made money hand-over-fist selling grain and meat to a hungry world during and after both World Wars. The only cause of disaster for people like my father was fiscal mismanagement of an unbacked paper currency.

In nations such as France, where revolutions and wars have created periodic upheavals, inflationary calamities have repeatedly caused similar experiences for Frenchmen. The paper *assignats* issued in the French Revolution in successive waves became totally worthless between 1790 and 1798, and resulted, according to one study, "in the complete financial, moral and political prostration of France—a prostration from which only a Napoleon could raise it."

Similar inflations ensued in France after both World Wars in this century, with a few other disasters in between in the 19th century. It is small wonder that Frenchmen nowadays hold about 150 million ounces of gold in private hoards. From generation to generation, sons have learned from the experience of fathers what happens to paper money in France.

There comes a point when the inflated paper currency no longer works—even under the threat of the death penalty—when there is any reasonable alternative available, such as gold or silver coins or a more stable foreign currency. The French Revolutionary authorities decreed death by the guillotine for anyone who refused to accept the depreciating *assignats* as legal payment in business transactions, but the system collapsed anyway.

It is no coincidence that the coin most Frenchmen hoard nowadays is the twenty-franc Napoleon. Andrew Dickson White, in his book *Fiat Money Inflation in France*, states that when Napoleon Bonaparte took over the French government, "the condition of fiscal affairs was appalling. The government was bankrupt; an immense debt was unpaid. The further collection of taxes seemed impossible . . . war was going on . . . all the armies had long been unpaid, and the largest loan that could for the moment be effected was for a sum hardly meeting the expenses of government for a single day.

"At the first cabinet council Bonaparte was asked what he intended to do. He replied, 'I will pay cash or pay nothing.' From this time he conducted all his operations on this basis. He arranged the assessments, funded the debt, and made payments in cash . . . . When the first great European coalition formed against the Empire, Napoleon was hard pressed financially, and it was proposed to resort to paper money; but he wrote to his minister, 'While I live, I will never resort to irredeemable paper.' He never did, and France, under this determination, commanded all the gold she needed. When Waterloo came, with the invasion of the allies, with war on her own soil, with a change of dynasty, and with heavy expenses for war and indemnities, France, on a specie basis, experienced no severe financial distress."

3

Inflation:
The global menace

Inflation, generalized and permanent, arbitrarily redistributes wealth in no relation to work and productivity. The Western world has lost control over raw materials, suffers monetary instability and soaring prices without an international set of rules of order being introduced to replace the system now in force.

—Nello Celio, former President of Switzerland
May 27, 1975

Politicians and others with more chauvinism than sense have one final argument in defense of the paper dollar. The United States dollar needs no gold backing, they say, because it is backed by the resources of the world's most powerful and productive economy. One would do better to hold specie than this specious argument.

At the time this book was started, in 1975, the United States Federal Reserve Board itself admitted that it was inflating the money supply at 6% a year (and fighting hard at that against Congress, which wanted the paper money supply to increase at an even higher rate). Later in the year the Board raised the rate of increase to 10%. At 6% or higher, compounded, you are going to double the money supply in somewhat more than a decade. Is the national economy going to double its productive capacity in ten years?

Over a period of many decades the American economy has demonstrated that it has been able to expand at an average rate of 4% a year. One may infer from this that if the money supply also grows at an average 4% annual rate, one can anticipate a zero rate of inflation.

It does not take any great intelligence to perceive that if the money supply grows faster than the 4% yearly increase in the national economy, then prices are going to be pushed higher by a growing quantity of dollars pursuing relatively fewer goods.

After the jolt of the Arab oil embargo in 1973, the growth of the American economy was practically zero; it even dipped into minus territory as the nation sank into the depressed conditions of 1974-75.

One might as well face it: with a zero to 4% growth rate while the authorities are intent on increasing the money supply by 6 to 10% a year, one is going to have inflation. You may still have the most productive and powerful economy in the world some years later, but prices will double and the dollar will halve in value.

The dollars you invest are yours and you can bet on the most-productive-economy theory if you like, but as a simple matter of prudence you would do well to hedge your bets.

Indeed you have already bet on it simply by holding your assets in dollars, and you have lost heavily—about 60% of your net worth if measured in Swiss francs, and much more than that if measured in gold. (The Swiss franc rose from 25 to 40 United States cents in recent years, while gold shot up from $35 to as high as $195 an ounce.)

The decline of the dollar is a story of growing delusions of grandeur in Washington, and its decadence will continue for as long as those delusions persist. The United States came out of World War II the richest and most powerful nation on earth. The American economy represented something like half the production of the entire globe. About three-quarters of the world's gold was buried at Fort Knox. All the war-torn nations of Europe were desperate for American dollars to rebuild their shattered economies.

All this American economic and financial strength was reflected in the monetary agreement signed at Bretton Woods, New Hampshire, in 1944. This pact created a new world monetary order based on two strong pillars: the American dollar and gold. The United States was the only country in the world to give an unconditional guarantee to buy or sell gold to all other nations at $35 an ounce.

American citizens were still forbidden to own gold, but this international guarantee by their government ensured that the dollar was tied to gold at a fixed price and could not sink uncontrollably like the paper currencies of other nations. The British pound was soon devalued from $4 to $2.80 per dollar in 1949. The French franc, issued in paper torrents to pay for a long war in Indochina, plunged to a rate of hundreds to the dollar. The American dollar and gold, in other words, were the unchanging standard against which all other currencies were measured under the Bretton Woods agreement.

Occupying, as it did, one of the twin thrones of this gold-dollar regime, the American government was ever more deluded into the belief that the American dollar was the kingpin of the global financial system, and that gold was just a psychological hangover from an earlier age, a "barbarous relic" as Lord Keynes called it. Over the years it became the official policy of Washington to phase gold out of the system altogether and to make the paper dollar, printed in Washington, the globe's single financial axis.

More and more paper dollars were issued through the 1950s and 1960s to pay for American domestic welfare programs, to build President Johnson's Great Society, to reduce unemployment and fend off recessions, to dispense foreign aid to just about every nation in the world, to fight wars in Korea and Indochina, and to prop up other allies against Communist expansion. Meanwhile American interest rates were held down by Washington to help the housing industry. As a result, billions of privately owned dollars fled abroad to earn higher interest rates in Europe—thus creating the Eurodollar market to compete with Wall Street.

With this unceasing outflow of dollars, the United States began to run bigger and bigger balance-of-payments deficits,
which meant that billions of dollars were piling up abroad. In
the 1970s this monstrous heap of dollars in the hands of foreigners—mostly foreign Central Banks—had grown to more
than $100 billion. Meanwhile, the United States' hoard of gold
had shrunk to a mere $11 billion.

Under the Bretton Woods system, Washington was thus legally obliged to meet a $100 billion gold claim when it had only $11
billion in gold available. When this sort of thing happens to a
company in business life, it announces it cannot meet its obligations and declares itself bankrupt.

The United States government, in effect, declared its bankruptcy on August 15, 1971, when President Nixon went on television to announce that the American dollar was now totally inconvertible into gold—for anybody from Joe Doakes on Main
Street to the Central Bank of Germany.

It was a long, tortuous process, with too many international
conferences of finance ministers, stopgap measures and financial contrivances along the way to detail here, but if you want
the exact date on which the era of reasonably honest money
came to an end in the United States, this was the day. On
August 15, 1971, the American dollar finally became a completely unbacked paper currency—no different in essence from
the Brazilian cruzeiro, the French franc, or the Argentine
peso—with all the latent potential for terminal debasement of
the eighteenth-century Continental or the French Revolution's
assignat.

As for the most-productive-economy-on-earth thesis, it has
not held up too well since then. In 1976, according to one com-
putation, the United States was only number six in per-capita
income—outranked by the United Arab Emirates, Kuwait,
Switzerland, Sweden and Denmark—and still slipping. West
Germany and Canada were only a step behind the United
States per-capita figure of $7,020. To a large extent this was a re-
flection of the diminishing value of the United States dollar
against other currencies.

So, as America inaugurates its third century of life, we stand in the opening years of a new era, the era of paper dollars in the United States, of paper currencies in the rest of the world—in a word, the era of global inflation.

It is a whole new ballgame now. For Americans the old world was the era of 3% yearly inflation and 4% bank accounts; the saver might not get rich, but at least he survived. The new era is of 12% inflation and 6% bank accounts, as in 1974. A few more years like this and your savings will be wiped out, perhaps sooner rather than later.

The old era was an era of growth stocks, of companies that paid no dividends because they plowed their profits back into a business that seemed destined to grow forever. The new era is already bumping against the upper limits of growth, with recurrent energy crises, gasoline lines, natural gas shortages, and oil embargoes. These are the early warning signs of a worldwide scarcity of natural resources.

The United States, once a resource-rich nation, has become an importer of oil, iron, bauxite, and other raw materials it needs for its very survival. The nation, to put it bluntly, depends on other states to stay afloat, and some of them, like the Arab oil exporters, are not averse to shooting off torpedoes when their own vital interests are at stake.

Your own personal survival in a cold winter depends in some measure on these unfriendly suppliers. It also depends on politicians, who love to promise benefits to everybody and hate to do unpopular things like raising taxes to pay for those benefits. The easy way out is to print more paper money, and politicians of whatever party, in whatever country (except a dictatorship, which doesn't care what the downtrodden citizenry thinks), will continue doing it. Under the present system, inflation is here to stay, and under present circumstances national insecurity is here to stay.

How are you going to survive financially now that the age of honest money and the almighty dollar is over? The decisions you make now will be the most important you have ever taken to protect yourself and ensure the safety of your family.

The essential thing to keep in mind is that a dollar bill is a piece of paper. You cannot take it to the United States Treasury and trade it in for gold, silver, or anything at all, except another dollar bill. This scrap of paper still has value only because people have some residual trust in the United States government.

But this trust is eroded more and more as inflation rises from 1% or 2% in the 1960s, to 5% and over in the early 1970s, to 14.4% in the final quarter of 1974, and perhaps even much higher than that in the years ahead. And the whole process of ever more inflationary paper money and credit, together with an ever-diminishing faith in the value of the currency—still at an early stage in the United States—tends to accelerate.

The reason is that when the first addition of paper money is made, the dollar loses value at a slower rate initially than the rate at which the amount of money in circulation increases. With the stimulation of extra spending money buying more goods, the economy gets a rosy flush. At this stage, the politicians are sure they have discovered the secret of preventing recessions, and, God forbid, a depression. Every time the economy starts deflating they pump some more money into it.

For a while this works, but when the remedy is repeated over and over, prices begin to catch up and even surpass the extra money in circulation. Then the country slides at an accelerating rate into the final stage of inflation. At this stage, a population hardened to incessant price rises begins to *anticipate* the new additions to the money supply. Housewives buy refrigerators *before* they really need a new one because they know that prices are *never* going to go down, and that the money that will buy a fridge this year will not buy one next year. Prices begin to rise at a faster rate than new inflationary money can be supplied, and there is a perpetual shortage of cash. Working people find that their wages and salaries are no longer keeping up with rising prices and that their real standard of living is going down. Businessmen call for yet more money and more credit to perk up their stagnant business.

But none of this does any good because the new money issues are always anticipated by a cynical community that has seen it all happen before. At this stage, you get the worst of everything—unbridled inflation, with prices rising monthly, weekly and even daily, at the same time as business sinks into recession or even a depression. The cure is still thought to be more money, and businessmen, labor leaders, and politicians all call for more cash and more credit.

"Stagflation" some people call it, and it is the typical bind of an economy running on fiat paper money. It is the bind in which the American economy is now caught and the one in which the British economy, somewhat further along the same road, is almost totally trapped. On the personal level, it is the bind of the Social Security pensioner in the Florida rooming house who survived the Great Depression and finds, to his dismay, that depressions ain't what they used to be. Now they come with inflation, too.

As inflating the money supply becomes less and less effective in stimulating the economy, the unemployment rolls start to mount; and this is the real kiss of death for any politician. No American yearns to be the Herbert Hoover of the 1970s. The remedy once again is to pump more money into the economy.

There is even a school of economic thought that contends you can make a tradeoff between inflation and unemployment. Professor A.W. Phillips of the London School of Economics invented the so-called Phillips curve, which illustrates the tradeoff graphically. Phillips studied wage rates and unemployment levels in Great Britain over nearly a century and found that when there is a lot of unemployment, workers who do have jobs don't press too hard for wage increases for fear of joining the dole. This damps down inflation. When there is no unemployment, workers push hard for raises and this stimulates inflationary policies.

Based on this concept, elaborate calculations were made in the United States and other countries to show, for instance, that if you had an unemployment rate of 8% you could get it down to 4% by inflating the money supply by, say, 6%.

The latest news on this theory is that in early 1976 the inflation rate in Britain was 25% and unemployment was still giving the British government the jitters with 1.4 million people, about 6% of the labor force, out of work. In the United States inflation went into double digits in 1974 without getting unemployment down below 8%. Some trade-off.

What appears inevitable in the end is a situation in which there is no either-or relationship between inflation and recession-depression. In the end you get both simultaneously.

We have seen what happened to other paper currencies in other countries at other times. The paper dollar will go the same way; it is just a matter of time. Almost certainly in your lifetime the extreme limit of depreciation will be reached, at which point it may be necessary to issue a New Dollar convertible once again into a specified quantity of gold.

We have mentioned the sudden, catastrophic type of inflation, as in Germany in the 1920s, the long secular debasement, as in Brazil, and the French rerun-style, in which the currency is ruined several times over in successive centuries.

These inflations, and whatever variety we have in the United States in the years ahead, need not be seen as the doomsday machines that some prophets of the financial world make them out to be. France still lives quite well; Germany is flourishing, and Brazil is booming.

The thing to grasp is that individual citizens—that's you and me—who put their trust in unbacked paper currency are the ones who are wiped out financially. They are the people who have their money in savings accounts, who have deductions made from their paychecks to buy government bonds, who purchase insurance annuities and contribute to pension plans that pay off at fixed dollar rates. The people who did this in the 1930s are being paid off in devalued dollars, and the people doing it now are likely to be paid off in practically worthless dollars.

Double-digit inflation is a warning to take your assets out of a paper currency that is becoming progressively more and more valueless. It is a warning to invest your assets where they cannot be eroded by inflation.

What are inflation-proof assets? The first and foremost is gold. This is the security of last resort, the last plank of salvation when inflation of paper money runs into double digits.

The rate of inflation may fluctuate up or down at varying rates in different countries at various times. In later chapters we shall see what other investments can make sense when inflation drops below 10% a year, or declines even further for a time, say as low as 2% or 4%, or when it is at a lower rate in some other countries than it is in the United States.

At such times it may be profitable to invest in American stocks or bonds for a few years, or even in foreign stock and bond markets. As situations change from year to year so do the problems and their solutions.

4

Gold: A safe refuge
when runaway inflation
hits double digits

For 41 years Americans were forbidden to own gold bullion. But even then there were shrewd people in the early 1970s, when gold was rising rapidly in price, who knew that you could own gold coins legally, provided they were minted before 1934. They bought coins when gold was worth $35 an ounce and sold when it hit $180 an ounce. Or perhaps they held on to them, foreseeing that the price might go even higher over the years as inflation raged on.

Now, since December 31, 1974, it is perfectly legal for American citizens to own gold in any shape or form and store it in the United States or abroad. Gold is one of the best things to own when the government is abusing its power to issue unbacked paper currency without limitation. No matter how many paper dollars the government runs off the printing presses, there is no way it can print gold. Your investment in gold is beyond the reach of the government's fiat money inflation.

The price of gold may then fluctuate from day to day, from month to month, and from one year to another. But as long as double-digit inflation continues, its price will continue to go up, just as the price of everything else goes up in inflationary times. Its long-term price trend in inflationary periods just has to be upward. Meanwhile, your dollars invested in government-insured savings accounts, Treasury bills or insurance annuities *must* decline in value as long as the rate of inflation continues at a faster pace than the interest rates you receive.

So you might consider gold as your first line of defense when inflation starts running into double digits.

Gold has been used directly as money ever since King Croesus of Lydia minted the first coins of pure gold 2,500 years ago. In the modern industrial age, gold was largely taken out of circulation and used as backing for paper money. Goldsmiths in England and elsewhere, the predecessors of today's bankers, issued receipts against the gold bullion held in their vaults. These notes circulated as dollar bills do today, and the goldsmiths soon discovered that not all the bills were presented for redemption at the same time. They found they could issue receipts promising to deliver, say twice as much gold as they actually held, secure in the knowledge that far less than one-half of them would be presented at one time. That is, a 50% backing was sufficient—as long as the people holding the notes were confident of the issuer's ability to deliver.

Once the public started doubting that capacity, there might be a rush to cash in while the going was good, and the goldsmith would then have to default on his commitment to the late-comers. Doubts did arise at times because there is always an insidious temptation for goldsmiths and bankers to issue more and more notes against the same gold backing. The situation is basically the same as the United States government faced in its capacity as the world's banker in 1971. And Washington reacted in exactly the same way: it defaulted on its promise to pay gold when there was a worldwide run on the bank.

The crucial point is public confidence in the bank. The United States Treasury's gold hoard hit a peak of about 700 million ounces in 1949. By 1974 the figure was down to 276 million ounces. But probably at no time could the United States have handled a really determined run on the bank by the holders of paper dollars thrusting forward their paper chits for redemption in gold.

Banking might indeed be considered as a sort of gigantic confidence game. For instance, John Smith deposits $1,000 worth of gold in Bank A, which lends the money to Jim Brown, who redeposits the $1,000 in the same bank pending a business deal he is planning. Two people now have a claim on the same $1,000 worth of gold, and the bank is not going to be able to pay them both off if Smith and Brown demand payment at the same time. This is still not the end of the matter, however, for the bank now has Brown's deposit, which it lends to Joe Bloggs. In next to no time, the $1,000 deposited by John Smith has been converted by the miracle of double entry bookkeeping into $3,000. Money has been created out of thin air. (Certain limits are set to this process by requiring banks to establish reserves. If the reserve requirement is 20%, for instance, the bank can relend only $800 of a $1,000 deposit. When the $800 is deposited in another bank, this second bank can loan out only $640, and this $640 is further reduced for the lending of a third bank. The upshot is that with a 20% reserve requirement $1,000 in new reserves expands the money supply by $5,000. With 5% reserves, the money created rises to $20,000.)

Eventually, in the example we have cited, the whole chain of transactions will be unwound when Joe Bloggs buys a second-hand car and the loans are repaid down the line. The bank has performed a useful function; business has been stimulated. But the whole series of events depends on Smith and Brown not claiming their money at the same time.

In a complex banking system, of course, with hundreds of banks, prudent reserve requirements, thousands of depositors, and millions of deposits, loans and withdrawals, everything averages out, and the bank is roughly in balance with the money it pays out and the money it takes in. That is, until people suspect for some reason that the bank cannot meet its obligations. Then they all rush to take out their money at the same time and the system breaks down.

It makes no difference, in this sense, whether the bank is

dealing in dollars that are fully redeemable in gold or in modern paper dollars that are totally unredeemable. The fundamental problem in both cases is that an inverted pyramid of credit has been built on a very small base and the whole thing can come crashing down.

If the paper dollar should ever be made redeemable into gold again, therefore, it would still be preferable to hold gold coins or gold bullion rather than banknotes representing this gold.

With unredeemable paper dollars now in circulation, the point is merely academic, but there may come a time when a President becomes so disgusted with the chaotic inflationary results of a fiat paper currency that he will decree a New Dollar, redeemable in gold at $300, $500 or $1,000 per troy ounce. Even at that price it is unlikely that the Treasury could ever deliver gold in exchange for anywhere near the total amount of paper dollars in circulation. Once again it would be a banker's con game.

The United States Federal Reserve System, which controls the American money supply, currently has the ultimate authority for creating money out of thin air. It does this in an extremely complicated way, by buying and selling government securities, raising and lowering bank reserve requirements and discount rates. And the dollars it creates multiply like rabbits. One dollar added to reserves on deposit with the Federal Reserve can in the end become $7. This is the ultimate con game in banking, and even if the dollar is put back on the gold standard, there is sufficient flim-flammery in the present system to cause inflation anyway by manipulation of the banking structure.

There is therefore no substitute for owning actual gold bullion or coins, even if the classical gold standard is restored.

Gold supply

When the inflation of paper money hits double digits and the political outlook points to further runaway inflation for a prolonged period, the monetary supply-demand equation is simple to estimate—the supply will get progressively closer to infinity and the value of money will simultaneously approach zero. Since the outlook for holding paper currency is so bleak, the next question becomes: What is the supply-demand equation for gold, as an alternative to paper?

The equation is better because the supply of gold is strictly limited by nature, not loosely regulated by politicians.

From the beginning of time until today, about three billion ounces of gold have been mined in the whole world. Most of this gold still exists in one form or another.

The amount of gold still to be mined around the globe has been loosely estimated at about 1.2 billion ounces, but this is an elastic figure. As the price of gold rises it becomes increasingly economical to work lower-grade ores. The quantity of gold potentially minable in the United States, for instance, is calculated by the U.S. Bureau of Mines at 237 million ounces, when the price of gold is less than $145 an ounce. The total would have to be revised upward when gold holds at a substantially higher price for a sustained period. The amount of gold still potentially minable in the rest of the world at relatively high prices is estimated at about 900 million ounces, mostly in South Africa, the Soviet Union, Canada, Australia, Colombia and Rhodesia. It looks therefore as though the amount of new gold coming into the market in the foreseeable future would be somewhere around 1.1 to 1.2 billion ounces, which would raise the total available supply to somewhat more than four billion ounces.

The potential supply is thus severely limited by nature. If it were not, we would have gold money inflation as well as paper money inflation. This has, in fact, happened on one or two occasions in history. When the Spanish conquistadores discovered the rich gold and silver mines of Mexico and Peru in the 16th century, Spain and most of Western Europe suffered a highly unusual form of inflation. This was caused by the massive inflow of precious metals, which vastly increased the spending power of the population without any corresponding increase in the production of goods.

About the only chance of this happening again is if someone were to discover a cheap way of extracting gold from seawater. According to one calculation, the oceans of the world hold about 600 billion ounces of gold. But this threat seems remote.

With current technology, only small quantities can be re-
covered and at a very high cost.

World production of gold in the mid-1970s is thought to be
around 45 million ounces a year. The figure is a guess because
the Soviet Union, a major producer, publishes no official
figures and the estimates of Soviet production are almost pure
conjecture. The Soviets are thought to account for about 17% of
world production, in second place behind South Africa, which
dominates the world gold market with around 65% of the world
supply. Canada produces about 5% and the United States 3% of
the world total. These four countries thus represent about 90%
of the newly mined gold coming onto the market.

Because of labor problems and the depletion of its richer
gold-bearing ores, South African output has been declining,
leaving the Soviet Union as the chief area of the world for a possible increase in world gold production. According to commodities expert Charles R. Stahl, "Within a decade the gold production of the Soviet Union may closely match that of South
Africa."

Russian gold sales, as well as production, are shrouded in
mystery. The Soviets apparently air-freight most of their gold
into the duty-free area at Zurich's Kloten airport and then sell it
through a Soviet bank in Switzerland. The Russians, says Stahl,
"play the market in an unashamedly capitalist fashion and can
be expected to exploit the American market for all it is worth"
now that Americans can legally own gold.

In fact, Pravda, the official Soviet newspaper, is a vigorous
supporter of the gold standard, joining hands, in this at least,
with financial conservatives in the West who demand an end to
the capitalist world's inflationary binge and a return to sound
money backed by gold. Stahl finds this weird ideological alliance of the political Left with the financial Right an ominous
development. The conservatives, he feels, are unwittingly playing into the hands of the Soviets with their gold crusade.

Stahl also takes a pessimistic view of the price outlook for
gold, based on the fundamentals of supply and demand, calculating that world consumption of the metal amounted to only 750
tons in 1974, about half of world production in that year. Gold
purchases by United States industry did in fact hit a ten-year

low in 1974, but this did not prevent the price of gold from soaring from $110 an ounce at the end of 1973 to nearly $200 at the end of 1974. Stahl's forecast is that gold will fluctuate between $125 and $185 an ounce for many years.

First National City Bank economists have also calculated that basic factors such as industrial demand and the cost of production would result in a "reasonable" price for gold of between $118 and $135 an ounce. Anything over that, said the New York bank, would be "mere speculative froth."

"Reasonable" however is not always an accurate characterization of human behavior. As *Barron's* magazine remarked, "All bets are off if the public gets really panicky over inflation. All sober statistical projections could be knocked into a cocked hat. Gold prices could skyrocket."

According to Merrill Lynch, "The prime force in the demand for gold is worldwide buying by small savers and investors who fear inflation and monetary uncertainty." But the output of gold is on such a comparatively small scale that "the value of new gold production equals only approximately one per-cent of the total annual private savings of the West."

Most of the world's gold trade is concentrated in London and Zurich, but analysts estimate that all of Europe's gold markets can absorb only about six tons of gold a day, which is about $35 million worth at the price of $180 an ounce. When more or less than that amount is offered, it is usually sufficient to swing the price sharply up or down.

One can imagine the volcanic upward pressure that would erupt in the gold price if the holders of the remaining 99% of Western savings lost all confidence in paper money in a global bout of inflation and scrambled to buy gold at the same time.

Exactly such a worldwide inflationary storm has been predicted by a leading Swiss banker. On February 19, 1975, Walter Frey, general manager of the Swiss Bank Corporation of Zurich, forecast that the price of gold would soar to unprecedented heights as "a new wave of inflation, worse than anything we have seen so far," sweeps across the world, and as Arab oil-producing countries and other buyers marshal their billions of dollars to buy gold as a protection against eroding paper currencies. Frey, however, is not exactly a disinterested party—his bank is one of Switzerland's three major gold dealers, who handle about 80% of South Africa's gold sales.

In Johannesburg, source of much of the world's gold and center of South Africa's 42 working gold mines, South African mining experts were confidently predicting in 1975 a gold price of $800 an ounce within ten years.

All of which, of course, depends on the course of inflation and the irrationality of human behavior should the runaway overissue of dollars and other paper currencies threaten the rapid destruction of present fiat money values.

It is to guard against the danger of a sudden, unreasoning stampede to buy gold in such circumstances—and to profit by buying early—that we concentrate on gold as the ultimate refuge for your investment funds whenever the annual inflation rate rises into double digits.

One other major factor to be reckoned with before doing this is the official gold holdings of the world's central banks, about 1.2 billion ounces. Surprisingly, the United States Treasury is still the biggest holder, with its 270 million ounces, more than twice as much as West Germany, which stands in second place.

For years this huge amount was totally immobilized because it was valued at the official price of $42.22 an ounce, and not a single nation in the world was buying or selling at this fictitious price. Then in 1974 countries almost bankrupted by the quadrupling of world oil prices—such as Italy—found themselves forced to borrow money abroad, which they did by offering government gold as collateral at around $120 an ounce.

This was the first hesitant official movement towards the real market price for gold. In January 1975 the United States Treasury, alarmed by the possibility of American citizens rushing to buy gold as soon as it became legal with the new year, auctioned two million ounces to the highest bidder and sold nearly half of this at around $165 an ounce. In June 1975 the Treasury auctioned another 500,000 ounces to the public at about $166 an ounce and threatened further sales from time to time. The huge frozen glacier of government-owned gold was now starting to melt and slide toward the free market.

In September 1975 the official $42.22 price was abolished and the International Monetary Fund was authorized to sell one-sixth of its 150-million-ounce gold hoard at free market prices for the benefit of the poorer nations of the world. This potential 25-million-ounce sale hung over the market, as did the threat of further U.S. Treasury sales. The Russians, plagued by a poor grain crop, were selling gold to buy millions of tons of wheat. All this combined to push the price of gold down below $130 an ounce in late 1975 and early 1976. For the time being, said Walter Frey, the price of gold was almost entirely in the hands of the world's central banks.

To many it seemed that the United States Treasury was decisively winning its anti-gold crusade. But there were powerful forces ranged against it. The big producers, Russia and South Africa, had the power to reassert themselves by withholding gold from the market. The nations that had borrowed against their government gold had a vested interest in keeping up the value of their collateral. So did the poor countries slated to benefit from the International Monetary Fund gold. Nations such as France were ideologically predisposed toward gold anyway.

The first International Monetary Fund Sale—780,000 ounces auctioned off on June 2, 1976, at $126 an ounce—caused scarcely a ripple on the world gold market. The London free market quotation was within a few cents of $126 the day before and the day after the sale. Buyers at the auction included the central banks of France and Switzerland and a Soviet foreign trade bank.

In the long run there remained the major peril we have been discussing in this chapter, the threat of double digit inflation. If runaway inflation is destroying the credibility of the world's paper currencies as it did in the 1974-75 period, there will come a time when governments will have to protect themselves in the same way as do private citizens. They will have to buy gold to provide more backing for their paper currencies.

Eventually, a worldwide bout of double-digit inflation might well be sorted out after a few years through a world financial conference, with a new agreed official price of gold, such as the $35-an-ounce standard fixed at Bretton Woods in 1944. But this time the price would be much, much higher—say $350 an ounce or more.

The big world gold rush could well have started when American private ownership was legalized on Dec. 31, 1974. It did not do so because of determined counter-efforts by Washington, and because most Americans still retained a good deal of faith in their paper dollars. But as the *Financial Times* of London observed, "There remains the distinct possibility that some time in the future rampant inflation or other grim happenings will finally spark off an American gold rush."

How to buy gold

There are various ways of investing in gold, each of which has its advantages and disadvantages. The alternatives include gold coins or gold bullion, which you can buy and hold in the United States or abroad, through banks or dealers. You can also buy gold bullion through the futures markets, and shares in gold mining companies can be bought through the stock market or through mutual funds. And there is at least one foreign government bond linked to the price of gold.

Gold coins

The most obvious place to start is your local coin dealer. He can offer you two types of coins, those sold for their rarity value and those sold mainly for their gold content. A rare $20 piece that sells among coin collectors for $5,000 is not really a gold investment; it is a numismatic item. Excluding the rare coins sold mainly for their numismatic value (a specialized field that is beyond the scope of this book) Table 1 shows some of the most popular coins your dealer can offer you.

The table is taken from *The Powell Monetary Analyst* (published every two weeks by Reserve Research Ltd., 63 Wall Street, New York 10005).

One very important omission from this table is the South African Krugerrand, which only became legal to own in the United States after Dec. 31, 1974. The Krugerrand contains exactly one troy ounce of gold (it actually weighs somewhat more than one troy ounce because it is made of 22 carat gold, or 11/12 pure gold, so the extra 1/12 is the weight of the alloy). This coin is turned out by the million by the South African Mint, without any pretention of numismatic rarity or value. It is bought and

Table 1

	Gold content (Troy oz.)	Intrinsic gold value	Average retail asking price (N.Y.C.) (for single coins)		Wholesale asking price (N.Y.C.) (dealer to dealer only)
		11/7/74	10/24/74	11/7/74	11/7/74
*U.S. $20 Double Eagle	.9675	$171.49	$295.00	$302.00	$294.00
U.S. $10 Liberty	.4838	85.75	175.00	170.00	164.00
U.S. $10 Indian	.4838	85.75	240.00	225.00	215.00
U.S. $ 5 Indian	.2419	42.88	125.00	125.00	107.00
Mexican 20 Pesos	.4823	85.49	90.00	98.00	95.00
Mexican 50 Pesos	1.2057	213.75	220.00	244.00	236.00
British Sovereign	.2354	41.72	58.50	63.50	61.50
Colombia 5 Pesos	.2354	41.72	46.00	49.00	46.00
French Napoleon	.1867	33.09	61.00	64.00	62.50
Swiss 20 Francs	.1867	33.09	60.00	64.00	62.50
Austrian 100 Corona	.9802	173.74	175.00	193.00	186.00
Austrian 20 Corona	.1960	34.74	36.00	40.00	39.00
Austrian 4 Ducat	.4429	78.50	81.00	90.00	87.00
Austrian 1 Ducat	.1107	19.62	21.00	23.00	22.50

Small price concession for purchases of 10 or more coins at retail.

*PMA "Best buy" now.

PMA gold coin index: 210
Two weeks ago: 203
Year ago: 126

Coin market comment: With this issue we institute a major addition to our table of coin prices: the gold content in troy oz. for each coin and their intrinsic gold value based on the London market price for gold as of the same day. By dividing the wholesale price by the intrinsic gold value, subscribers can determine the premium being paid for each. For example, the Austrian 100 Corona is selling at a 7% premium, computed as follows: $186.00 (wholesale price) ÷ $173.74 (gold value) = 1.07 or 7% over par. Our Best Buy this week is the U.S. $20 Double Eagle, which is lagging behind such bullion coins as the British sovereign and the Mexican restrikes. On February 26th, $20 Double Eagles sold as high as $350 at wholesale with bullion at $177.25 in London but are now 16% below this level with bullion back to the same price. We do not recommend purchase of the Hungarian 100 Corona restrikes now being offered by some dealers - these coins are being produced primarily for the U.S. consumer market and have virtually no market in Europe at present.

sold simply for its gold content, and therefore sells usually at a very small premium above the current price of gold bullion. Since gold is quoted around the world in American dollars per troy ounce (you will find the daily quotation in the *Wall Street Journal* in a regular item headed "Gold and Silver") it is easy to discover whether the price your coin dealer is quoting you for Krugerrands is a reasonably fair offer or not. It should certainly not be more than 10% above the day's gold bullion price.

The other coins listed in the table tend to sell at higher premiums above their gold content. The premiums fluctuate widely and may, in fact, double the gold content value of some coins such as the United States $20 Double Eagle. The small premium of the Krugerrand and the simplicity of calculating the value of its one-ounce gold content have made the South African coin one of the most popular around the world in recent years.

If there is no reliable coin dealer where you live, you can buy gold coins by mail order from banks and dealers in big cities. Try to deal with one from out of state—you may save yourself a sizable sales tax on the purchase. If you order from a New Jersey address, for example, a dealer in New York City would not have to charge you an 8% New York sales tax, which would have to be added to the bill of a client walking in off the street in New York.

One such firm which can handle mail orders from across the country is Perera Fifth Avenue, Inc., 630 Fifth Avenue, New York 10020. Perera has a gold line (212-586-2175) that you can telephone 24 hours a day for the latest gold prices. Another possibility is the Girard Bank, Girard Plaza, Philadelphia, Pa. 19101, which responds to queries for the latest gold quotations at 215-471-GOLD. In Chicago you have the First National Bank of Chicago, 1 First National Plaza, Chicago, Ill. 60670 (telephone 312-732-5890). Other banks and dealers in gold coins are also available in other major American cities.

If you buy gold and take it home, you will have to store it yourself. The cost of this is minimal. A bank safety deposit box renting for $18 or so a year will hold gold coins worth many thousands of dollars. (One hundred British sovereigns, which are coins about the size of the current American 25-cent piece, will cover about a letter-size sheet of paper when laid out side by side, and are worth about $5,000 when gold bullion is around $165 an ounce.)

Gold bullion

You can also buy gold bullion rather than coins from your local coin dealer. It usually comes in sizes of ½, 1, 5, 10, 100 or 400 troy ounces, or 1 kilo (32.15 troy ounces) and is usually certified 99.5% fine.

But with bullion, things become trickier. Coin dealers rely on their own expertise to detect counterfeit coins and will buy your coins back from you after a mere visual inspection. But when it comes to gold bullion they are considerably more cautious and may require that your gold bars be assayed before they will take them from you. Assaying is an expensive process, involving a complex chemical analysis. The Girard Bank, for example, charges an assayer fee of $75 to $150.

You might as well buy Krugerrands, which are almost the equivalent of gold bullion, and avoid the assay problem. But if you insist on bullion, you should be twice as cautious as the dealers are. Some firms have their own trademarked wafers and ingots on the market, and if the firm is not well-known in the trade it may be difficult to persuade other firms to buy these items from you. You will then be a captive customer of a firm that may or may not offer you a fair repurchase price. It is safer to stick with bullion stamped with the names of the really big refiners that have nationwide or even a worldwide reputation, for instance, the United States Assay Offices and Mints, United States Metal Refining Company, American Smelting and Refining Company, Engelhard Industries, Handy & Harman, Matthey Bishop Inc., Johnson Matthey Chemical Limited, Sheffield Smelting Company Limited, the Perth Mint of Australia, Metallurgie Hoboken of Belgium, the Royal Canadian Mint, Rand Refinery Limited of South Africa, the Swiss Bank Corporation, and the State Refinery of Moscow.

Even here you will have the expensive assay problem when the time comes to sell your gold bars if you have taken delivery of them.

If you keep your gold in a safe at home it will cost you about

2% of its value annually to insure it against loss. Similar insurance will cost much less if it is stored in a bank safe deposit box—about 50 cents per $1,000 value per year.

You avoid the trouble and expense of assaying altogether if you do not insist on taking delivery of your bullion. For instance, you can buy gold bullion from the Girard Bank, which waives the assaying requirement if you store your gold in the bank's vaults. When you want to sell, the authenticity of your gold is then accepted without question. The minimum amount the bank will accept for storage is ½ ounce and the storage fee is 1% annually of the value of your gold, which is based on the London market price plus 5%. You can save yourself a 6% sales tax if you order from outside Pennsylvania. This bank will store gold coins for you as well as bullion. It stresses that, in either case, gold in its vaults does not come under Federal Deposit Insurance Corporation guarantees (the FDIC is the government agency that insures bank checking and savings accounts up to $40,000 in participating banks).

A prominent Wall Street firm is in the gold business through Dreyfus Gold Deposits, Inc., 767 Fifth Avenue, New York 10022. In this case, you have to make an initial purchase of at least $2,500, after which you can add as little as $100 at a time. Dreyfus bases its bullion price on the daily settlement price of the nearest futures month quoted on the New York Commodity Exchange, one of the major United States futures markets for metals. Dreyfus charges you a 3% commission whenever you buy or sell, plus a storage fee of 10 cents a month per ounce of bullion you own. You can arrange to have your gold delivered to you if you want. If not, it is stored for you in Delaware, a state which has no sales tax.

Merrill Lynch (1 Liberty Plaza, New York 10006), the biggest stock brokerage house in the United States, with branch offices in all 50 states and some foreign countries, offers a plan in which it will store your gold bullion for you. The bullion may be purchased through any Merrill Lynch branch office throughout the United States. It comes in ½, 1, 5, 10, 50 and 100 ounce bars fabricated by Handy & Harman, a major American gold refining firm, with the Merrill Lynch logo stamped on each. Merrill Lynch bases its daily quotations on the morning fix of the

London gold market, but may vary them during the day. To the quotation it adds a sales commission of $2 per ounce plus 5% of the first $5,000 worth purchased. Amounts over $5,000 pay $2 per ounce plus 2%. The sales commission is computed in the same way and is subtracted when the customer sells his gold back to Merrill Lynch. The sales commission when buying or selling thus works out to about 6% for smaller amounts and comes down to 3% on larger quantities. The sales tax depends on the point of delivery—8% if delivered in New York City, for example.

You can store your gold bullion free with Merrill Lynch at the time of writing. If you take delivery of it, one unusual feature of the Merrill Lynch plan is that the firm makes no assay charge when buying back its own gold bars from its customers. You would probably incur such an assay fee, however, if you sold your Merrill Lynch bars to another dealer.

In Canada, the Bank of Nova Scotia, a major financial institution with branches throughout the country, offers a gold certificate of 10 ounces, with a minimum purchase of 20 ounces. The storage fee is about $11 a year per 100 ounces. The bank pledges to keep on hand all the gold that its certificates represent. And with this the wheel has come full circle, back to the days when goldsmiths gave paper receipts for the gold in their safes.

Gold futures

The sort of bullion purchase we have mentioned so far makes sense when you are buying a small quantity of gold, up to 30 ounces or so. Once you get into bigger amounts it may be more economical to buy through the futures markets, of which there are five in the United States and one in Canada. You then pay a commission to a commodity-futures broker, which is generally smaller than the commissions and markups charged by the banks and dealers mentioned so far.

The size of the gold contract you buy varies on each market. On the Chicago Board of Trade it is 96.45 ounces (3 kilos). On the New York Mercantile Exchange and Chicago's Mid-America Commodity Exchange the contract is for 32.15 ounces (1 kilo). The Commodity Exchange Inc. in New York and the Chicago International Monetary Market both have 100-ounce contracts. In Canada, the Winnipeg Commodity Exchange has two different contracts, one for 400 ounces and the other for 100 ounces.

All these markets are primarily for speculators who want to make big profits fast and are willing to take high risks. But they offer opportunities to the conservative investor, too, if he can resist the urge to operate on margin and overextend himself. There are two ways to buy gold bullion on the futures markets: one is to buy a contract in the nearest delivery month and accept delivery of it; the other way is to buy a contract in the farthest possible month and keep rolling it over into ever more distant dates, so that you may never actually take delivery.

In either case your first step is to find a commodities broker—Merrill Lynch, Bache, E.F. Hutton & Co., Reynolds Securities, or any other reputable brokerage firm in your area. You open an account, making whatever deposit is required to do so.

Taking the roll-over method first—in which you buy a contract in the farthest possible delivery month—let us say it is a contract on the New York Mercantile Exchange, simply because trading on this market allows deals farther into the future, about a year and a half, than any of the others. On the New York Mercantile Exchange you could buy a gold contract in April 1977 that would fall due in September 1978. Each contract is for 32.15 troy ounces. (This curious figure is explained by the fact that it equals exactly one kilo, a popular gold weight measure abroad.) When the price of gold is at $170 an ounce, the total value of each 32.15 ounce contract is $5,465.55, but at the time of writing the minimum margin required by the Exchange is only $500 per contract. This means that most speculators are putting up less than 10% of the purchase price, which gives them great financial leverage. If the price of gold goes up to $200 an ounce, for example, the contract will be worth $6,430, which means a profit of $964.45 (less brokerage commissions of about $40) on a $500 investment. Not bad, but it is counterbalanced by high risk. If the price of gold goes down a few dollars the $500 investment will be entirely wiped out, unless you can supply the additional margin required. If you cannot, you will be sold out by the broker. This is speculation, not investment.

If you buy a contract you have to be prepared to meet margin calls from your broker, and if you want to be absolutely sure of not being sold out against your will at a bad time you must have the full purchase price of the contract available at all times. The ideal time to buy is when gold is not in the news limelight and when the gold bullion price is just coasting along at a considerably depressed level from the peak of the most recent monetary crisis and gold-buying fever. You now have 18 months to wait, during which you could cash in at any time by selling your contract whenever the price rises high enough to give you a good profit. During that year and a half—as long as the dollar remains a currency officially inconvertible into gold and inflation is rising into double digits—gold will tend to rise in price. During this year and half, also, there very probably will be one or more events in the world that will send the price of gold soaring, at least temporarily. There is no way of knowing beforehand what the event will be: perhaps another Arab-Israeli war, an Arab oil embargo, a massive shutdown of the South African gold mines, a big devaluation of the dollar or pound sterling, a Russian invasion of Yugoslavia, or a Communist electoral victory in Italy or France. It really does not matter what particular event causes the rush for gold. The important thing is to be holding a gold contract when it happens.

If neither inflation nor dire world happenings have pushed the gold price up dramatically as the expiration date of your contract approaches, you sell it anyway and buy another contract a further 18 months into the future. You thus roll over your investment every year and a half until something happens to make people rush to buy gold.

The other method of buying gold in the futures markets will not give you the feeling that you are constantly backed up against a deadline. In this case you buy a contract in the nearest delivery month, and when the time comes, you take delivery of it, making full payment in cash. Let us suppose that in this case you buy a 100-troy-ounce contract on the Commodity Exchange Inc. in New York. If the price is $150 an ounce, you will get a delivery notice, a bill for $15,000 and a depository receipt. This receipt certifies that you own a 100-troy-ounce bar of .999 fine gold bearing the serial number and identifying stamp of an Exchange-approved refiner. It is held in one of six depositories approved by the Exchange—Chase Manhattan Bank, First National City Bank, Iron Mountain Depository Corporation, Irving Trust Company, Republic National Bank, and Swiss Bank Corporation. All these are located in New York City. You can hold your gold there as long as you pay the storage charge, which is minimal, ranging from $24 to $36 a year for each 100-ounce contract.

Provided you do not remove the gold from the depository, it is accepted automatically as a good delivery on the Commodity Exchange, and so you will incur no assay charge when you sell, which you do by selling a futures contract in the nearest delivery month on the same Exchange.

Taking delivery of gold through a futures contract is also one way of avoiding the sales tax if you do not remove it from the depository. Spokesmen of the commodity markets say the exchanges have "no policy" as regards the sales tax, brokers do not collect it, and so few contracts come down to actual delivery that the government apparently does not bother to enforce collection.

As this is written, it is hard to finance gold bullion held in this way. Banks are discouraged by United States authorities from financing such an "unproductive" asset as gold. So you will have to pay all cash for your bullion, unless your broker agrees to finance your holding, which he is not likely to do. Most brokers prefer in-and-out traders who generate plenty of commissions rather than owners who keep their gold immobilized in a vault.

You can, of course, remove your gold bars from the Exchange-approved depository if you wish, but you will then face storage and insurance risks and costs of your own, and may also incur an assay charge when you sell, as well as the local sales tax.

One other way of acquiring gold bullion is to buy it from Uncle Sam. The United States Treasury, which for 40 years insisted that gold was worth only $35 an ounce, is now willing to sell its gold from time to time at whatever price the traffic will bear, which has been about five times the old official price. The first Treasury auction was held Jan. 6, 1975, when about 750,000 ounces were sold to private investors at an average price of $165. Another 500,000 ounces were auctioned to the public on June 30, 1975 at around the same price. True to its contention that gold no longer has any part to play in the world's monetary system, the Treasury seems determined to part with its gold hoard and has promised further auctions at unspecified future dates.

If the price rise from $35 to $165 seems to you an outrageous profit for the government, just remember that the Treasury refused to sell any gold to American citizens at $35 an ounce for 40 years. Now that it *is* willing to sell its bullion at a much higher price, you might reflect that when you buy you are giving the Treasury paper dollars and the Treasury is giving you solid gold. Over a period of years you are likely to get the better end of the bargain.

These Treasury sales are sporadic, and apparently timed to embarrass the supporters of monetary gold, such as the government of France. If you want to be alerted to the auctions ahead of time, write to the General Services Administration, Metals Branch, Office of Stockpile Disposal, 2000 L Street, N.W., Washington D.C. 20036 and ask to be put on the mailing list for gold auctions.

Inflation, taxes, confiscation

We have been talking about gold primarily as a way of protecting your assets in a period of runaway inflation. Your gold coins or bullion will yield you no dividends or interest, but the rising price of gold will easily compensate for that. When inflation is running into double digits, say 12% a year, it is almost impossible to find a safe investment in the stock or bond markets that will give you the 18% yield you need to preserve your capital against erosion and provide some income as well. Indeed, it is not even necessary for inflation to hit double digits most of the time. *Fortune* magazine found in 1976 that no conventional financial asset kept pace with inflation over the 1965-75 decade, only at the end of which were double digits attained. Even with reinvestment of dividends or interest, investors in stocks, bonds, and Treasury bills all ended 1975 poorer—in terms of real purchasing power—than they were ten years before.

You will not have to worry about paying income tax on your gold bullion investment. However, you *will* be liable for capital gains taxes when you sell your gold at a higher price, as measured in inflationary dollars. The way you choose to buy gold bullion or coins will affect the completeness of the paper records of your transactions for tax purposes. Many coin dealers like to deal on a cash and carry basis, cut their paperwork to a minimum, don't identify buyers or sellers on their sales slips, and some may keep no records at all on small transactions. Banks and brokerage firms are more closely regulated by the authorities, are required to keep their books strictly, have to keep microfilms of checks above $5,000, and must report to the U.S. government such things as their clients' dividend and interest payments.

Many gold investors are also uneasily aware of the possibility of confiscation. In 1934 President Roosevelt required all American citizens to turn in their gold holdings to the government at the then official price of $20.67 an ounce. He then raised the gold price to $35 an ounce, making a nice profit for the government but not for the investors who had their gold expropriated.

Some gloomy people even foresee the possibility of a war, which the United States might lose, and then a situation like post-war Germany in which the pre-World War III dollar would simply be abolished altogether. The advantages of holding gold at such a time—preferably with no traceable record of its purchase—would be obvious. This means holding gold coins in a secret cache at home or holding them in safekeeping in some neutral nation abroad.

Buying and holding gold abroad

There are banks overseas, in Switzerland and other countries, that consider themselves under no obligation to report anything to United States government authorities, leaving this entirely up to you. Swiss banks, in fact, will resist any kind of foreign official prying into their customers' accounts, since they are liable to criminal prosecution themselves if they violate the strict Swiss banking secrecy laws. They will only make revelations of a client's affairs under a Swiss court order proving criminal conduct by the customer, which is to say practically never, unless something like a kidnapping, extortion or bank fraud is involved. Tax evasion is not included by the Swiss in this category.

There are hundreds of banks in Switzerland, many of them eager to deal with foreign customers. One which buys, stores and sells gold bullion or coins for its customers is the Union Bank of Switzerland, Bahnhofstrasse 45, 8021, Zurich, Switzerland. This is a giant bank, one of the three biggest in Switzerland, but it is not at all snooty about accepting small clients. Once you open an account it may, for example, take your order for 10 British sovereigns, worth perhaps $500. When dealing with a Swiss bank you have no need to worry about counterfeit coins, because the Swiss bank is the actual seller of the coins or bullion to you, and it cannot very well claim any of the items are counterfeit when it buys them back from its own vaults later on.

The Foreign Commerce Bank, Bellariastrasse 82, 8038 Zurich, is another Swiss bank that can correspond with you in English. Most of its sales literature and all of its bank documentation are in English, so there are no language problems. This is a smaller bank, but it aims at a rather more well-heeled clientele and it probably can give you more personal attention than one of the Swiss Big Three. Foreign Commerce Bank has a minimum investment of $2,500 in gold bullion or coins, charges a brokerage commission of ½% on sales and purchases, and collects a storage and insurance fee of 0.20% per year for gold coins and 0.25% for gold bullion which it keeps in safe custody.

Buying and holding gold in a Swiss bank thus offers significant advantages. Your gold is in a neutral nation that is unlikely to be involved in any war; you do not have to worry about buying counterfeit gold; you avoid paying United States sales taxes when buying gold; you do not have your gold made inaccessible if there should ever be a general bank holiday in the

United States (as occurred in 1933, when American banks were closed for weeks); you do not have to worry about theft as you would if you kept your gold at home in a safe. One major disadvantage is that an airmail letter may take four days to get to Switzerland, and the reply another four days to reach the United States. In unsettled times the price of gold can move dramatically in four to eight days, so you would be well advisted to specify in your letters the minimum or maximum price at which you want to buy or sell.

One final possibility in buying gold is to open a bank account in which your balance is not denominated in American dollars, Swiss francs or any other currency but reckoned directly in gold. Such an account is offered by Bankhaus Deak, Rathausstrasse 20, A-1010, Vienna, Austria—another neutral nation. A similar account may be opened with Deak National Bank, Fleischmanns, N.Y. 12430. In this case you might consider that you have cut the umbilical cord to all the world's paper currencies and are on your own private gold standard, standing entirely apart from the global monetary inflation.

Gold mining stocks

If you bought gold at $100 an ounce in 1973 and sold it at $150 an ounce in 1974, you had a 50% gain. For the mine that produced the gold, the percentage gain was probably much greater. If its cost of production was $50 an ounce, for instance, the same advance in the selling price doubled its profits, from $50 to $100 per ounce. For more than 40 years there were gold mines that sold gold at the officially fixed price of $35 an ounce. They managed to stay in business, and some even prospered. Now they are selling the metal at a free market price that has ranged from $128 to $195 in 1974 to 1976. Their costs of production have risen with inflation, but most of that increase went into fatter profits.

This financial leverage has given investors in gold mining stocks fantastic gains. ASA Ltd., a closed-end trust, quoted on the New York Stock Exchange, rocketed from a low of $4½ per share in 1960 to a high of $104½ in 1974. This trust has a portfolio of about two dozen South African gold mines. With a more than twenty-fold gain in fourteen years, it beat the much-touted

growth stocks at their own game in the same period, outperforming even IBM, Polaroid and Avon, the darlings of the
growth-stock cult.

Before you jump to buy gold shares, however, it is well to recall that this is by no means the same thing as buying gold bullion or coins. It is a totally different investment.

If you buy the shares of an individual mine, such as Homestake Mining, the largest United States gold producer, you run
all the business risks to which that company is liable. The mine
may be flooded. Management may make mistakes, such as
promising (it has actually happened) a big part of any gold price
increase to the workers in labor contract benefits.

You could buy Campbell Red Lake or Dome Mines Ltd., two
of the biggest Canadian gold mining companies, or any number
of Canadian penny gold mining stocks. Some of these had Canadian government subsidies, which they forfeited when the price
of gold went up. Some have long lives ahead of them with big
reserves of ore still in the ground, while others are likely to be
worked out in a few years. Among the penny stocks, fraud, misrepresentation, and manipulation of stock prices are perennial
problems.

In South Africa you have the choice of dozens of publicly
owned gold mines, many of which are traded in the United
States. You buy these through your United States stock broker
in the same way as you buy any American stocks.

ASA Ltd. (NYSE) is a pre-packaged portfolio of individual
South African mines. It tends to exaggerate the price swings of
gold mining stocks, selling at a premium over its net asset value
when the gold bullion price is soaring, and sinking to a discount
when the gold price is slumping on world markets.

Anglo-American Gold Investment, quoted over-the-counter in
the United States, is the world's biggest concentration of gold
mining assets. The company has holdings in many of the major
South African mines, with a total value of about $1.5 billion.

Buffelsfontein is South Africa's biggest uranium producer as
well as a major gold mining company.

Gold Fields of South Africa is a big outfit with holdings in
major South African mines.

Individual South African mines available to American investors include Hartebeestfontein, Kloof, President Brand, President Steyn, St. Helena, Vaal Reefs, West Driefontein, Western Deep Levels, and others. Many of these mines have an added attraction in the fact that one of their secondary products is uranium, the price of which has increased as dramatically as the price of gold in the early 1970s.

South African gold mines are thus in a strong position, but South Africa presents its own special political perils. The risks include the disaffection of a majority black population kept rigidly apart from the ruling white minority by the segregationist apartheid policy, and an atmosphere of unrelenting hostility fomented by black African states in the United Nations and other international bodies. This is a country where white miners are paid salaries eight times higher than their black fellow employees. Many black miners are immigrants from neighboring black states, and to compound the potential risk of social strife, black nationalist regimes have now taken over the former Portuguese colonies on South Africa's borders. They can be expected to give aid and comfort to any black subversion against the South African government.

If you bet too heavily on South African gold mining stocks, it is not beyond the bounds of possibility that some day the South African racial and political situation may blow up, with the mines sabotaged, closed down, or nationalized. The price of gold could then shoot up due to the lost South African production, but even so you would be a big loser if the price of mining shares went down the drain.

Because of the extraneous risks involved in buying gold mining shares, it would be wise to recognize two things. First, buying gold shares is not the same thing as buying gold itself. It may be more profitable but it involves extra risks. And secondly, it is only prudent to diversify those risks as much as you can. This means buying ASA Ltd., with its portfolio of two dozen different mines, rather than any individual South African gold mine. It means buying shares in American and Canadian mines, say Homestake and Campbell Red Lake, so as to avoid being entirely exposed to the peculiar risks of South Africa. As further measures of diversification one could buy shares of gold mining companies active in other areas, such as Rosario Resources, a company quoted on the New York Stock Exchange that produces silver and gold in Central America and in the Dominican Republic.

For the investor who has no time or inclination to pick his own stocks, there are also mutual funds which specialize in gold mining shares. They include International Investors Inc., 420 Lexington Ave., New York 10017; United Services Fund Inc., P.O. Box 2098, Universal City, Texas 78148 (a no-load fund); SAFIT, a Swiss-based mutual fund with a portfolio of about 60 South African companies, more than half of them in gold mining (sold by the Union Bank of Switzerland, Bahnhofstrasse 45, Zurich).

Gold: An "unproductive" investment?

One common objection to gold is that it is a "non-productive" investment, that it does nothing for the economy. To people who think this way there is something reprehensible about keeping gold under the mattress, in a bank safety deposit box, or in a wall safe at home. One is then withholding potentially productive capital from the nation's economic lifestream.

Ignore such reasoning. It starts out from the idea that it makes no economic sense to dig gold out of one hole in South Africa and then bury it again in another hole at Fort Knox. If the gold lying unused in Fort Knox builds public confidence in the value of the American dollar and thus promotes a stable means of exchange, then it is performing a useful function. Once the gold is not there, the chances of hyper-inflation grow immeasurably greater. And in times of runaway inflation your attempts to make "productive" investments in stocks and bonds will reduce your capital towards zero in short order. The economy, meanwhile, will go to pot anyway, with you or without you. It might as well be without you.

The ultimate standard for judging the usefulness of your investment is the satisfaction it gives you. If gold gives you peace of mind at a time when paper money is depreciating daily, then invest in gold. There are things that economists cannot measure and do not even attempt to measure. About half the nation's work is done by housewives who get no pay at all for doing the most essential work of all—raising the next generation, cooking, cleaning, shopping, washing, nursing, teaching, housekeeping. Ask an economist how his calculations of the gross national product would work out if housewives were paid $200 a week, $300 a week or $500 a week. (According to the Social Security Administration, the average American housewife's economic value was $4,705 a year in 1972.) Ask him what would make a bigger difference to the GNP: removing all the housewives from the economy or subtracting your investment in "unproductive" gold. And then ignore his answer anyway. What happens to a mismanaged and miscalculated economy is beside the point. What is relevant is what happens to you.

French peasants apparently know this. Witness their atavistic distrust of paper money. So do the French middle classes, perhaps through a more conscious study of the history of their country's currency. Frenchmen hold billions of dollars worth of gold bullion and coins as a sort of financial fallout shelter against the periodic catastrophes of paper money.

The French government is well aware of this and pays constant lip service to the essential role of gold in the world monetary system. It also issues paper currency incessantly as all governments do, but it is aware of the problem as other governments are not. France even offers a government security that pays interest and is made inflation-proof by being valued in gold coins.

French Pinay bonds

A curious hybrid combining the features of a gold-coin investment with those of a fixed-interest paper security is the Pinay bond, which was issued in the 1950s by French Finance Minister Antoine Pinay and paid 3½% interest on its nominal value of 100 francs. It has now been converted into the Emprunt 4½ 1973—the 4½% Loan of 1973.

This security is indexed to the price of the gold Napoleon 20-franc coin, and is thus protected against the depreciation of paper currencies. The interest rate is not so indexed, however, and became minuscule as the rising price of the gold Napoleon carried the price of the bond up with it to seven or eight times its face value. (The Napoleon sold for about $13 as recently as

1971, and in mid-1976 fetches around $50). Interest on the bond is paid on June 1 each year and is exempt from French income tax.

You might consider this as a gold investment on which you receive a small return instead of paying the small storage charges you would incur by buying gold bullion and storing it in a bank.

The bond has other interesting features, however, arising from the fact that the Napoleon sells for a premium above its gold content of about one-fifth of a troy ounce.

The premium on the coin market is usually around 30%, but it sometimes rises higher and in fact went as high as 115% in mid-1976. You might find it appealing to reflect that if this premium were maintained for three months or so, the French government would in effect be obligated to pay you the current price of gold bullion plus a 115% markup for your bond. This might be a good time to sell.

On the other hand, you may well pause before buying these bonds when the Napoleon is selling at a 115% premium over its gold content. The premium may well drop to 30% again and bring the price of the bond down with it. (The premium is easy enough to calculate. You multiply the dollar price of the Napoleon by five to get the price per gold ounce, $250 when the coin costs $50, and compare the result with the current dollar price per ounce of gold bullion.)

The French government calculates the price of the bond twice a year, May 15 and November 15, by taking the average price of the Napoleon on the previous 100 business days, multiplying by 100 and dividing by 36. This is the official price for redeeming the bonds for the next six months.

There is also a market price, which fluctuates, is usually lower, and is quoted daily on the Paris Stock Exchange, where you can buy or sell your bonds like any other stock or bond. The price here is, of course, determined by the free market forces of supply and demand.

The Emprunt 4½ 1973 is redeemable by equal annuities on June 1 each year to 2001, but from July 1, 1983, onward the French government may redeem all or part of the loan. France has no restrictions preventing foreigners from buying these bonds, and Americans may thus deal freely in them as far as

French foreign exchange regulations are concerned.

You could buy or sell through a French bank or stockbroker. One way to go about it would be through Credit Industriel et Commercial, (CIC) one of the biggest commercial banks in France. Write to the bank's trust department, Departement des Etudes Financieres et de la Gestion, 33 Avenue Hoche, 75008 Paris. Or else contact one of the bank's many branches throughout France. These branches offer the same sort of services that a commercial bank in the United States provides and on the same sort of scale. It is not necessary to be a millionaire—transactions of $500 or $1,000 are welcome.

Also, an account with any branch of Credit Industriel et Commercial or any other big French bank may be useful to you in dealing in other French bonds and stocks, as well as Eurobonds—all of which are covered in later chapters of this book. The bank's trust department could steer you towards a branch that is able to correspond with you in English.

5

Silver: Another asset
to protect you
against runaway inflation

Silver may give you even better protection than gold if the
present paper monetary system collapses into runaway inflation in the years ahead. But it presents some problems for the
investor. Above all, it is bulky and troublesome to store in your
own vault or safe in any significant amount.

For more than 40 years, Americans who wanted to buy
precious metals were not allowed to own gold bullion and had
to buy silver bullion instead. As it turned out, the gold ownership ban ended in the United States just as inflation showed
signs of hitting the runaway stage in 1974. In Great Britain,
however, the unhappy subjects of Her Majesty Queen Elizabeth II were still forbidden to own gold bars or imported gold
coins, and British inflation was running above 25% a year. A
British citizen who wanted to protect himself against the constant devaluation of his pounds sterling by investing in precious
metals had to invest in silver or perhaps in platinum.

This was one reason why silver prices tended to do better
than gold in 1975, and probably will continue to do so for as long
as the British pound gallops towards inflationary extinction and

the British gold ban remains in force.

According to many experts, the outlook remains much brighter for silver than for gold—for the simple reason that worldwide demand for silver has been constantly outstripping the supply for years.

Commodities expert Charles R. Stahl says, "The largest profit potential among the precious metals is in silver; the second best in platinum, and gold is a poor third."

Stahl, publisher of *Green's Commodity Market Comments*, a fortnightly market newsletter (565 Fifth Avenue, New York 10001), predicted in mid-1975 that "over a period of two to five years, I can see silver prices as high as $8 to $10 per ounce" (more than double its price at the time). Stahl reasoned that "unlike gold, silver is a commodity in short supply. Year-in, year-out, the world yearly consumption exceeds the yearly production. In 1974, the gap amounted to 208 million ounces." In 1975 the production fell short by 155 million ounces, according to Handy and Harman, a major American precious metals firm.

Since the 1950s the industrial demand for silver has been increasing at a rate of about 6% a year, but the supply has not kept pace. By 1974 silver production in the non-communist world was 240 million ounces, while consumption was nearly twice as much at 448 million ounces. In 1975 the figures were 235 million and 390 million ounces.

Obviously, a yearly deficit of 150 to 200 million ounces implies not only a constantly rising price—it means that eventually we are going to run out of silver. However, the deficiency has been made up in recent years from other sources than newly mined metal. The United States government sold off a large part of its huge silver stockpile; some silver scrap is recycled; private investors have been tempted by rising prices to sell off some of their hoards; and silver coins have been melted down.

In the end, of course, the existing supply will be exhausted if the yearly shortfall continues, and then the mining of new silver will have to supply the entire market. It is the anticipation of this situation that keeps the price of silver rising.

The price of silver, like the price of gold, was held at an artificially fixed level for years by the United States government.

Then, as its silver stocks dwindled and the floods of paper money rolled on, Washington lost control of the situation. On May 18, 1967 the United States Treasury withdrew its standing offer to sell silver to all comers at $1,2929 per troy ounce.

The price of silver zoomed 100% on a tide of speculation, then lost nearly all that gain two years later, beginning a series of wild fluctuations that over the years, however, have shown a consistent upward trend. In February 1974 silver bullion hit an all-time high of $6.70 per troy ounce. In 1975 it dropped to a range of $4 to $5 an ounce.

Silver supply

Silver is found mostly near the earth's surface, down to a depth of about 200 feet. The deeper you dig, the thinner the silver-bearing veins become, which means that in the course of centuries the silver lodes in the Old World have been pretty much exhausted. Spain was famous for its silver mines during the days of the Roman Empire, and Asia Minor produced great quantities in even more ancient times, but those mines are just about worked out.

The big producers nowadays are all in the New World. Mexico is the leader, with 42 million ounces mined in 1975, followed by Canada with 38 million, Peru 36 million, and the United States with 34 million ounces. These four countries produce two-thirds of the non-communist world's newly-mined silver.

But the days are long gone when the Spanish conquistadores shoveled the metal out of the South American silver mountain at Potosi and American miners spaded it out of open pits from the fabulous Comstock lode in Nevada. The chances of making such rich finds diminish year by year.

Meanwhile, about 75% of the silver being mined today is only a byproduct of mines that are in business mainly to produce copper, lead, tin and zinc. What this means is that the supply of new silver is relatively inelastic and unresponsive to price increases. If the price of the mine's main, base metal product does not go up, even a steep increase in the price of silver still may not make it worthwhile to increase production since silver represents only a small percentage of total sales. An economic recession or depression thus tends to cut back the supply of new silver because it reduces the industrial demand for base metals.

There is also a fair chance of the silver-producing countries getting together to push up the price of silver by means of a producers' cartel. In 1975 Mexico and Peru started negotiations to set up an association of silver producing and exporting countries. They were following the example of worldwide cartels already formed by nations that produce bauxite, coffee, copper, tin and other commodities. The big league in this global monopoly game was of course the Organization of Petroleum Exporting Countries, which managed to quadruple the price of oil in 1973. However, it seemed doubtful that the silver producers could achieve such success. One of the main concerns of Peru and Mexico seemed to be that the United States government would dump its remaining stockpiled silver on the market (about 148 million ounces) and drive the price down as a sort of sideshow to the Treasury's anti-gold campaign.

Silver hoards

Probably the world's biggest silver hoard is in India, where Hindu women own most of their personal wealth in the form of silver jewelry. There is no accurate figure of the amount of silver in India, but according to one estimate it may amount to a staggering five billion ounces. This would be the equivalent of more than 20 years of world production and could obviously have a huge impact on the price of silver if it were all disgorged at one time. This seems unlikely, however. A traditionalist society accustomed for centuries to measuring personal wealth in gems and precious metals is not about to let go of its time-honored financial security when the paper rupee is ravaged daily by the inflationary policy of a socialist government.

For many years the Indian government banned the export of silver, but millions of ounces were apparently smuggled out anyway when the price began to rise. Contraband silver shipments out of the Indian subcontinent hit an estimated high of around 25 million ounces in 1973. The Indian authorities realized they were losing a lot of customs revenue and in 1974 legalized exports. The outflow then rose to perhaps 60 million ounces through legal and illegal channels. This may have been one of the major reasons why the world price of silver dropped from a high of $6.70 in early 1974 to around $4 an ounce some months later.

Silver demand

The United States is the world's biggest guzzler of silver, using up 173 million ounces in 1974—more than a third of world consumption. West Germany, Japan and Great Britain are next in line, with about 143 million ounces consumed among them.

Photography accounts for about 27% of United States demand for silver, but the metal is also widely used in radio and electronic equipment, appliances and computers. Electronic usage represents about 21% of demand. The use of silver in jewelry has spurted sharply in recent years as the price of gold soared, but jewelry still takes only about 3% of total American demand. Sterling silverware accounts for about 13% and electroplated tableware about 8% of the total. Makers of silver medallions and commemorative coins are also important users of silver, with about 12% of the total. In some other countries regular silver coinage is important, too. Canada, which was preparing silver coinage for the 1976 Olympic Games in Montreal, used fifteen million ounces of silver for coins in 1974. West Germany used seven million ounces and Austria four million in the same year.

The supply-demand equation

In the silver market, as in all things, the future is always an unknown quantity. The growth of the photographic industry was unforeseeable in 1900, when the consumption of silver for photo film was practically zero. The future probably is even more unpredictable now since the pace of technological advance is quicker. Perhaps some genius in the Kodak or Agfa research laboratories will figure out a way of recording pictures without using any silver at all.

Perhaps new uses—say the solar energy industry—will require even more silver than photography does now. According to Dr. A.F. Hildebrandt of the University of Houston Solar Energy Laboratory, energy from the sun may produce up to 20% of United States energy needs by the year 2000. And silver is the ideal metal for this industry of the future. Silver-backed mirrors would collect the sun's heat in a system requiring about 32,000 ounces of silver per square mile of mirror area. A system providing 20% of U.S. energy needs would require 500 million ounces of silver—about 15 years' worth of current United States production. A pilot plant is scheduled for 1979, and full-scale production may come by 1985. But all this is conjecture and speculation; it will not affect the price of silver today.

The rationale for buying silver at this time is the same as it is for gold. Both are scarce materials and it is hard to envisage any sudden inflationary expansion of the supply. As long as gold and silver are scarce and difficult to dig out of the ground, they are a better bet than paper money, where there is no limitation on the supply of dollar bills except the self-restraint of the politicians in charge of the money supply. As George Bernard Shaw once noted, "If you have a choice between gold and the good sense of the gentlemen running the government, you would do well to vote for gold."

The same argument applies in spades to silver, since consumption is constantly, chronically outrunning production.

How to invest in silver

You have several ways of investing in silver. You can buy silver bullion in the United States or abroad, silver futures contracts in London, New York or Chicago, silver coins, or shares in silver mines. Each has its advantages and drawbacks. In general terms you might say that bullion is for the wealthy conservative investor, futures are for well-heeled speculators, coins for the small investor, and shares for the man who already knows his way around in the stock market.

Silver bullion

Silver bullion is bulky. The Commodity Exchange Inc. in New York, one of the biggest silver futures markets in the world, accepts only bars of 1,000 or 1,100 troy ounces. A 1,000 troy ounce bar is about 13 inches long, 4½ inches wide, 4½ inches high and it weighs about 68½ avoirdupois pounds. You would need a good-sized bank safety deposit box to store one of these bars, which would be worth $5,000 when the price of silver is $5 an ounce. So you are immediately involved with storage problems and costs that do not arise when you own gold, a much more compact form of wealth.

Even if you store your silver at home and are willing to run the risk of burglary and theft, you will need a large safe to store any significant quantity of silver bullion.

Engelhard Industries, a major American refiner of precious metals, sells ingots of .999 pure silver in sizes of 1, 5, 10, 25, 50, 100 and 500 troy ounces. They are stamped with the Engelhard hallmark, weight and fineness. The smaller the size you buy, the higher your proportionate cost of mail and delivery charges, so you will pay a lower price per ounce for a larger size ingot. The address is Engelhard Minerals & Chemicals Corp., Pine & Dunham Streets, Attleboro, Massachusetts 02703.

ASARCO, another major American producer of silver, sells refined silver bars of 50, 100, 500 and 1000 troy ounces. They are guaranteed 99.9% pure silver. Deliveries take about two weeks. The address is 150 Charles Street, Newark, New Jersey 07101. The price is as quoted daily in the *Wall Street Journal* plus an overage of 60 cents per troy ounce, plus 5 cents an ounce for handling and shipping, plus freight charges and sales taxes.

The accumulation of charges means that the price of silver will have to rise substantially before you can make a profit.

You can also buy silver from the United States government whenever Washington decides to auction off surplus silver from its stockpile. The minimum amount the government will sell you is usually 5,000 troy ounces, for which you have to pay all cash—an investment of $25,000 when silver is at $5 an ounce. For further details write to the General Services Administration, Office of Information, 18th & F Streets, Washington, D.C. 20405.

In each case you are going to have a storage problem, and a resale problem, both of which you can avoid by buying through the futures markets.

Silver futures

Silver was the most heavily traded commodity on American futures markets in 1975. The main reason, analysts said, was a growing number of speculators seeking refuge against worldwide inflation.

Silver bullion futures are traded in the United States mainly on the Commodity Exchange Inc. in New York and the Chicago Board of Trade. In both markets the contract is for 5,000 troy ounces of silver, and the delivery dates run about a year and a half into the future. In New York, trading is for delivery in the current calendar month and the two following months, as well as January, March, May, July, September and December, covering altogether a seventeen-month period.

There is heavy speculative trading in both markets, with hundreds and even thousands of contracts changing hands daily. The key word here is *speculation*. The minimum original margin required on the New York Commodity Exchange is $1,000 for a 5,000 ounce contract, which is worth $25,000 when the price of silver is at $5 an ounce.

The price per contract thus has only to rise $1,000, to $26,000, and you have doubled your money. It has only to fall $1,000, to $24,000, and your $1,000 margin is completely wiped out.

The silver futures market is not only a wild and woolly place where speculators make and lose fortunes in a matter of days; it has also become a playground for Texas oil billionaires, who operate on an awesome scale that makes the short-term risks even scarier and more unpredictable. In 1974 Nelson Bunker Hunt, heir to a Texas oil fortune, reportedly had $200 million invested in silver futures contracts. He was reported to have actually taken delivery of 40 million ounces of the metal, which was more than half the silver stored in the New York Commodity Exchange licensed depositories and vaults, and the equivalent of more than one year's production of all United States silver mines. With so much hanging on the buy or sell decisions of one man, the silver futures market becomes an unpredictable affair indeed over the short run.

The only interest these futures markets have for us at this point is that they provide a reasonably economical way of buying silver bullion at the going price if you are buying at least 5,000 ounces at a time. You can then buy a futures contract in the nearest delivery month, pay cash for it and accept delivery. Hardly any futures speculators ever take delivery of their silver—they just cancel it out by selling a futures contract. Practically all their deals are mere paper transactions in which no silver actually changes hands. More than 95% of all futures contracts are cancelled out in this way, with only cash changing hands from the winning speculator to the loser.

However the silver bullion contracted for is in storage in warehouses approved by the exchanges. In the case of the Commodity Exchange, all its licensed warehouses are located in New York City, which is the largest United States silver trading center.

The licensed depositories or vaults (Chase Manhattan Bank, First National City Bank, Iron Mountain Depository Corp., Irving Trust Co., and Republic National Bank) are in fact bank vaults that are judged by the Exchange to be sufficiently well-guarded to insure against theft. The Exchange also makes periodic random tests to insure that the silver contracted for is there and that it meets the minimum standard of .999 fineness.

You can keep your silver in these warehouses for a small storage fee (about $90 a year for each 5,000 ounce contract), receiving a depository or vault receipt as proof of ownership. Or if you are able to make some better storage arrangement yourself, you can insist in physical delivery of your bullion. A buyer located far from New York can even execute an Exchange for Physical, or EFP, which means he sells his futures contract to a silver supplier, who in turn provides him with the equivalent amount of bullion, thus avoiding the expense of transportation and handling from the Exchange warehouse. An EFP can be arranged through a commodities broker and is a common transation by which silver fabricators take delivery of the silver they need for their manufacturing operations. By leaving your silver in the Exchange depository, you avoid the necessity of paying the local sales tax—a considerable amount in New York, where this tax is 8%. Apparently this tax loophole was left because so few futures contracts come down to actual delivery that the authorities never got around to taxing them.

In order to trade on the futures market you have to sign a "margin agreement" with a brokerage house and deposit the necessary margin funds for your anticipated trading. From there on the broker handles all the technical details of the futures transactions, presents confirmations in writing of each purchase and sale, and provides you with regular monthly statements of your transactions.

If you are active in the stock market, your own stockbroker may be able to help you, as many stock brokerage firms are also in the commodities field. Some of the biggest firms in the business are: Bache & Co., 100 Gold Street, New York 10038; Merrill Lynch, 1 Liberty Plaza, New York 10006; E.F. Hutton & Co., 1 Battery Park Plaza, New York 10004; and Reynolds Securities Inc., 120 Broadway, New York 10005.

All of them have branch offices throughout the United States and some in foreign countries as well.

Thus you can buy a silver bullion futures contract in the nearest delivery month on the New York Commodity Exchange, 81 Broad Street, New York 10004, or the Chicago Board of Trade (141 W. Jackson St., Chicago, Ill. 60604) which can give you further details on their operations.

You can make full payment for it and take delivery, but in reasonably normal times—that is with inflation under the double digit level—this is not a particularly recommendable investment. Craig Dixon, a commodities executive with Loeb Rhoades and Co., observes that "you'd have to be crazy to buy silver bullion outright and store it in the Exchange warehouse. You'd lose the interest on the money you have tied up and you'd pay storage charges. In normal times you might as well buy the farthest delivery on the futures market and keep rolling your investment over every year and a half."

In this case, of course, you would only invest a small margin payment of your own funds and get high leverage to jack up your profits. The storage and insurance costs would remain about the same, as they are built into the price of the futures contract through a generally increasing premium that rises for the more distant deliveries. The risk of a futures contract is higher because you have to be prepared at all times to meet a margin call—otherwise your broker may sell you out against your will at a very bad time when the price of silver drops temporarily. And with a contract expiring at a definite date, there is always the feeling of being backed up against a deadline, the fear of losing in the short run even though the price of silver rises in the long run. Also, to avoid being wiped out, like most speculators, by a small, transitory downturn in the silver price, you would have to keep sufficient funds available to meet possible margin calls far in excess of the minimum margin payment.

Whether you hold silver bullion or a silver futures contract, in times of reasonable price stability in the economy you are betting on the fluctuations of a metal that is merely one more industrial commodity. In times of high inflation, however, the odds rise in your favor. This is because you are betting that silver—a commodity with a finite supply—will increase in value against a potentially infinite tide of paper money that is demonstrating its growing worthlessness precisely through double-digit inflation.

Remember that we are discussing silver here, whether in bullion form or as a futures contract, strictly as a means of protecting your assets against the ravages of double-digit inflation.

Financing your purchase at such a time will not only force you to pay double-digit interest rates; it will also subject you to the vagaries of the inflation rate, thus adding an extra risk. Let us suppose, for example, that you have bought a futures contract through the New York Commodity Exchange, have decided to take delivery of it and are considering whether to finance your holding. The bank involved—let us say one of the Exchange's depositories, Chase Manhattan or First National City—will handle all the details of storage and insurance for you for a small fee. You are now the outright owner of 5,000 ounces of physical silver—five bars of bullion, certified 99.9% pure, with the stamp and serial number of the United States Mint or some refining company with a worldwide reputation. Your carrying charges are very low—about 25 cents a day, or $90 a year, on a contract worth $20,000 or so in 1976.

At the time of writing it is next to impossible to get financing for silver holdings from American banks—they are actively discouraged from such deals by the United States authorities. But at some time it may become possible. We are considering a time of double-digit inflation.

If you finance your silver holdings—borrowing say 50% of the price from the bank (or whatever percentage the bank will lend you at that time)—your interest payments will increase your carrying charges. The prime rate of interest will be in double digits, and the bank will charge you several percentage points above the prime rate. In Britain, where the inflation had already reached in 1975 the type of situation we are considering here, London banks were charging more than 20% to finance silver holdings.

It is true that you get more leverage this way and that your interest costs are tax deductible, but your risks are significantly increased. By borrowing to finance your silver bullion you are in effect betting on a constant increase in the rate of inflation, which may not be a safe bet. If you pay 20% interest, anticipating a 30% inflation over the coming year, a drop in the inflation rate to 10% will hurt you badly, even if it is only a temporary drop.

The safest course is just to own the bullion outright, and it is also the cheapest, involving minimal storage charges. When the time comes to sell, your natural outlet is the same futures market where you bought the bullion, as you are holding silver that has already passed inspection in an approved warehouse and is therefore a good delivery on the Exchange. All you have to do is call your broker and tell him to sell a contract in the nearest delivery month.

Commodity brokers tend to deride the idea of owning silver bullion outright at any time. "If you think the country's whole financial situation is going to come apart," says Dixon, "then you might as well take your bullion out of the Exchange warehouse and put it in a hole in the ground of your own."

Of course, nothing is really impossible. It is, at least, conceivable that the government could confiscate all the silver held in exchange warehouses, or that calamities such as war or revolution could destroy all semblance of financial order for a time. Not very likely perhaps, but in the aftermath of such a catastrophe, it would be nice to have some silver bars stashed away in the cellar to ensure one's financial recovery when things got going again.

Some investors whose view of the future is positively cataclysmic may have taken this precaution. Others have found a similar solution—owning silver abroad.

Owning silver abroad

Whatever you can do with silver in the United States can also be done overseas, particularly in London, one of the world's largest and most active silver markets.

Owning silver abroad is useful for people who want the United States government to know as little as possible about their wealth and financial operations. London commodity brokers make a point of not passing on information about their customers' business to the tax authorities of foreign countries, including the United States. This is in their own self-interest, as a good deal of their trade comes from abroad.

London banks also advance up to 80% of the purchase price, but the interest rate is high—more than 10% in dollars in 1976 and 20% or more in the inflation-ridden pound sterling.

In London, as in New York or Chicago, the advantage of owning bullion in storage in this way, as opposed to a contract in one of the silver futures markets, is that you have no deadline for selling your silver. Forced selling dates always seem to come at the most awkward moment, when prices are going through a temporary sinking spell.

The cost of storing your bullion in Europe is small. A bank will usually charge around ¼% per year for storage and insurance of your silver in its vaults.

Purchase and storage of silver in Europe is the most convenient method for those who want no record of their transactions available to the United States authorities, but Washington keeps an eye on money entering and leaving the country. Financial institutions are required by the Treasury to keep records for five years of all transfers into or out of the United

States of more than $10,000. Up to 1974 the cutoff was only $5,000, which seems to indicate that the authorities are out to catch big fish, such as narcotics dealers and mobsters. There is apparently not too much official interest for now in the thousands of people who quite legitimately move a few thousand dollars in and out of the country. But this may change in the event of an American economic crisis or if the international situation turns ugly.

For the time being, transfers abroad of less than $10,000 are less likely to attract official scrutiny. There are other precautions, such as buying silver through a Swiss bank. A bank in Switzerland buys the silver on the London market through a customer's account that is shielded from the United States authorities' possible inquiries by the strict Swiss bank-secrecy laws. All that the silver broker in London knows—and the British tax authorities as well—is that the purchase was made by a Swiss bank.

It is then up to the American buyer of the silver to decide whether he is going to declare the ownership of the bullion to the Internal Revenue Service when he completes his yearly income tax form.

The precaution of buying silver abroad is not only for Mafia bosses and others who want to keep their ill-gotten gains from Uncle Sam. There also are people who fear that buying silver in the United States will leave a written record, such as a futures contract or a warehouse receipt, that will defeat the whole purpose of buying the precious metal in the first place.

In a sudden national emergency the United States government might well demand that citizens hand over all their silver to the government at a price arbitrarily and probably unfairly fixed by Washington.

An outbreak of war would not be necessary for this to happen. Uncle Sam did precisely this in peacetime with regard to gold when President Franklin Roosevelt banned gold ownership by Americans in 1934. All citizens were required to turn in their gold at $20.67 a troy ounce, and then the government decreed the new official price to be $35 an ounce. Those who had bought gold as a protection against the uncertainties of paper money were stripped of their own legally owned wealth by their own government through a measure whose legality was upheld by the Supreme Court, despite a constitutional ban against the issue of fiat paper money by the government. Some habitually law-abiding people, once impoverished by governmental acts of this nature, tend to regard the laws and the Constitution with some skepticism when it comes to protecting their assets.

In other sections of this book we have given the names and addresses of a few of the biggest Swiss and British banks, some of which may also serve the investor in silver bullion and perhaps put him in touch with a reputable silver broker. Among smaller institutions, the Foreign Commerce Bank, Bellariastrasse 82, CH 8022 Zurich, Switzerland, is one foreign bank where the English-speaking investor can buy, sell, or hold silver bullion without running into any language problems. Statements, correspondence, and transactions with this bank can all be handled in English. The minimum purchase is $5,000 worth of silver, and there is a 1% commission on purchase and sale. Storage and insurance are provided by the bank at 0.15% per year on the average value of the silver holdings stored in the bank's vaults. The bank will finance up to 50% of a silver bullion investment, with a minimum loan of $5,000. The interest rate depends on the prevailing money market conditions at the time. The bullion comes in bars of 100, 250, 500 or 1000 grams (1000 grams, or one kilo, is equal to 32.15 ounces).

Silver coins

For the investor who wants to keep at least some of his silver in his own possession, rather than in a foreign or American bank or a commodity warehouse, silver bullion has disadvantages. It is bulky to store, is sold in large lots, and is hard to buy at a fair price in smaller amounts. It may also be hard to sell when you want to get rid of it, and you may well incur an expensive assaying fee before a buyer will take it off your hands. You also run the risk of fraud, and it would be prudent to avoid any silver bars which do not have stamped on them the hallmark, weight and fineness of a leading refiner, such as

ASARCO, AMAX Inc., Anaconda, Cerro, Engelhard Industries, International Nickel, U.S. Smelting, or the United States Mint.

You can avoid at least some of these problems by buying silver coins instead of silver bullion. There is a large and organized trade in United States dollars, half-dollars, quarters and dimes minted in 1964 or earlier. Up to that year these coins contained 90% silver. Since 1965—and it is a sad commentary on the debasement of the United States currency—they generally have been made of base metals, although some Kennedy and Eisenhower half dollars were produced with a 40% silver content.

Among the advantages of owning U.S. silver coins are that you can buy them in small amounts (a dime or a quarter at a time, if you want, from your neighborhood coin dealer); the U.S. government stamp on them is a first-class guarantee of their silver content, and they are easier to sell than silver bars. Nobody is going to require an assay of your coins when you sell them.

These are simply "junk" silver coins, in the sense that they have no numismatic value. Rare silver coins bought mainly as collectors' items are beyond the scope of this book. Collectors' items are what they are, rather than investments, and they require a degree of expertise not usually possessed by the average investor.

An uncirculated 1804 silver dollar might fetch $250,000, and an 1893 Morgan silver dollar $30,000, but you have to know what you are doing in this field or else depend on a numismatic expert whom you can trust. A $250,000 rare coin is obviously much more of a temptation to counterfeit than a plain old silver dollar that sells for $3 because of its silver content. And once you get up into those stratospheric price levels you are not really talking about a silver investment anyway.

However, in the long run, silver coins have a better chance of appreciating in value than silver bullion. They can always be melted down into bullion, and the coins remaining then become scarcer, which raises their numismatic value. So there is a marginal numismatic aspect to your investment in bulk silver coins, provided the pieces are in mint, uncirculated, or extra-fine condition, the grades prized most by collectors. Heavily worn coins are unlikely ever to appreciate in numismatic value.

The disappearance of silver coins has been fairly rapid. In the past decade about 400 million ounces of silver in coin form have been melted down, and there are now only about 500 million ounces left in the form of United States coins, according to one trade estimate.

One further advantage of silver coins should be mentioned. At the depths of the Depression in the 1930s, silver bullion fell to 24.5 cents an ounce. Such a decline is unlikely now because of inflation and the constant outrunning of silver supply by demand. But silver coins have a built-in price floor, which silver bars do not. This is because United States silver dimes, quarters, half-dollars and dollars are still legal tender. They cannot drop below their face value. So if the price of silver falls below $1.40 an ounce—the point at which the coins' face value equals their bullion value—you can still use them as cash. Silver bullion does not give you such protection, which, however, is likely to be of merely theoretical importance.

How to buy silver coins

The United States coins with a 90% silver content are easy to recognize. The date—1964 or earlier—is not the only identifying mark. The coins minted since 1965, as you can easily verify by checking your loose change, have a coppery sheen on their milled edges. They are a metal sandwich of copper and other base metals with an intrinsic value of about 1/25th of their face value, in other words, practically worthless scrap metal.

Your first concern when buying or selling silver coins is to make sure you are getting a fair price. There are two easy ways of doing this.

One way is to calculate the price of their silver content. The coins usually sell at a small premium above this, say 3% or so.

The price of silver is quoted daily in the *Wall Street Journal* in an item headed "Silver and Gold Prices." The quotations are given by Engelhard Minerals and Handy & Harman, two major refiners and fabricators of precious metals. *Barron's* magazine also carries each Friday's quotation under the same heading.

All you need to know then is that the United States coins minted through 1964 contained:

Dollar	0.77345 troy* ounces of silver
Half dollar	0.36168
Quarter	0.18084
Dime	0.07233

* The troy ounce is equal to 1.097 avoirdupois ounces in everyday use.

The older and more worn coins have some wastage of course. In a $1,000 bag the average will work out to about 715 to 720 ounces of silver.

Another, even simpler way of checking the value of your silver coins is to glance at the daily quotations on the silver coin futures markets.

Silver coin futures

Silver coin futures are traded on two big commodity markets, the New York Mercantile Exchange and the Chicago International Monetary Market. The standard unit is a bag of dimes, quarters, or half dollars of pre-1965 coins with a total face value of $1,000. The futures contract in New York is for ten of these bags and in Chicago it is for five bags.

These futures markets are mainly for in-and-out traders who are also out-and-out speculators, not investors. By offering highly leveraged margin contracts, they provide all the wild risks of sudden fortune and sudden death that are to be found in the futures markets for silver bullion. But the silver coin futures markets present an additional risk as well: the volume of trading is much smaller and the market is less liquid than in silver bullion futures.

Our only interest in the silver coin futures markets at this point is that they do give the general market consensus on the fair going price for your silver coins.

In the *Wall Street Journal* and in *Barron's* magazine you will find a table that looks like Table 2 in the section on commodity futures trading.

Table 2

N.Y. Mercantile Exchange
Silver Coins (10-$1,000 Bags)

SeaHi	SeaLo		WkHi	WkLo	WkLa	Prv	OpInt
4300	2965	Oct	3222	3066	3195a	3210	1,055
4040	3020	Jan	3305	3145	3270a	3295	1,507
3890	3085	Apr	3380	3230	3345	3380	854
3960	3125	Jul	3450	3320	3425a	3465	668
4010	3395	Oct	3435	3430	3415a	3650	655
4164	3525	Jan	3624	3525	3575a	3635	114

Sales: 446

The figures on the first line of the table show that bags of silver coins for delivery in October 1975 with a face value of $1,000 sold for as much as $4,300 and as little as $2,965 in the past year and a quarter (Season's High and Low). During the past week the High was $3,222 and the Low was $3,066 per bag. The final quote was $3,195, compared with $3,210 the previous week. The Open Interest is 1,055, which means simply that there are 1,055 contracts in existence for delivery in that month. (The table is from *Barron's*—the *Wall Street Journal* carries the daily figures, which you can also get from the New York Mercantile Exchange by calling 212-966-2323 for a recorded message 24 hours a day.)

As October 1975 is the closest month for delivery, it has to be the closest approximation to the current or spot price for immediate delivery. You now know that a coin dealer who quotes you around $3,195 per $1,000 bag (or 31.95 cents for each silver dime) is quoting you a fair price that is in line with current market prices.

If you want to work out the price per troy ounce of silver, the Chicago Exchange calculates that every $1,000 bag of silver contains 715 troy ounces of silver. This exchange also has a futures market for Canadian silver coins minted in 1966 or earlier, which contained only 80% silver (Canadian coins minted since then are generally made of base metals, like their U.S. counterparts). The figure for each $1,000 bag of Canadian coins is thus only 585 troy ounces of silver.

There is one way a non-speculator can make use of the coin futures markets. You buy a contract, pay all cash for it, and take delivery of it. The minimum purchase would be five $1,000 bags (the standard contract on the Chicago market) or ten bags (the standard New York futures contract). In this way you would be sure to get the fair going price and eliminate the markup a coin dealer would charge you. If you leave the bags in the exchange warehouse, you get a warehouse receipt and pay the storage and insurance charges until the time comes to sell them through the futures market once again or take physical possession of them, if that is your choice.

The New York Mercantile Exchange's authorized warehouses or depositories are all in the New York area. They are Chase Manhattan Bank, First National City Bank, Iron Mountain Depository, Irving Trust Co., National State Bank of Rahway, New Jersey, and Republic National Bank of New York. Their storage fees vary but are generally around $1.50 a month for ten bags (including insurance). Some charge a $1 fee if you want to remove your bags, which you should do by renting an armored car, as ten bags are both heavy and valuable. In addition to the trouble and expense of the armored car service, you will then have storage problems of your own, and your bags will have to be recertified if you ever bring them back to the Exchange warehouse. Recertification means the contents are rechecked by an Exchange-approved certifying agent, who will charge about $5 per bag for the service.

It saves a lot of trouble and expense to leave the coin bags in the Exchange depository. You could then use your warehouse receipt as collateral if you try to get bank financing for your coins. At the time of writing, loans of this type are hard to get, as they are discouraged by the government authorities.

Silver mining stocks

If the outlook is for a rising silver price, then the shares of silver mining companies should be a good investment, too. This may seem logical, but buying silver stocks is not the same thing as buying silver bullion or coins. It is a totally different investment.

When you buy shares in a company you assume all its business risks, which may be considerable. You are betting on the capability of its management, which may be poor. You take on extraneous risks which have nothing to do with silver. Most silver mining companies also produce base metals, and in a recession the demand for these drops sharply, so the company may do poorly even if the price of silver rises. Spreading your money over several companies is also a wise measure. In 1972 a disastrous fire shut down the Sunshine Mining silver operations for seven months. In 1973 the company was shut down for another four months by a strike.

ASARCO, quoted on the New York Stock Exchange, is the largest silver producer in the world, with an annual output of around 7.5 million ounces. This company illustrates the difficulty of investing in a pure silver-mining operation, however, because silver is only a by-product of its copper, lead and zinc mines. These base metals are among the first to show a downturn whenever a recession starts contracting industrial demand, and so ASARCO's stock tends to rise and fall with the nation's general business cycle rather than with the price of silver.

Hecla Mining, another New York Stock Exchange listing, produces about 3.8 million ounces of silver a year—about 11% of United States production—and silver generates about half its gross annual revenues. Hecla has major silver properties in Idaho. This is usually a volatile stock and its price is more closely tied to the price of silver than ASARCO.

Sunshine Mining, also listed on the New York Stock Exchange, started out as a silver company, and still produces about two million ounces a year, but it has diversified into electronics and other products, which now provide the major part of its income.

Callahan Mining Corporation (NYSE) has a 50% interest in the Galena silver and copper mine in Idaho, which is operated by ASARCO and which provides the bulk of Callahan's income. Callahan is also active in oil exploration and manufacturing operations.

Rosario Resources (NYSE) produces about 3.4 million ounces of silver yearly, mainly from its properties in Honduras and the

Dominican Republic. In the latter country, Rosario has also re-opened a gold mine that was originally discovered in the time of Christopher Columbus from which it anticipates a yearly output of about 350,000 ounces. The company has other mining interests in Nicaragua, Mexico and Canada.

Texasgulf (NYSE) owns a rich silver mine in Timmins, Ontario, and produces several million ounces yearly, but this is mainly a by-product of its copper output. More than 80% of Texasgulf's income is from base metals. The company is also one of the world's biggest sulphur producers.

On the American Exchange you have Day Mines Inc., which gets about half its income from silver and the other half from lead, zinc, copper and gold.

All these companies are ranked B+ to B (Average to Below Average) by Standard & Poor's, which is not an overwhelming recommendation, but they are among the most substantial stocks available in the silver mining field.

There are also many penny mining stocks quoted in Canada and over-the-counter in the United States, which are mostly out-and-out speculations. As this area has been noted for its fraudulent promotions and stock manipulations, the prudent investor should avoid it.

Medallions, mints, and private exchanges: Investors beware

The silver futures markets, as we noted, are generally set up for speculators, not investors. Their primary appeal is to the gambler, the crap-shooter, the impatient get-rich-quick mentality.

There are two other areas the conservative investor is well advised to stay away from. One is the purchase of silver medallions and commemorative coins, which is usually just a lousy investment, and the other is the acquisition of margin contracts through private firms, a practice that has been the object of anti-fraud measures by the Securities and Exchange Commission.

The issue of medallions and commemorative coins has become a veritable craze in the last few years. They are struck by privately owned mints, by foreign governments, even by Com-

munist regimes, to record almost every conceivable occasion—the death of former President Harry Truman, the death
of a baseball star, a moon landing, the anniversary of a state
joining the Union, a visit by Queen Elizabeth to Hong Kong,
Mother's Day, Flamingo Day in the Bahamas, and many other
events and non-events around the globe.

These coins and medallions may be fine if you are a collector
of such items—an expensive hobby—and if you have an emo-
tional involvement, say, in the Philippine commemorative coin
glorifying the tenth year of the Presidency of Ferdinand Mar-
cos. As an investment they usually make no sense at all.

Their silver content is minimal in relation to the price. They
are sold as works of art, but many of them are tasteless. They
are advertised as "limited editions" to give them scarcity value,
but the incredible profusion of different issues means that the
market is flooded with them. Scarcely one of them has appreciated in resale value from its original sales price, and many
sell at a deep discount if they can be sold at all.

Perhaps the best way to invest in this business is to buy the
shares of the companies that manufacture them, who have been
doing a land office business in recent years and will probably
break all records with commemoratives of the Second Centen-
nial of the United States in 1976. Perhaps the biggest firm in the
field is the Franklin Mint of Franklin Center, Pennsylvania,
which in addition to its own commemorative medallions and ingots has struck silver coins for the governments of Panama, the
Bahamas, the British Virgin Islands and other foreign states.
Franklin Mint shares are quoted on the New York Stock Exchange and are rated B+ by Standard & Poor's. The price per
share rose from 25 cents to $35 between 1960 and 1976.

Private exchanges

Silver bullion and silver coins are heavily advertised in the
press by a number of outfits that sometimes call themselves exchanges but are, in fact, private firms that have nothing to do
with the organized commodity exchanges of New York and
Chicago, where a free public auction determines the price.

These private firms are a different kettle of fish. They sell you silver bars or bags of coins, which you can buy for cash or on margin and leave in storage with the firms. They charge you interest on the margin contracts as well as storage fees. They may or may not, at their pleasure, buy back your silver at prices they determine. If the silver bars have the stamp of some obscure exchange rather than of a well-known refining firm, you will find it hard to sell them elsewhere and will incur expensive assay charges.

Since they hold you as a captive customer, there is nothing much you can do if they do not offer you a fair repurchase price when you want to sell. Some of them do in fact offer unfair and arbitrary repurchase prices to their customers, according to the Securities and Exchange Commission, which accused a number of these "Exchanges" with misrepresentation and fraud. Some were investigated and found not to be holding the bullion and coins that investors had purchased and supposedly stored with them. There were firms that did not even have any of the depositories they had advertised. The biggest firm in the business made sales of more than one billion dollars before the SEC cracked down.

The summing up

There is no substitute for knowledge. It is the uninformed investor who is conned by glib salesmen into buying high and selling low. He is swindled by hucksters who play on his fears and stimulate his greed for fast profits. If you are well informed on the silver market and have a realistic evaluation of its possibilities, you will save yourself much grief.

You can keep yourself up to date on silver production figures and other data by reading such specialized journals as *American Metal Market* (7 East 12th Street, New York, 10003) and by asking for literature from the Office of Mineral Information, Bureau of Mines, Washington, D.C. 20240. The Silver Institute, 1001 Connecticut Avenue, NW, Washington, D.C. 20036 provides useful data. Brokerage houses also put out interesting folders on silver from time to time. Clip their advertising coupons in the newspaper and resist their invitations to gamble on the futures market.

Further information on investing in silver may be obtained from *Silver—How and Where to Buy and Hold It* by Franz Pick (Pick Publishing Corp., 21 West Street, New York 10006), a short, very expensive ($45) but interesting study of ways to invest in silver for the wealthy investor.

The author, publisher of a well-known annual reference work on the currencies of all the nations in the world, takes a dyspeptic view of all paper currencies. Pick finds that "a major contribution to present and future silver price trends will be the terminal disease of the American currency. All indications are that the greenback will continue to dwindle in value until a monetary caesarian or an exchange of ten old units for one new unit is decreed. It is probable that with every new decline of the dollar, silver will attract additional owners as a valuable hedge against the expropriation of United States dollar owners. Nobody knows how many hundreds of millions of ounces of silver coins are still hoarded in pickle jars by American housewives. These pieces are a very cheap hedge for the middle-class housewife."

And with this we return to our starting point. Silver offers you good protection against runaway inflation, when prices at the supermarket are being raised every few days, when your 5% savings account is being eaten up by 20% inflation. In the end, if the American dollar reaches the terminal stage predicted by Pick, the old pre-1964 quarters and dimes that contained 90% silver may well be the best currency to hold for purchasing everyday necessities. Already in 1976 the pre-1964 dime you parted with so blithely from your loose change 12 years earlier was worth 30 to 40 cents because of its silver content.

But as long as the government keeps firm control of the paper money supply, holding inflation down below the double-digit level, the attractions of silver as an investment tarnish rapidly. The price fluctuates wildly, like that of any other commodity. And the costs of storing, insuring, and financing a silver investment eat up a big chunk of any profits you make. Silver, like gold, is a foul weather friend, good to have when financial storms are brewing and paper currencies are sinking in a sea of inflation.

6

Fixed interest investments
when inflation drops below double digits:
From Treasury bills to commercial paper

> Experience shows that neither a state nor bank ever has had the unrestricted power of issuing paper money without abusing that power.
>
> —British classical economist David Ricardo, in 1817

For too many years, like the City of New York, we have been trying to burn the candle at both ends, living off our inheritance and mortgaging our future at the same time. Whether we can prevent the nation from falling into the same plight as our greatest city is now the central issue before us.

Americans are rightfully concerned about the fiscal plight of the largest and richest city of the land because they know that the philosophy that has prevailed in New York—the philosophy of spend and spend, elect and elect—first took root and flourished here in Washington D.C.

As a nation, we began planting the seeds of fiscal irresponsibility long ago. Forty out of our last forty-eight budgets have been in deficit, and fourteen out of the last fifteen.

> —Treasury Secretary William E. Simon,
> as reported by the Associated Press, June 26, 1975

In all states, therefore, the issue of paper money ought to be under some check or control; and none seems so proper for that purpose as that of subjecting the issuers of paper money to the obligation of paying their notes either in gold coin or bullion.

—David Ricardo

The United States national debt is the biggest single borrowing in the history of man. It is increasing at an accelerating rate, and its growth seems to be unstoppable.

These facts are the first thing to keep in mind before investing in the most highly rated securities available in the United States: those backed with the full faith and credit of the Federal government. This is the ultimate in safety. The risk of the United States government defaulting on its bonds and other financial obligations, according to respected bond-rating services, is negligible.

The danger of loss through inflation, however, is considerable. And the longer the term of the government security you buy, the more the danger grows. Purchase of a 25-year government bond practically guarantees you the loss of a major part of your capital when Uncle Sam—keeping full faith and credit with you—repays his debt to you with depreciated paper dollars in the early years of the next century.

A few figures starkly contrast the size of the Federal debt and the gold stock held by the United States Treasury.

Every business day the Treasury issues a statement of its cash position, which on June 19, 1975 included the following two lines

Total debt $527,268,000,000
Gold assets $ 11,620,000,000

The Federal government's total debt of $527 billion thus amounted to about $2,500 for every man, woman and child in the country. The gold stock of $11.6 billion would cover about 2% of the outstanding debt. To be fair, the Treasury's gold was valued at the absurd official price of $44.22 per troy ounce. At the real free market price on that date it was worth about four times as much, around $45 billion, but still less than 10% of the total national debt.

To lean over backwards even further in pursuit of fairness, the only people really interested in the Treasury's gold backing are so-called gold-bugs and other financial conservatives who perversely insist that the bank should hold enough bullion in its vaults to guarantee redemption of the paper chits and IOU's (banknotes, bonds and bills) it has issued. Everybody else seems to be quite willing to accept the Treasury's promise to re-pay on the strength of two things—Washington's power to tax the American people until all the government's needs are met, and the Treasury's ability to borrow even more money to pay off previous debts. Both propositions have certain limits.

At the time of the Treasury statement quoted above, the Treasury Secretary was William Simon. (The date was picked quite arbitrarily, and the basic situation will most probably be the same on the date you read this book, even though the government officials and the figures are different.) Simon was a fiscal conservative as Treasury Secretaries go, but he had a problem.

The problem was that the Secretary needed more money to keep the government going, and he wanted to abolish the statu-tory limit on the federal debt. But Congress wouldn't let him do it. The current legal limit was $531 billion—just a shade over the $527 billion debt already outstanding. With government spend-ing at its current rate, the Secretary could see the debt shooting up through the limit to $617 billion by mid-1976, putting him in an impossible legal position in a matter of weeks.

The House of Representatives had just voted down Simon's proposal, and this was his angry reaction: "Who voted in that majority against raising the ceiling? And who had the temerity to lecture us on the horrors of a large national debt? Why many of the very same people who have been voting to increase the size of the federal budget and increase our federal deficits. Americans must only look with sorrow and anxiety at these political theatrics."

There do indeed appear to be self-contradictions on both sides of this argument. In fact, according to the *Wall Street Jour-*

nal, "the battle over the debt limit is more political than substantive. Most Congressional Republicans traditionally have voted against debt-ceiling bills to protest government spending and did so again, even though the Ways and Means Committee bill before them had the Ford administration's backing."

The gravity of Mr. Simon's problem could be gauged from another item in the *Wall Street Journal:* "The federal government, already expecting to borrow about $1.5 billion a week this calendar year (1975) may have to step up that frantic borrowing pace for 1976. Treasury Secretary Simon said the Treasury's cash requirements could reach $84 billion by 1976."

This estimate was on the low side. According to a statement by President Ford, made incidentally just after signing a seven billion dollar tax cut, the spending programs planned by the Democratic Congress could bring the 1976 federal budget deficit to "the enormous total of $100 billion. Deficits of this magnitude are too dangerous to permit and threaten another vicious spiral of runaway double-digit inflation."

A deficit of $60 billion, said the President, a lifelong fiscal conservative, "is as far as we dare go."

Shortly after this, on January 21, 1976, President Ford sent Congress a budget proposal for fiscal 1977 containing a deficit of $43 billion. "The fiscal problem," commented one Wall Street economist, "is fast approaching a crisis stage. In a span of only two years, the privately held federal debt will have expanded by $138.3 billion—or more than it had in the entire period since World War II. With such a record, it is not surprising that the Ford administration is trying to reverse the spending tide."

Barely two months later, on March 16, 1976, President Ford signed a bill increasing the federal government's debt limit to $627 billion. And in the meantime Treasury Secretary Simon was back before Congress pleading for a further increase in the debt ceiling to $645 billion. He said the Treasury would have to borrow "upward of $90 billion" in the next year and a half. In June 1976 the House voted to increase the limit of the national debt to $700 billion.

Mandatory budget deficits

Why does a President with a balance-the-budget mentality go

along with $60 billion deficits, and why does a penny-pinching Treasury Secretary push for unlimited federal debt at the same time he predicts the dire consequences of such a debt? The answer is simple. They have to.

At this late stage of the game there is no other way out, because rising federal expenditures are mandated by laws that in some cases were passed a generation ago. These laws regulate payments to Social Security beneficiaries, to people on welfare, to the unemployed, and to other beneficiaries of government income redistribution.

These benefits, called transfer payments, in 1950 represented 20% of federal expenditures. They now account for 50%, and if they grow at the same pace, they will take 80% of the government's tax income by the year 2000. By that time, according to Roy Ash, a former director of the Office of the Budget and Management, "the contributors—the people who are paying the bill—will be virtually slaves." Already, says Ash, more people are receiving transfer payments than are paying taxes. When the people with a vested interest in getting money out of the system outnumber those putting money into it, the political implications are pretty obvious—the votes will be on the side of more welfare, more unemployment benefits, and more government food stamps.

Eventually, of course, such a system will destroy itself. The critical point will come when the minority still working to support the system gives up and joins the free-loaders. Whether such a point will ever come is an open question. The current trend may be stabilized when it verges on the intolerable, or perhaps even reversed.

Whatever the future may bring, the problem at this point is simply that these social welfare payments are growing year by year, and there is presently no way the government in power—whether it be Republican or Democrat, liberal or conservative—can reduce them. This means that 50% of the federal budget is now irreducible by any means. Any reduction will have to come from other, presumably more expendable sectors, such as national defense or the administration of justice.

The most likely outcome is that there will be no reduction anywhere in federal spending. The government is now spending 30% of everything the United States produces, and the ratio will rise to 60% of the gross national product if the present trend is not stopped. So says Stephen S. Gardner, Deputy Secretary of the Treasury. Each government spending program, he says, "is relatively uncontrollable, with a strong constituency to support it. In 1975, the federal deficit is half as large as the total deficit of $160 billion for the previous 10 years." In the first four months of 1975 alone, Congress introduced over a hundred spending bills.

Back in 1965 the government food stamp program was costing $36 million a year, and less than 500,000 people were using this government subsidy to buy cheap food. By 1975 the program was costing more than $5 billion yearly, and 19.5 million people were on this gravy train. The eligibility requirements were so loosely defined that even families earning as much as $16,000 a year could be eligible for food stamps in some cases. According to an official forecast, perhaps as many as 58 million Americans might eventually be eligible.

The growth of government spending in all areas has been so prodigious that by 1974 it amounted to more than five times the net profits of all American corporations. More people were working for the government than were employed in all the nation's factories.

"It should be clear to everyone by now," said Boston-based investment adviser David L. Babson, "that government activity has become so vast, so self-serving and so politicized that it is beyond effective control. In fiscal 1966, federal, state and local government spending was 38% as large as the private sector. We estimate that in fiscal 1976 the figure will reach 57%.

"The ten-year increase in transfer payments to welfare recipients from $36 billion to $165 billion," said Babson, "is partly due to the fact that most benefit schedules have been boosted faster than the cost of living has gone up. The number of recipients has soared by over 50% since 1966. Over 50 million adults—nearly all non-working—receive income support of some kind from Uncle Sam. Another 15 million are employed at various levels of government. So let's compare those 65 million people who have a vested interest in bigger and bigger public outlays with the 71 million who work for private enterprise. It is almost a one-to-one situation: nearly one public beneficiary for each tax-supporting private worker."

By mid-1975 the United States Department of Commerce reported that transfer payments—consisting mainly of welfare, unemployment, social security and veterans' benefits—were running at an annual rate of $178 billion. At the same time, it added, dividends to stock owners were being paid at an annual rate of only $34.5 billion, while persons receiving fixed interest on savings were getting $120 billion yearly. Farm income was running at $30.5 billion yearly.

In other words the people on welfare, social security, unemployment and military retirement—none of them particularly productive groups—were getting nearly as much money from the government as the nation's investors, savers, and farmers combined were getting from their productive investments and labor. Obviously a massive transfer of wealth was taking place. Nobody wants to play Scrooge to a social security pensioner, a man out of work, or an abandoned mother with five children to care for. The point is that wealth is flowing massively from the productive people into the hands of the unproductive. And there are limits to such a process in any society.

"Most politicians," Babson concludes, "do not understand that the growth in government spending must bear a reasonable relationship to the expansion of output and income in the private economy. If public outlays rise at a more rapid rate, then tax rates must eventually be raised and/or additional government debt has to be created. Both alternatives are the major long-term causes of inflation."

Who is to blame?

We have already noted the recriminations between Congress and the President and members of his administration over the growing public debt. The inflation this indebtedness causes brings into action another governmental body, the Federal Reserve Board, a nominally independent agency that is in charge of controlling the United States money supply. When the inflation rate gets too far out of hand, the Federal Reserve tries to put a brake on the money-printing presses for a while. If you issue less paper money, you tend to get less inflation. Unfortunately the economy slows down, too, for lack of funds, and the stock market plunges for the same reason.

This causes more recriminations. Here is investment adviser John Wright of Bridgeport, Connecticut, commenting on the situation in April 1975. The Federal Reserve Board's open market committee, which controls the Board's monetary policy, has, he claims, "already brought this great nation to its lowest point in 40 years. The twelve committee members (two ex-professors, two ex-commercial bankers, seven career Federal Reserve bankers, and one ex-corporation executive) have and exercise the absolute power to determine prosperity or recession for the nation and liquidity or bankruptcy for its businessmen."

Wright berated "the foot-dragging failure of this committee to provide any significant support for the deficit financing requirements of our governments. We are now once again witnessing the incredible spectacle of a little group of willful men effectively frustrating the will of the people of the United States as expressed through a newly elected Congress."

The men in charge of the money supply thus not only have the politicians but also the business community putting pressure on them for more and more money to perk up the economy.

Now listen to a voice from the Federal Reserve Board on the results. According to Dr. Henry C. Wallich, a member of the Federal Reserve's board of governors: "We are in this fix because we have followed the advice of the Keynesians for years. Whenever we have slowed down the money supply growth to fight inflation, unemployment starts rising," said Wallich, as reported by the *New York Journal of Commerce.* "Keynesians then told us to postpone the fight against inflation and increase the money supply sharply in order to fight unemployment now. But this solution to today's unemployment creates tomorrow's inflation. We followed the advice of the Keynesians each time (from 1965 onward) and each time the tradeoff between unemployment and inflation got worse. As a result, (in April 1975) we have peak rates of unemployment, and very high inflation, too."

In other words, unemployment is supposed to cure inflation and inflation is supposed to cure unemployment, but neither of them do, and so we are stuck with the worst of both worlds.

You may blame whomever you dislike most for causing this mess: Congress, the President, Democrats, Republicans, liberals, conservatives, politicians in general, welfare cheats, Communist conspirators, Keynesian economists, the American people, or the Federal Reserve Board.

Our concern is to recognize the mess for what it is and to take the necessary measures for survival.

Safety: What is it?

In considering interest-bearing investments, your first consideration must be safety against default, and United States federal securities offer you this in the highest available degree. Uncle Sam will not pay you off in gold, but he will print all the paper dollars that are needed to pay off his debts in full. If issuing more paper dollars causes more inflation, that is too bad, but for every $100 you pay in you will in due time be paid $100 back, even if the purchasing power of those dollars is then only $80. Of that you may be sure.

Secondly, you must have safety against inflation, and here you can get no guarantees from Uncle Sam. Until the United States government starts issuing inflation-indexed bonds to protect you, you must protect yourself against inflation. This means watching the cost-of-living figures, the handiest measure of inflation and the one that affects you most directly.

It is senseless to invest in United States government securities yielding 5% when the inflation rate is 10% a year. You have a negative interest rate of 5%—which means that you are paying the government 5% for the privilege of lending it your money. Your capital is melting away in your hands. The interest rate you are getting must be, at the very least, a few percentage points above the rate of inflation. If it is not, you should start thinking about buying gold, silver, land, housing, or some other tangible asset with the money you have in fixed-interest investments.

Thirdly, neither you nor anybody else in this uncertain world has any way of predicting what the inflation rate is going to be next year, or the year after, to say nothing of 25 years ahead.

The trend in the United States has been toward higher and higher yearly rates, from 2% in the 1960s to 10% and higher in the 1970s. In the 1980s you might well face a rate of 20% to 30% a year, as has already occurred in Britain, Japan, Italy, and other countries. But there is no way of knowing the exact rate ahead of time, and it will fluctuate from one year to another. If you can buy United States government securities yielding 8% in 1975 when the inflation rate is around 6%, this may be a reasonable way of preserving your capital. But it will make no sense at all in 1977 if the inflation rate is 10%.

As long as inflation-indexed bonds are not available (they should be investigated immediately when and if the government puts such things on the market), the only way to protect yourself against the unknown future risks of higher inflation rates is to invest on the shortest term possible. The safest investment for you is one maturing in a week, a month, or three months. Six months is not so good. One year is riskier. Five years is already a high danger area. Twenty years you should not even consider.

Investors are not absolute morons, and as a result of inflation the maturity of the United States national debt has been getting shorter and shorter. As the inflation rate rose, investors were only willing to lend money to Uncle Sam for shorter and shorter periods. By mid-1975 the average maturity of federal securities had dropped to two years and eight months, an all-time low. Only ten years before the average maturity was five years and four months. The amount of Treasury bonds maturing in twenty years was down to seven billion dollars, a minute part of the total national debt, and also near an all-time low. Treasury bonds maturing in ten to twenty years totalled less than fifteen billion dollars.

The overwhelming mass of the $527 billion national debt was due in less than 10 years, and the government was paying higher and higher interest rates year after year as a result of the rising inflation rate. As a consequence of the ever-shortening maturities and ever-higher interest rates, the United States government's yearly interest payments rose to more than $30 billion in 1974 and around $32 billion in 1975. This was about $150 for every man, woman and child in the country. It was also about half of the projected federal budget deficit in 1975-76.

Still, there are degrees of safety, and the next step down from federal securities is a significant step downward. As Deputy Secretary of the Treasury Stephen S. Gardner noted in April 1975, the federal government was still better off than other borrowers, like the City of New York. It could always print money if the need arose, he pointed out. New York City could not, nor could New York State or any other state or municipality in the country. New York City at that time was insolvent, unable to meet payments on its six billion dollars of short-term debt, rebuffed by Washington in its desperate search for funds to pay its debts, and surviving on temporary handouts from the New York State government, because banks and other private investors refused to lend the city another penny until it found some way of living within its means.

The federal government and New York City were not alone in their fiscal woes. Sam I. Nakagama, chief economist of Kidder, Peabody & Co., a major Wall Street financial house, noted in May 1975 that "the huge federal budget deficit is not the only fiscal crisis affecting the nation's financial markets. No less worrisome are the budget problems faced by states and municipalities across the country. The serious budget bind confronting New York City has attracted the most attention, but its problems are hardly unique except in magnitude. Among 67 cities surveyed earlier this year, two thirds stated they anticipated revenue shortfalls and expected to cut services and/or raise taxes."

All of this was bad news for the nation's banking system. In New York alone, the city's seven major banks held about $1.25 billion worth of city obligations in their portfolios. A city default would cause serious trouble for seven of the country's biggest banks. They also held about $2.25 billion in New York State securities, and if the city dragged the state down with it, the New York banks would be in a financial hole that was more than twice as deep. Across the country another hundred banks would be seriously damaged by a New York City default, banking authorities found in a survey.

In any event, the banking system's problems were already serious, "with an overhang of very shaky loans the most visible one," said *Business Week* in April 1975. "The odds are now against a tidal wave of bank failures, here or abroad. But there will probably be further casualties, and another bank or two may join the list of failed giants that already includes U.S. National Bank of San Diego, Franklin National of New York and Security National in Long Island. The United States has just come through the wildest boom in all of its economic history, and roughly one dollar of every three dollars borrowed in the economy came from a bank. Banks or bank holding company subsidiaries funded everyone that needed money in the past decade. They used up their own deposits and they sold certificates of deposit and holding company commercial paper, and borrowed federal funds to keep the game going—creating loan/deposit and capital/asset ratios that were simply intolerable. Many of the risks the banks assumed were simply not worthy of being financed. The risks got so great that banks in 1974 had to charge off an unprecedented $1.8 billion to cover loan losses, and there are still billions of dollars in loans that are in considerable trouble—$10 billion to $12 billion in loans to real estate investment trusts alone."

According to Federal Reserve Governor Wallich "it would be difficult to argue that while all this was going on, the degree of risk in the banking business was going anywhere but up. It is clear today that the degree of protection provided by bank capital is less than adequate."

Doomsday

You will note that in this chapter we have taken great care to attribute everything to reasonably responsible sources. We have quoted statements from the President of the United States, the Secretary of the Treasury, other ranking government officials, such as governors of the Federal Reserve Board, and economists of leading financial houses, as well as such respectable financial publications as the *Wall Street Journal* and *Business Week*. If these statements paint a picture for you that takes on the alarmingly lurid hues of an impending economic doomsday, remember that those words come from people in authority and from observers of noted respectability.

The author is not in the business of predicting the economic end of the world, but there are people who are quite willing to predict at least the end of the present monetary world. One of these is monetary expert Franz Pick, publisher of *Pick's Currency Yearbook*, a $120 reference work bought by a who's who of financial bigwigs and economic researchers, ranging from Dutch bankers to Yale University.

According to Pick, the end is only a couple of years away now. "Within the next year or two (1976-77)," he says, "and after the collapse of the present untenable system of paper money relying on more paper as monetary reserves, new currency values are going to be created. There is one way, and one way only this can be done—by using the old remedy of repudiating present government debts, and perhaps also private debts, along with the calling in of present banknotes for an exchange against new units. As far as the United States monetary system is concerned, it will necessitate an exchange of 10 present greenbacks, or maybe even 20, against one new 'hard' dollar based on gold. The outlook remains gloomy for all monetary units of the Western world. They will resemble the eggs that have to be broken in order to make a new currency omelet."

Pick's predictions have always been on the gloomy side in the two decades that he has been publishing his *Currency Yearbook*. Obviously, if you share his pessimism, you might as well read this book no farther than the chapters on buying gold and silver.

It takes no predictions at all, however, and not too long a memory either, to recall that banks failed across the United States in the Great Depression—more than 9,000 of them between 1930 and 1934. These were about half the banks in the country. The other half were forced by the government to close their doors temporarily in the banking holiday of March 1933. It would be prudent at least to take precautions against getting caught in a similar recurrence by keeping some cash at home for spending money and perhaps a bank account in Switzerland for additional safety.

How safe is the United States banking system?

What protection do you have today against a banking disaster like the calamity of the 1930s? For one thing you have the Federal Deposit Insurance Corporation (FDIC), a government agency that insures all accounts in participating banks up to a maximum deposit of $40,000. In June 1975, for instance, the FDIC stepped in with $11.5 million to protect the assets of de-positors in the Bank of Picayune, Mississippi, which was de-clared insolvent.

That was nice for the people with accounts in this small town bank, but Picayune might just be the right word for it. As of June 1975, the FDIC reported that it had a $6.2 billion deposit in-surance fund to make good the losses of depositors in failed banks. It could also count on another $3 billion from the Treasury any time it needed the money, making a total of $9.2 billion.

That was less than 1.2% of the $800 billion deposited in FDIC-insured accounts in the nation's 14,500 banks.

We quote now the words of Frank Wille, chairman of the FDIC: "Many of the doubts concerning the FDIC's ability to deal with a number of large bank failures focus on the fact that the deposit insurance fund is but a small fraction of the total de-posits insured by the FDIC. This is factually correct, but it has always been the case and is nothing new. Except for the startup years it has ranged between 1.2% and 2% of all insured de-posits. Even the most skeptical observers of the American fi-nancial scene concede that our deposit insurance system has worked smoothly in the past. Their concern is for the future. The ultimate question they raise is whether the FDIC could cope with a wave of large bank failures or a general banking emergency. While I have indicated my belief that the FDIC has adequate financial resources to handle, even within a single year, bank failures several times the combined magnitude of U.S. National Bank, Franklin National Bank and American Bank and Trust, a massive breakdown of our entire banking system, which I do not believe is even remotely possible, could be a different story."

Listen carefully. The man in charge is obviously trying to put the best possible face on it, but he has just told you that in the event of another wholesale run on the banks such as occurred in 1933, the FDIC might well be powerless to prevent a general banking collapse.

However, says Mr. Wille, "were that nonetheless ever to hap-pen, I have no doubt that Congress would act promptly to provide the FDIC with such additional borrowing authority or funds as might be needed."

Perhaps so, but even if Congress did come through, the only way it could repay depositors their lost funds would be by printing more paper money or authorizing more paper credit. Which means more inflation, and on a massive scale.

The FDIC chairman complained that "much of what has been said in the popular press about the vulnerability of the banking system is exaggerated and badly out of balance in its perspective. I would concede, however, that over the past ten years the degree of risk in the American banking system has increased. Nonetheless, I consider the present level of risk well within tolerable limits."

This was in mid-1975, a time when the FDIC had a list of about 180 "problem banks," more than 50 of which it considered to have "serious problems." The New York financial crisis later in the year added another 100 banks to the list.

By February 1976, Wille was reporting that the FDIC had nearly 350 banks on its "problem" list, and that about half of these banks were "serious" problems. In the same month, the comptroller of the currency—another regulating authority—declared 275 banks to be "problems." These banks had total assets of about $200 billion and held 42 percent of all national bank deposits. The Federal Reserve Board also said it was keeping an eye on 128 banking institutions for possible financial trouble. Supervision of the banking system by the FDIC, the comptroller, and the Federal Reserve was described by Federal Reserve Board Chairman Arthur Burns himself as "a competition in laxity."

It seems a fair comment considering that the former chairman of the Franklin National Bank testified under oath that he spent two years warning the authorities of impending disaster without getting them to take any remedial action. The bank collapsed in May 1974 and was the biggest bank failure in United States history.

Sixty-three savings and loan associations with assets totaling nearly $5.6 billion were listed as "problem institutions" in February 1976 by the Federal Home Loan Bank Board, which supervises 4,079 savings and loans across the country. The

troubled institutions held about 1.7 percent of all assets of insured institutions. (Deposits in savings and loans are insured in
the same way as bank deposits.)

By the time you read this book the list of problem banks and
savings and loan associations may have grown or shrunk. In any
event, the prudent thing to do is to hold no accounts above
$40,000, the insurance limit, and to spread your money in accounts
with several banks. An even more prudent precaution would be
to have one of these bank accounts in Switzerland—in dollars,
or even better in Swiss francs—ensuring you access to at least
some of your funds even if all American banks were closed for
a time.

It might be worth noting at this point that the FDIC has never
yet had to face a nationwide banking crisis. It was created as a
result of the banking crisis of the 1930s and has yet to meet its
first major test. In the meantime, in the four decades from Jan.
1, 1934, to Dec. 31, 1974, it has had to rescue 508 banks, which
either failed or required financial assistance. The biggest was
Franklin National Bank, with $1.4 billion in deposits the day it
closed. In each case, the FDIC has either arranged for a solvent
bank to take over the failed bank, or it has paid off the depositors itself, starting payments within five to seven days of the
bank closure.

"Riskless" investment and the "Prudent Man" rule

Now that we have examined the potential risks of what are
supposed to be "riskless" investments—there is, of course, no
such thing under heaven—let's review the basic ground rules.
Your investment has to yield at least a few percentage points
above the prevailing rate of inflation. If there is no such interest-bearing investment available, then it is time to be buying
gold, silver, land, real estate, or some other tangible asset that is
not vulnerable to the constant, abusive over-issue of paper
money and credit. The shorter the term of your fixed-interest
investment the safer you are. The longer the term, the more certain will be your loss to the erosion of a depreciating paper
currency.

When you get down to the practical matter of choosing the
best and safest places to put your money, the logical place to

start is with the "Prudent Man" rule, which is accepted as a legal rule of thumb in most states. You will find this rule essential if you are named executor of an estate or are held legally accountable in any way for the investment of somebody else's funds as a guardian or trustee.

Back in 1830, Harvard College sued Francis Amory, one of its trustees, because it thought he was not making as much income on the College funds as he might have done. The case wound up in the Supreme Court, where judge Samuel Putnam found in favor of Amory and wrote in his decision: "All that can be required of a trustee to invest is that he shall conduct himself faithfully and exercise a sound discretion. He is to observe how men of prudence, discretion and intelligence manage their own affairs, not in regard to speculation, but in regard to the permanent disposition of their funds, considering the probable income as well as the probable safety of the capital invested."

Nowadays, the practical conclusions to be drawn from this rule are spelled out for you in detail in most states by the state's "legal list" of securities. This list is sent out by the state banking authority to bank savings and trust departments, pension and retirement funds. If you restrict your investments to this list you will come under the "Prudent Man" rule and avoid the danger of being considered a wild-eyed speculator with your own or other people's funds.

Each state has its own list—there are currently about 600 approved securities on the Massachusetts list, for example—and each list is usually updated every month or so with additions and removals. You may get your list from your state banking department, usually for a fee of about $3. When you receive it, do not conclude, however, that anyone is urging you or advising you to buy these securities or telling you that you will do well with them. The authorities are not endorsing these securities in any way; they are just telling you that they are legal to buy for a trustee. If they turn out to be high on safety and low on income, remember that this was exactly the complaint Harvard College filed against Mr. Amory.

It would be too complicated to go through 50 state lists in this book, so here instead is a brief rundown of all the major types of fixed-interest investments available. They may or may not be on your state list, and they are listed approximately in declining order of safety. (After this short summary we shall go into the details of each one in the next chapter.)

United States Savings Bonds. They can always be redeemed at par value, so they do not fluctuate in price, and they are backed by the full faith and credit of the United States government. The only risk is from the depreciation of the paper dollar as a result of inflation.

Savings Accounts. Do not despise your plain old ordinary savings account with your local bank or savings and loan association. In normal times it has one shining virtue that many sophisticated higher-yielding investments do not: it is always worth $100 for every $100 you put into it. Not even Treasury obligations can claim that. It is also insured up to $40,000 by the FDIC or FSLIC. And if there should be a general banking collapse in which even the insurance goes under, none of the other investments listed below is going to be in much better shape than your insured savings account.

United States Treasury Bills. These are the shortest term investments you can make in government obligations. They come in maturities of three months, six months or one year. Backed by the full faith and credit of the United States government, they are the most liquid of all money market instruments and are in fact virtually the equivalent of cash that bears interest.

United States Treasury Notes. Somewhat longer term than Treasury bills, they mature in from one to seven years. They are also backed by the full faith and credit of the federal government, but the longer term means you assume a greater risk of loss through the depreciation of the dollar and from price fluctuations should you try to sell them in the open market before their full term is up.

United States Treasury Bonds. These are the longest term Treasury securities. Their maturities run to 25 years, and the longer the maturity the greater the risk of loss for you through inflation and the declining value of the dollar. At the quarter-century mark you might figure that the inflation risk far outweighs the protection of the government's full faith and credit guarantee.

United States Agency Obligations. Similar to Treasury

obligations, they are issued by agencies such as the Federal Land Banks, Banks for Cooperatives and the Government National Mortgage Association. They come in maturities of from one month to twenty-five years. Some are backed by the full faith and credit of the United States government, while others are guaranteed only by the issuing agency. So far, the difference has been merely academic, as none of these agency bonds has ever defaulted. They have usually provided somewhat higher yields than Treasury obligations. The longer the term, of course, the greater the risk of loss to you through inflation.

Treasury bills, notes and bonds as well as some federal government agency obligations are exempt from state and local taxes. Municipal bonds, mentioned below, are free from federal taxes.

Municipal Bonds. This term covers a dense thicket of different obligations issued in profusion by states, cities, school districts, counties, highway authorities and other local governmental bodies. There is a big step down in safety here, because none of these political entities can print their own money to pay off their debts, as the federal government can. New York City's insolvency is a glaring example of this danger. However, you can protect yourself by buying an insurance policy against default of interest and principal, as we shall see farther ahead. The degree of risk varies widely among the thousands of different issues, and the relative safety of each one is graded by bond rating services, from top-quality gilt-edge down to speculative. Many issues are also small and lack liquidity—you will find it hard to sell them at a fair price. As with other securities, the shorter the maturity of the municipal bond you buy the less risk you run from the worst ravages of inflation. The safest municipal you can buy is a big issue with a short maturity and a top-notch rating that you insure against default.

Bank Certificates of Deposit. The negotiable bank certificate of deposit usually pays a significantly higher rate of interest than a plain savings account. The snag is that certificates are usually issued in amounts of $100,000 or more, only $40,000 of which is covered by FDIC insurance. Certificate maturity usually ranges from one month to one year.

Bankers Acceptances. They are issued by a corporation guaranteeing payment in a trade deal, are guaranteed once again by the bank "accepting" the note, and are also secured by the goods involved in the business deal. This triple guarantee has so far offered good protection, as there is apparently no record of any investor losing money through a default on a bankers acceptance. The usual term of an acceptance ranges up to nine months.

Floating Rate Bonds. Issued by a number of large banks, the interest rate they pay is adjusted every six months or so in line with the current yield available from Treasury bills. Typically they pay 1% more than Treasury bills to compensate for the greater risk. Usually you can be sure of taking your money out at 100 cents on the dollar every 6 months. However, they are not covered by FDIC insurance, as they are not considered deposits but investments in the bank itself.

Corporate Bonds. The bond issued by a corporation is just as safe as the company that issues it, which means anything from very safe to wildly speculative. Bond rating services have a grading system to indicate the amount of risk involved in each case. If the company gets into financial trouble, the bondholders get priority over the common stockholders when the concern's liabilities are paid off. *Convertible bonds* are a hybrid between a stock and a bond that guarantee a fixed rate of interest and also give you a chance of making capital gains by converting the bonds into common stock—a big plus if the common stock price starts soaring.

Preferred Stock. Like bonds, they give you a fixed rate of interest, but unlike bonds, they have no fixed maturity date. They also rank after bonds should the time ever come to settle creditors' claims against a failed corporation. The numerous individual issues of preferred stock are also graded for relative safety by the rating services. Convertible preferred offer the same advantages as convertible bonds.

Commercial Paper. Unlike bondholders and preferred stock owners, the buyers of commercial paper have no claim on the assets of the corporation issuing it. The paper is an unsecured obligation in which you are offered no collateral. Its usual maturity is short, from one to nine months. In the stack of fixed-interest investments it ranks lowest in safety. Because of the higher risk, commercial paper usually pays the highest interest rate. The paper of different issuing companies is also graded for risk by the rating services.

Investment Packages: Money market funds and bond funds

All these various securities, from Treasury bills down to commercial paper, can also be bought pre-packaged by investment companies that manage a whole portfolio of different issues of bonds, bills, acceptances, or preferred stock. The two main types available are money market funds and bond funds.

Money Market Funds. These are mutual funds that specialize in holding short-term obligations, such as Treasury bills, bankers acceptances, and certificates of deposit, with an average maturity of a few months to only a few weeks. Their individual portfolios vary greatly. The more conservative funds invest exclusively in United States government securities, while the more speculative look for a higher yield by buying commercial paper.

Bond Funds. These are investment trusts that put your money into a portfolio of longer-term bonds. They allow you to diversify your investment into several dozen municipal, corporate, or convertible bonds—depending on which type the fund specializes in—while making a single package investment. Because of the longer average maturity of their portfolios, they expose you to more danger from the long-term ravages of inflation than the short-term money market funds.

Now, after this brief survey of the different securities available, it is time to look at each one in more detail for the nuts and bolts of investing. How do you actually go about buying and selling Treasury bills, bankers acceptances or commercial paper?

7

Fixed interest investments:
The nuts and bolts of beating
single-digit inflation with safety

On Tuesday August 6, 1974 the Federal Reserve Banks in New York, Richmond, and other cities were mobbed by thousands of people. In New York there was a line several blocks long and four-to-five persons wide. This was not a panic-stricken run on the banks. It was more like a gold-rush, a mad scramble to get United States Treasury notes with a 9% coupon, the highest rate since the Civil War.

At that time the highest rate you could get from a bank savings account was 7.5%, provided you committed your funds for at least five years. An ordinary savings account paid only 5%. United States Savings bonds were held by law to a top rate of 6%, also provided you held them for five years.

The Treasury note issue being offered that August day had a maturity of only 33 months. On shorter term bills, the Treasury was paying even higher rates—in excess of 10% on one-year bills. In the first week of February 1976 the Treasury offered $3.5 billion worth of 8% notes and drew down an avalanche of orders totaling $29.2 billion from investors.

The interest rate fluctuates week by week and month to

month on Treasury bills and notes, and it is not always that high. But there are times when it is well worth raiding your ordinary savings account to buy them, and times to consider other high-yielding investments, such as municipal or corporate bonds. They have all one common drawback, however—from Treasury bills down to commercial paper, they all fluctuate in price. United States Savings bonds and a bank savings account do not. They are loss-proof.

United States Savings Bonds

Since the worth of United States Savings Bonds is about $65 billion, they are evidently one of the most popular forms of investment in the United States. Americans who have invested such massive amounts in their government should always keep in mind, however, that their Savings Bonds are a good way of increasing or at least preserving their capital only when the inflation rate is down to 6% a year or less. The government holds the yield on Savings Bonds down to 6%. When it issues paper money at such a pace that the cost of living rises more than 6% a year, it is surreptitiously taking more out of the Savings Bond owner's pocket than it is paying him in interest.

Savings Bonds come in two types, Series E and Series H, each of which has different features.

Series E Bonds are the most convenient to buy in small amounts. The minimum purchase is only $25, and the maximum amount you can buy is $10,000 in any one year. They yield 4.5% the first year and 6% yearly if held to their five-year maturity. There is an additional ten-year extended maturity period in which you can go on collecting interest. They can be purchased through a bank or a savings and loan association or a payroll deduction plan as well as through the Treasury, Federal Reserve banks, and some post offices. There is no need to pay any commission. The interest is discounted, which means the $100 bond you buy costs you only $75, and the amount you get back depends when you cash it in—the full $100 if you wait out the full five-year maturity, proportionately less for a shorter period. The difference between the price you pay for E bonds and the redemption value you get is interest, on which you pay federal income tax but no local or state income taxes. You can redeem your bonds at your local bank at any time two months after the date of issue, but you cannot sell them or use them as collateral for a loan.

Series H Bonds have the same tax status as E Bonds, but are different in other ways. They come in higher denominations—you can buy H Bonds with a face value of $500, $1000 or $5000. Your interest is added on, not discounted from the price. You pay the full face-amount of the bond, and the Treasury mails you an interest check every six months until you redeem the bond or until it matures in ten years. H Bonds also have an extended maturity period of an additional ten years in which you can go on collecting interest. The yield is 5% the first year, 5.8% the next four years, and 6.5% the second five-year period, giving you an average of 6% over the ten-year maturity.

The bonds are also bought differently from E Bonds. H Bonds are issued only by Federal Reserve banks and their branches, or by the Office of the Treasurer of the United States, Securities Division, Washington DC 20222. You can order them through your bank. The most you can buy in one year is $10,000 worth. You can redeem your H Bond at full face-value at any time after six months from the date it was issued. You cannot sell it, transfer it, or use it as collateral.

When you invest in Series E or Series H Savings Bonds, you are in effect betting that the rate of inflation will be 6% or less per year for the next five to ten years. This may be a dubious proposition.

Bank savings accounts

We have already noted why we put an FDIC-insured bank account near the top of our safety list. It is the only investment, apart from United States Savings Bonds, that guarantees you repayment of $100 for every $100 you put in, any time you want it. That can be an unbeatable advantage if you need your money in a sudden emergency.

The only danger is a wholesale bank crash in the United States, and you can guard against that in part by having one of your savings accounts with a Swiss bank in Switzerland (not an American branch of a Swiss bank). We shall give names and addresses of Swiss banks in the chapter on foreign investments.

The only other precaution to be taken is, of course, to keep your account under the $40,000 that is the maximum insured by the FDIC.

Like United States Savings Bonds, your savings bank account provides adequate protection against erosion of your capital only when the inflation rate is around 6% or less. The reason is the same: government regulation. In this case the name of the game is Regulation Q, the measure through which the Federal Reserve sets a ceiling on the maximum interest rate which banks can pay on savings and time deposits. The ceiling is varied from time to time, but it tends to be held low by economic and political consideration. Savings banks take in deposits on which they pay interest and then relend the money at a higher rate of interest to finance home mortgages. The higher the interest rate they pay their depositors, the higher the interest rates they have to charge on their mortgages to home-buyers, which is bad not only for home owners but also for the construction industry and real estate interests. Commercial banks also use your savings account to finance business and industrial firms which have a vested interest in low interest rates and considerable political clout. Politically, your role as a savings depositor is to provide cheap credit for business, industry and housing. As long as the government controls the process through Regulation Q, it is not likely to be a rewarding role. At the best, your savings account interest might just about keep level with a low-to-moderate rate of inflation. In recent years it has done considerably worse than that. Because of Regulation Q, the really big money started fleeing the United States about a decade ago in search of higher interest rates overseas, thus creating the multibillion Eurodollar market (which we shall discuss in a later chapter).

Treasury bills

Treasury bills are the first way to get around Regulation Q with any funds you have available for a short-term investment of up to one year. They are sold at a discount and redeemed at face value when they mature, so the difference in price is the interest you earn.

Three-month and six-month Treasury bills are sold every

Monday afternoon at 1:30 P.M. at the nation's twelve Federal Reserve banks across the country. Write to the nearest bank and ask for a "tender form" on which to submit your application. If you do not have the address of the bank nearest you, write to the Bureau of Public Debt, Treasury Department, Washington D.C. 20220 and ask for the latest information on buying Treasury bills, notes and bonds, as well as the addresses of the Federal Reserve banks.

Before making up your mind to apply for a bill, you can find out the interest rate Treasury bills are currently yielding by buying Tuesday's edition of the *Wall Street Journal*. This will tell you the results of the previous Monday's bill auction. If the yield then was 8%, you could usually expect to get ¼% more or less than that at the following week's auction of 90-day bills.

One-year Treasury bills are sold about every four weeks on dates announced in the press a few days before the auction. For one-year bills the yield may vary considerably more from month to month than for the shorter-term bills. It has even been known to vary as much as 2% from one month to the next.

All the Treasury bills are auctioned off by the Treasury to the highest bidder. This means that you may not get anything if your bid is not high enough. You can get around this problem by submitting a "non-competitive bid," which means you will be sure of getting your bill at the average price of the auction.

What you do in this case is send in a certified or cashier's check for the face amount of the bill. The minimum is $10,000, and you can make additions of $5,000 above that. When the Federal Reserve bank has figured out the average bid, let us say $9,300 for a $10,000 one-year bill, it will mail you a check for $700. You have thus bought the bill at a discount and are, in effect, getting your interest in advance. It also means you are getting a higher real interest rate, because you only put up $9,300 instead of the full $10,000. In August 1974, bills that nominally yielded 9.5% were in fact yielding 10.5% because of this discount feature.

If you deal directly with a Federal Reserve bank, you will not be charged any commission, and the bills you have bought will be mailed to you by registered post at the Treasury's expense in about ten days. The important thing to note here is that

Treasury bills are bearer securities—they are not registered in your name or anyone else's. If they are stolen, the thief can sell them with no questions asked—they are practically just as good as cash to him. If you keep a bill at home, it is like having $10,000 in cash lying around. A safe or a bank safety deposit box would be a reasonable precaution.

You can avoid this security problem altogether by buying through a commercial bank or stock broker, who will keep the bill in safe custody for you. In this case, however, you have to pay a commission. One large broker, for instance, has a flat fee of $25 per order, whether your purchase is $1,000 or $100,000. As soon as a broker has the safekeeping of your bills, the question arises whether your broker is any safer than your home safe. More than a hundred members of the New York Stock Exchange have gone bankrupt since 1969. Fortunately, even if yours goes belly-up, you are now protected up to $50,000 by the Securities Investor Protection Corporation, an agency similar to the FDIC, which was created by an act of Congress mainly as a result of those bankruptcies. If your account is bigger than that, some brokers offer insurance of their own for even larger sums. Merrill Lynch, for example, provides an extra $250,000 insurance to cover losses in the event that your securities cannot be found or cannot be identified.

With such short-term investments as Treasury bills maturing in three months to one year, the chances are that you will hold them to maturity and redeem them at full face-value. However you can sell them—at a gain or a loss—in the secondary market if you need the money unexpectedly before the bills mature. We shall get to that a little further ahead.

Treasury notes

The investors who flocked to buy Treasury notes yielding 9% in August 1974 locked in their 9% yield for nearly the next three years, and, considering the absence of risk, they probably did as well or better than most people investing in stocks or bonds at that time. Even so, when you buy these notes, which traditionally matured in from one to seven years (the maximum maturity was raised to ten years in March 1976), you are assuming a greater risk of loss through inflation in such a time-span than you run when you buy the short-term Treasury bills.

Treasury notes are auctioned at regular quarterly sales held on February 15, May 15, August 15, and November 15, as well as on other dates announced by the Treasury. For the smaller investor they are easier to buy than the $10,000 Treasury bill because the minimum amount is usually only $1,000, or sometimes $5,000. Once in a while it is hiked to $10,000.

You also have the choice of buying a note made out to the bearer or registered in your name. The bearer note is more easily stolen, but it is also easier to sell if you have to raise cash before the note matures. Another difference from the Treasury bill is that the interest rate is not discounted in advance. You pay the full face-value of your note and then collect the interest semiannually.

Otherwise the procedure for buying Treasury notes is basically the same as that outlined for Treasury bills, and you will probably find the "non-competitive bid" the most convenient way of doing it. If you buy through a broker, a typical commission might be $18.75 for a $5,000 note and $31.25 for a $50,000 note. The bigger the purchase the lower the proportionate cost of the commission.

Every once in a while the Treasury takes fright at the billions of dollars pouring out of bank savings accounts, savings and loan associations and credit unions to take advantage of the higher yields available from Treasury bills and notes (the Regulation Q syndrome again). It then raises the minimum purchase to $10,000 to keep the little guys out. This happened in 1974, for example, when the yield on Treasuries started hitting 100-year records. The government's problem is that such high Treasury yields drain money out of the mortgage market, making housing loans unavailable to most people, knock the construction industry for a loop, and do all kinds of other damage to the economy. The savings banks and the savings and loans also complain loudly in Washington that they want their little customers back.

The result is sheer discrimination against the little guy, of course—which means you and me and anyone else with less than $10,000 to throw around—but nobody puts it that crudely.

According to a Treasury spokesman quoted by the *New York Times* during the 1974 flap, the object of raising the minimum investment was to protect the small investor. "These investments are not designed for the individual because of their inherent market risk—they trade at fluctuating prices," said the Treasury man.

You may find this statement surprising, coming as it does from the spokesman of an institution that tends to emphasize its own rocklike soundness rather than its speculative nature. But it is true.

As the *Times* noted, "Right now, all outstanding issues of Treasury notes and bonds are selling for less than 100 cents on the dollar—some as low as 70 cents—because the interest rates they pay are lower than current rates."

It is the old story. Double-digit inflation breeds double-digit interest rates. If you were unfortunate enough to buy Treasury notes away back when inflation and interest rates were at 5%, the value of your Treasury note is going to go down, even with all the full faith and credit of the United States government behind it. Uncle Sam will pay you off in the end, of course, at the full 100 cents on the dollar he promised. But it is just too bad if you have to sell at a loss before your note matures.

As the Treasury official remarked, "It's not like a savings account. There's some risk involved."

Treasury bonds

United States Treasury Bonds mature in periods ranging up to 25 years. If you are rash enough in these inflationary times to buy a fixed-interest security maturing a quarter-century ahead, you will want to know that Treasury bonds are sold on the same dates as Treasury notes. Like the notes, you can have them in bearer form or registered in your name.

In 25 years you will be paid off at 100 cents on the sadly depreciated dollar, which in the last 25 years has lost nearly 50% of its purchasing power according to the consumer price index of the United States Bureau of Labor Statistics. And if you should need your money back before the 25 years are up, you may do even worse. You will probably have to sell the bond at considerably less than 100 cents on the dollar.

There is one thing, though. This is one place where the Treasury makes no effort to discourage the little man. Even when it was raising the minimum investment in Treasury notes to $10,000 in the 1974 crunch, the Treasury was still selling a 25-

year bond issue at the same time in minimum lots of $1,000.

The Treasury in fact has a severe marketing problem in selling long-term bonds. Away back in World War I, Congress passed the Second Liberty Bond Act, which clamped a 4¼% interest ceiling on long-term Treasury bonds. This ceiling is still in effect—except for $12 billion worth that the Treasury is allowed to issue without regard to the 4¼% ceiling. As it is impossible to sell 4¼% bonds nowadays, even with the full faith and credit of the United States government behind them, and the unrestricted interest issues are constantly backing up against the $12 billion limit, the Treasury is lobbying vigorously to raise the exempted issues limit to $20 billion.

Big deals in the secondary market

If you think the Treasury is discriminating against the little guy by making the minimum bill purchase a whopping $10,000, you should see what happens after the Treasury auction when the bills are traded in the secondary market. This is where you have to go if you want to sell your bill before it matures. The "round lot" or minimum trading amount here is $100,000, and most big banks and corporations deal in lots of a million dollars.

If you sell bills worth less than $100,000, you will have to deal through a bank or broker, and you will probably lose at least 1½% on the spread between bid and asked prices. The spread goes to your friendly bank or broker, who will also charge a $25 fee for his services.

Since you can only deal directly with the Federal Reserve Banks when they are issuing new bills or redeeming them at maturity, you have to resign yourself to the loss of money in commissions and price markdowns if you are forced to sell on the open market before your bill, note, or bond matures. The price of the security will also fluctuate, probably downward.

Presumably, when you buy three-month, six-month or one-year Treasury bills, you are using funds you will not be needing in the short time before your bill matures. However, emergencies do arise at the most unexpected times, so it is worth keeping in mind that if you should have to sell your bill before it matures you would incur selling expenses that might nullify the advantage of the higher interest the Treasury bill is paying you.

If you really need the cash, it might even pay to use the bill as collateral and borrow the money you require rather than sell the bill before maturity. Most banks and brokers will lend you up to 90% of the value of the bill.

Trading on the American Stock Exchange

Because of the $100,000 lots involved, the bulk of trading in government securities was confined until recently to the big financial institutions. Then, in 1975, the American Stock Exchange in New York set up a trading system of odd lots for the little fellow where Treasury notes and bonds can be bought in lots ranging from $1,000 to $99,000. The smaller lots are not the only advantage—trading expenses are cut, also, because no certificates actually change hands. On the Amex all transactions are recorded simply by bookkeeping entries.

Trading on the Amex started in January 1975 and caught on rapidly. By the end of the year, all 75 Treasury bond and note issues were listed. The Exchange added all the federal government agency securities in 1976, and more than 250 federal government issues were then available to small investors on the Amex. As the Treasury auctions new issues, they automatically begin trading on the Amex too. Treasury bills, however, presented problems because of their very short maturities and were not yet listed by the Amex.

Treasury issues are traded on the Amex in bearer form only. You can get delivery of your certificate if you insist, but there is not much point in doing so since they are held in perhaps the safest possible place, the Federal Reserve Bank of New York. The records registering your ownership are held by the broker you deal with, and your account with him is covered up to $50,000 by the mandatory insurance of the Securities Investor Protection Corporation—perhaps also by additional insurance that your broker may carry voluntarily for his customers.

Further details of the Amex trading system, in which Treasury securities can now be bought as quickly and conveniently as stocks or corporate bonds, may be obtained from the American Stock Exchange, 86 Trinity Place, New York 10006.

You will find the daily quotations of Treasury bills, notes, and bonds, as well as the federal agency obligations, in a table in the

Wall Street Journal headed "Government, Agency and Miscellaneous Securities." These quotes are for round lots of $100,000 to $1 million. Your odd lot on the Amex might go for a ¼ point less or cost you a ¼ point more if you are buying, and the brokerage commission could range from $1.25 to $5.00 per bond.

United States agency securities

About 40 federal government agencies also issue securities similar to the Treasury bills, notes, and bonds discussed above. Their maturities run from less than one year to twenty-five years. Some are backed by the full faith and credit of the United States government, while others are guaranteed only by the issuing agency. In either event they are considered second in safety only to Treasury obligations. None have ever defaulted. Some are exempt from state and local taxes, others are not. The minimum purchase you can make runs from $1,000 in some cases to $10,000 or $25,000 in others.

The agencies have been piling up debt at a dizzy rate, and the total is approaching $100 billion, more than ten times the $8.8 billion outstanding in 1960. It might be worth noting that their securities are exempt from registration with the Securities and Exchange Commission, as are the securities of the federal government itself, the city of New York and other state and municipal borrowers. This means they are not obliged to present the full disclosure statements required of non-governmental corporations, so any financial trouble is liable to come without warning. If New York City had been required to make the registration statements required of publicly owned corporations, a lot of investors would have avoided buying city bonds.

As regards price, you run exactly the same risks that you incur with Treasury obligations. The trading price of agency securities may drop below the price you paid for them if you sell before maturity. And if you cash them in at maturity, you will be paid off in depreciated dollars—the longer the maturity the bigger the depreciation.

The main advantage of agency securities is that they yield somewhat more than Treasuries. Kidder, Peabody & Co. notes that sophisticated investors, aware "of the government's strong responsibilities for these instruments and attracted by their higher yields, often find agencies preferable to direct issues of the Treasury." The difference in yield has been as much as 1% at times. In August 1974, for example, when three-month Treasury bills were yielding 9%, comparable federal agencies were returning 10%, while the interest on bankers acceptances and commercial paper was around 11.5% and bank certificates of deposit 12%. At other times, however, the difference in yield between Treasury and Agency securities has been more like 0.3% on short term issues and 0.5% on long-term issues.

Agency securities can be divided into three main groups: a half dozen government-sponsored enterprises, a half dozen federal agencies owned outright by the United States government, and the Federal Financing Bank, which handles the borrowing of the remaining three dozen or so agencies.

Government-sponsored enterprises were originally owned by the United States Treasury but were later transferred to ownership by the public or the particular organizations they served in the fields of farm credit and housing. They raise funds under supervision of the Treasury but are not guaranteed by the government. Government-sponsored enterprises include the following.

Banks for Cooperatives borrow money and relend it to farmers' cooperative associations. The minimum purchase is $5,000 and the bonds are offered monthly, usually with six-month maturities, but occasionally with maturities as long as five years. These bonds are not guaranteed by the government but they are backed 100% by collateral and the resources of the thirteen Banks for Cooperatives. They are subject to federal taxes, exempt from state and local taxes.

Federal Intermediate Credit Banks provide funds for other banks and financial institutions, which in turn make loans to farmers. Securities are issued monthly by the twelve Federal Intermediate Credit Banks, with maturities ranging from nine months to five years. The minimum denomination is $5,000. Like the Co-op bonds, these FICB bonds are backed only by collateral and the resources of the issuing banks, not by the government itself. Their tax status is also the same as the Co-op securities.

Federal Land Banks borrow money mainly to make long-term real estate loans to farmers. FLB bonds are similar to Co-op and FICB bonds in that they are backed only by the twelve Federal Land Banks and by collateral in the form of farmers' mortgages, not by the government itself. They are also subject to federal taxes but exempt from state and local taxes. FLB bonds are issued four to six times a year in maturities of one to fifteen years. The minimum denomination is only $1,000—the smallest minimum purchase of any of the government-sponsored enterprises.

The Federal Land Banks, the Federal Intermediate Credit Banks, and the Banks for Cooperatives all come under the supervision of the Farm Credit Administration, an independent agency of the United States government, from which further information may be obtained by writing to Information Division, Farm Credit Administration, Washington D.C. 20578.

Federal Home Loan Banks (FHLB) are a network of 12 district banks that supply credit to about 4,500 savings banks and savings and loans associations, which in turn provide mortgages to home buyers across the United States. The Federal Home Loan Banks issue short-term discount notes of 30 to 270 days maturity (big-ticket items on which the minimum purchase is $100,000) as well as interest-bearing notes of less than one year's maturity and bonds that mature in more than one year (both of which have a minimum denomination of $10,000). These securities are not liabilities of the United States government. They are secured by the combined assets of the twelve Federal Home Loan Banks (about $22 billion) and indirectly by the assets of the 4,500 home-financing institutions (which amount to about $300 billion). There are nearly 50 issues outstanding, with a total value of $22 billion. FHLB securities are issued in February, May, August and November at coupon rates that reflect money market conditions at the time. The interest rate is subject to Federal taxes but not to state and local taxes. Further information may be obtained from the Federal Home Loan Bank Board, 320 First Street N.W., Washington D.C. 20552.

Federal Home Loan Mortgage Corporation (FHLMC), also known as "Freddie Mac," raises funds to buy home mortgages from savings and loans associations and savings banks when these institutions need more money to finance new housing in tight money periods. FHLMC securities are all big-ticket items: *mortgage-backed bonds* with maturities of 12 to 25 years and a minimum purchase of $25,000; *participation certificates*, with a minimum purchase of $100,000, which are backed by pools of individual mortgages and the guarantee of the FHLMC itself; and *guaranteed mortgage certificates*, which also have a minimum denomination of $100,000 and carry a FHLMC guarantee that it will buy back the mortgage certificates at par after 15 years. Freddie Mac securities are all subject to federal, state and local taxes.

Federal National Mortgage Association (FNMA), otherwise known as "Fannie Mae," is a publicly owned entity—its common stock is listed on the New York Stock Exchange. Fannie Mae's job is to raise funds to buy mortgages from savings and loans, banks and insurance companies, when credit is tight and these institutions find it hard to raise funds. Fannie Mae raises money by issuing several kinds of securities: *discount notes*, which mature in 30 to 270 days and require a minimum investment of $50,000; *debentures* maturing in 3 to 25 years, with a minimum required purchase of $10,000; and *mortgage-backed bonds*, with a minimum $25,000 investment. All these securities are subject to federal, state and local taxes.

The six government-sponsored enterprises we have listed above account for about three-quarters of the total debt of the federal agencies, with a total of more than $76 billion outstanding. The agencies listed below account for the remaining quarter and are owned outright by the United States government.

Government National Mortgage Association (GNMA), or "Ginnie Mae," provides money for housing programs where established home-financing facilities are inadequate. This is a new type of government security, set up in 1968, and is backed by mortgages on property as well as the full faith and credit of the United States government. Ginnie Mae bonds are mainly for big institutional investors, however. The minimum amount you can buy is $25,000, to which you can then add $5,000 at a time. By mid-1975 nearly $18 billion worth of these securities were outstanding, of which only 1.3% were held by individual investors. Ginnie Mae issues three kinds of securities, all of which are subject to federal, state and local taxes: *mortgage-backed securities*, with a minimum purchase of $25,000; *participation certificates*, with a minimum investment of $5,000; and *modified pass-through securities* (minimum investment $25,000), which are created when a mortgage bank assembles a group of individual mortgages into a pool of at least $1 million. The pool is guaranteed by GNMA, and the GNMA mortgage-backed certificates are then sold to investors. The attraction of the Ginnie Mae security is that it offers the investor about the same yield as he could get from a mortgage, with much less paperwork, plus, of course, the government guarantees. The securities are sold by banks and thrift institutions throughout the country. Further information may be obtained from GNMA, Department of Housing and Urban Development, Washington D.C. 20410.

Export-Import Bank (Exim Bank) raises funds to finance trade between the United States and foreign countries. The securities it issues are backed by the full faith and credit of the United States government, but their interest payments are subject to federal, state and local taxes. Exim Bank securities come in three types: *short-term discount notes*, with a maturity of 30 to 360 days and a minimum required investment of $100,000; *participation certificates*, with a minimum purchase of $5,000; and *debentures*, with a maturity of three to seven years, on which your minimum investment is also $5,000.

Farmers Home Administration (FHDA) borrows money to make real estate and housing loans to farmers. It issues two kinds of securities, both of which are guaranteed by the federal government and are also subject to federal, state and local taxes: *insured notes* and *certificates of beneficial ownership*. These are big ticket items that usually are sold to big institutions in $500,000 lots, but the *certificates* may also be bought with a minimum $25,000 investment. You will have to wait a year for your interest, however. FHDA securities pay interest annually.

Federal Housing Administration (FHA) provides government insurance for home mortgages and it issues a peculiar type of security to raise funds when any of these mortgages go into default. Each security is an individual case, since it conforms to the yield, maturity, and amount of the particular defaulted mortgage it covers. This is certainly the smallest investment you could make in any of the federal government agencies—you could theoretically buy one of these securities for as little as $50, although a more usual denomination is $1,000. As there is very little trading in these small-ticket items you would have to reckon on holding them to maturity. The interest they pay is subject to federal, state and local taxes, but they are guaranteed unconditionally by the United States government.

Tennessee Valley Authority (TVA) securities are not backed by the United States government, but they have first claim on the TVA's net income from its sales of electric power in the Tennessee River Valley. There are two types of TVA securities (both subject to federal taxes but not to state or local taxes): *short-term notes*, which are of no interest to the average investor as they sell in lots of $1 million; and TVA *bonds*, where the minimum purchase is only $1,000.

U.S. Postal Service has one bond issue outstanding, which is *not* guaranteed by the United States government. The minimum denomination is $10,000, the issue matures in 1997 and is callable after 1982.

Federal Financing Bank was created in 1974 to handle borrowing by dozens of smaller federal agencies, which are lumped together under one umbrella organization, making it easier for them to raise money efficiently. This notable institution appears to be the final solution to bureaucratic overstaffing. It consists of one small office and a part-time director, and it has no full-time employees. Its loan portfolio is more than $18 billion. To put it unkindly, the Federal Financing Bank is a gimmick which enables a horde of government agencies and other bodies to borrow money without the debt ever showing up on the federal budget deficit. When it was on the verge of default, New York City turned at once to this bank, which bought $600 million worth of City paper. Federal Financing Bank bonds have a minimum denomination of $10,000 and are sold several times a year in much the same way as Treasury bills. You can put in a non-competitive bid at the nearest Federal Reserve Bank and get the security at the average price of the auction, just as you do with Treasury bills.

Buying and selling federal agency securities

In fact the procedures for buying many of the Federal Agency securities mentioned in this chapter are similar to those for buying Treasury bills, notes, and bonds. You can get information on forthcoming sales from your broker, bank, a Federal Reserve bank, or the Agency itself on the date, terms, and conditions of the sale.

Once the Agency securities are issued they are traded largely on the over-the-counter market by securities dealers who specialize in government securities. The quotation spreads are usually larger than the spread on United States government securities, and this disadvantage may well nullify any benefit from the larger yield the Agencies provide as compared with Treasury bills, notes, or bonds. The smallest spread is likely to be found in the Agency securities traded on the American Stock Exchange, now that the Amex has started trading in odd lots of these securities. Buying and selling through the Amex is probably the most convenient way to buy, sell, or hold these securities, as it eliminates a lot of paperwork and allows you to trade in smaller quantities. The Amex launched trading in Federal Agency securities, with 39 issues of the Federal Land Banks, in November 1975, and added the other agencies later on.

Municipal bonds

In 1975 the average price of tax-exempt bonds was bumping down around an all-time low, and the Dow Jones municipal bond index—which is of course the inverse reflection of the low price—was flirting with its highest-ever reading of 7.24%, set in December 1974.

If you had bought a representative portfolio of municipal bonds in 1964—a time of relatively low interest rates—your bonds would have been worth in 1975 about 60 cents for every dollar you invested.

The advantage of these bonds, and the main reason they are still being sold in spite of drastic price declines and growing fears of default, is precisely the tax-exempt feature. A municipal bond yielding 6.5% will give you the equivalent of 10.8% on a taxed investment if you are in the 40% tax bracket; it will yield you 13% if you are in the 50% bracket. And 13% covers a multitude of other sins for many people.

One unpleasant side-effect of inflation is that it pushes more and more people into higher and higher tax brackets without any corresponding increase in their standard of living. This is another reason why tax-exempt municipals, once the private preserve of the yacht and caviar set, are now an attractive loophole even for hard-pressed wage-earners.

However, the step down from Federal government securities to municipal bonds is a big one. It is like the difference between lending money to a man who can print his own money to pay you back and one who can't. If the man who can't runs out of cash, you're stuck with a bad debt.

New York City—the horrible example

That the danger is not merely theoretical was demonstrated in 1975 by the nation's biggest and richest city. "Day of Reckoning Arrives for New York As Money Runs Out," read a front-page headline in the *Wall Street Journal* on May 20, 1975.

"The city's controller, Harrison Goldin, called off a $280 million note auction for yesterday," the *Journal* story added, "because no buyers were in sight. Instead, he sat down in secret with banking syndicates to try to negotiate a loan that would keep New York on its feet until June 11. He failed." Only a last-minute advance of $400 million from New York State enabled city hall to meet its debt and payroll obligations for the month of May.

Desperate appeals for help to higher authorities went unheeded. Federal help, said President Ford, "would only postpone New York's coming to grips with the problem." The Federal Reserve Board, too, was stony-hearted. "I would strongly caution against any proposals that would provide direct access to central bank credit by hard-pressed governmental units," said the Federal Reserve Vice Chairman, George W. Mitchell. "The result could be a debasement of the nation's money and a ruinous domestic inflation." If New York City asked for money, he warned, "the Federal Reserve would have to turn it down."

Treasury Secretary William Simon was even more callous to the city's plight. If New York had to default on its debt and declare itself bankrupt, said the Secretary, then so be it. The impact on the national economy would be "negligible."

The city at this time owed $6 billion in short-term debt, and other observers were considerably more jittery than Simon. Contractors were refusing to provide the city with supplies, except in return for cash. Foreign bankers were nervously considering withdrawing funds from New York City banks if the situation worsened. Communist propaganda from Moscow was having a field-day, pointing to the bankruptcy of New York, the world center of 'monopoly capitalism,' as a dire warning of the final crisis of the capitalist system. The dollar weakened on foreign exchange markets. In the eyes of the world, United States prestige was on the line and a huge international monetary crisis would ensue if it allowed New York to default.

"New York's gathering financial storm," reported the *Wall Street Journal* at the height of the crisis, "caused the interest return on some of its near-term notes to be raised to an astonishing 60% on an annual basis in the resale market. But there were few, if any, buyers, dealers said."

No records of ownership of its bonds are kept by New York City, but apparently the major part of its bond and note issues were in the hands of individual investors. These small bondholders, typically around retirement age and depending on the securities for their income, held about $5 billion worth of notes and bonds as the city approached default in late 1975. They were estimated to number anywhere from one hundred thousand to several hundred thousand persons, among them Mayor Abraham Beame himself, who said he held $90,000 in city obligations.

All these investors, who had been seeking steady, safe income, now found to their dismay that the purchase of tax-free municipal issues was not the solid, conservative investment they had imagined. In 1975, as the yield on New York securities soared higher and higher, many middle-income families joined the ranks of the wealthier New York bondholders, attracted by the irresistible allure of a 9% tax-free yield. The city obligingly accommodated these little people on its trip to fiscal disaster by lowering the minimum city note denomination from $25,000 to $10,000.

Municipal bonds are exempt from registration with the Securities and Exchange Commission, which requires all private business promoters to make full disclosure statements of the possible risks to investors before they issue stock to the public. As events unfolded in New York, the SEC quietly started an investigation to establish whether city officials, banks, and brokers had defrauded investors by selling them New York City securities. Worse was still to come. Federal, state, and city officials would soon be proposing solutions that bondholders might reasonably consider as subjecting them to fraud, extortion, and blatant violations of their constitutional rights.

As Sin City teetered from one threatened day of default to another, New York State finally came to its aid and set up the Municipal Assistance Corporation, "Big Mac," to divert stock transfer fees and other taxes from the profligate politicians of the Big Apple into the hands of investors. Big Mac issued $1 billion in tax-exempt bonds paying interest rates up to 9.5%, but even the best selling efforts of 365 securities dealers and banks across the country left about a third of the bonds unsold on the day of issue. An outraged Mayor Beame found it "incredible that this agency, an instrument of New York State, is forced to sell bonds at an interest rate exceeding 9%. There isn't a safer security in the tax-exempt market." Since Beame had been city comptroller before becoming mayor, in the years that New York was digging itself into its financial hole, perhaps investors viewed the bonds as diners might consider a restaurant where they knew that Typhoid Mary was still running the kitchen.

As the crisis deepened through mid-1975 at least one large brokerage house vigorously touted New York City securities as "the second safest investment in America," urging investors to take advantage of sinking prices because "the city's bondholders are required by law to be paid off first—before the policemen, before the firemen, before even the mayor himself collects his salary." By the end of August there was considerable doubt about this. City Counsel Bernard Richland warned that the city's first priority if it defaulted would be to pay municipal workers and keep city services functioning. Holders of city securities would have to wait for their money he said.

In September the politicians moved to make it legal, presenting a bill in Albany to suspend the "first lien" rights guaranteed to New York bondholders by the state constitution. While the state politicians were making their little plans, there now was action on the federal level, too. In October President Ford insisted he would veto any federal bailout of New York City, but he had now thought up his own solution to the problem. Once the city was in the hands of the bankruptcy court, said the President, the bankruptcy law would be changed so that "the court would be empowered to authorize debt certificates covering new loans to the city, which would be paid out of future revenues ahead of the other creditors." In other words the city would go on borrowing money from new investors, leaving its old creditors to whistle for their money.

New York Governor Hugh Carey objected that Ford's plan would send not only the city but New York State into default as well. This seemed likely to happen in any event, since the state, now hopelessly entangled in the drowning clutches of its major city, was unable to sell any new bond issues to skeptical investors and was facing a $200 million budget deficit. The same brokerage house that had touted New York securities a few months earlier now vigorously advertised the merits of selling or swapping New York securities so as to establish tax losses, proudly pointing to the fact that it was perhaps the biggest and most experienced dealer in New York City paper.

In November 1975 some of the best legal minds in the country came up with a solution that quite obviously excelled everything that had gone before—since the critical problem was to avoid a default, why not declare a moratorium instead? "Default," explained one legal expert, "is a failure to do what the law says you have to do. A moratorium is an adjustment of the law in the face of a fiscal emergency." In both cases investors do not get their money when they are supposed to. The moratorium ax was to fall on the city revenue anticipation notes, the shortest term problem and thus the most pressing. These were notes the city sold to investors at a 10% interest rate, pledging the tax money it had not collected yet but hoped to extract from the owners of rent-controlled buildings and other sources. Building owners were abandoning their properties at the rate of 20,000 apartments a year at this time because the controlled rents were insufficient to cover their taxes and other expenses.

The holders of these dubious short-term notes, said Governor

Carey, would be required to trade them in for Big Mac bonds with a fifteen-year maturity. If they did not like to tie up their money for so long they would have to accept a 6% interest rate instead of 10% and they still would not be allowed to cash them in at maturity, perhaps not even for several years.

"The Municipal Assistance Corporation," said Big Mac in its newspaper advertisements, "has no taxing power. The 1975 bonds do not constitute an enforceable obligation, or a debt, of either the State or the City and neither the State nor the City shall be liable thereon. Neither the faith and credit nor the taxing power of the State or the City is pledged to the payment of principal or interest on the 1975 bonds." Big Mac bonds were soon trading at a deep discount from par value—about 65 cents on the dollar.

It could be that extortion and fraud are rather strong epithets to use in a case like this, but investors in New York City paper did have the distinct feeling that they were being shabbily treated by the powers that be.

This was indeed an oblique confirmation of the principle that power comes out of the barrel of a gun. The crucial fact for city, state, and federal politicians was that while certain classes of people are liable to riot in the streets, bondholders generally speaking do not. One million welfare clients tearing the city's supermarkets apart as soon as their welfare checks stopped coming; policemen walking off the job when the paychecks stopped; firemen walking away from their engines as the city went up in flames—these were the pictures that a city default conjured up for the politicians, and it was all just too awful to contemplate. If anyone had to give, it would have to be the investors in city securities.

One unhappy buyer of New York City notes went so far as to challenge the constitutionality of the Big Mac solution in the courts. The moratorium, a New York State Supreme Court Justice blandly declared, violated neither the federal nor the state constitution since priority must be given "to the public interest over strict compliance" with contract obligations.

At all events, the solution was satisfactory to President Ford, who dropped his opposition to federal aid and pledged $2.3 billion in short-term loans for the city.

Such was the course of events in New York and, human

nature being what it is, an investor in municipal bonds can anticipate something roughly similar in any other city that goes into financial difficulties. A holder of 25-year bonds might reflect that the process does not take all that long. It took New York City a little more than 10 years to dig itself into its financial hole. It posted a $100 million deficit in 1964, and the shortfalls widened steadily from there on until, in 1975, the gap between municipal income and expenses was $1.5 billion, 13% of the city's entire budget. The projection for 1976 as the crisis erupted in 1975 showed interest payments alone of $2 billion. This was the total amount of the whole city budget only fifteen years before. All of this was covered up by bookkeeping that could fairly be called imaginative and innovative to a high degree. Capital expenditures and current expenses became inextricably confused with each other, and pension fund calculations were based on actuaries' tables that had not been updated since 1913. These and other financial maneuvers, unkindly called "gimmicks," finally became unworkable as the situation became more desperate.

With all the publicity given to New York's financial woes, other cities across the country found it increasingly difficult to raise the money they needed, and they had to pay sharply higher interest rates to attract investors. The mere threat of a New York City bankruptcy caused jitters in a financial market that every year raises $22 billion in new capital for local governments across the United States.

The municipal bond market and bond ratings

The municipal bond market includes state securities as well as city obligations, and the bonds of school districts, highway and tunnel authorities, county governments, and other local bodies. All in all, there are something like 150,000 tax-exempt municipal issues available. New York accounts for a large share—perhaps 20% of the dollar amount of the whole.

You can exclude the vast majority of these thousands of issues from your consideration as possible investments. Many are small issues for which there is no ready market and where the spread between the bid and asked price will wipe out any advantage of a big tax-exempt yield when you try to sell your bonds before maturity. Some are not rated by the bond-rating services, and they, too, should be excluded, in case you find yourself holding the bonds of a penniless mini-New York away out in the boondocks.

So you are left with the bigger and more liquid issues, where the rating services give you some idea of their investment quality. There are three main bond-rating services: Standard & Poor's, Moody, and Fitch. Standard & Poor's divides rated bonds into seven groups. These groups are listed below, from highest to lowest.

> *AAA Prime* (This is the highest quality—comparable to U.S. Government bonds.)
> *AA High Grade*
> *A Upper Medium Grade*
> *BBB Medium Grade*
> *BB Lower Medium Grade* (This is the lowest investment-grade security. From here on down you are dropping into speculative territory.)
> *B Low Grade*
> *D Defaults* (Either interest or principal or both are in arrears.)

Standard & Poor's publishes a monthly *Bond Guide,* with the latest ratings and other details, to which you may subscribe for $50 a year (Standard & Poor's Corp., 345 Hudson Street, New York 10014).

Moody has a slightly different rating system in which issues rated from AAA to Baa are considered as investments rather than as speculations. Fitch's service is a smaller outfit which rates a fewer number of issues.

The ratings are not infallible, however, nor are they immutable. Your BB investment may be pushed over the borderline into a B speculation from one month to the next. Some critics even find the rating services excessively generous in their appraisals of financially shaky borrowers. New York City got an A rating from Standard & Poor's in December 1974—coupled with a warning about balancing its budget—just a few months before the city ran out of money.

Barron's magazine finds that the rating agencies "shy away from downgrading municipalities, particularly if it means a drop below investment grade, because banks would then be barred from buying their bonds. . . . While no rating service will admit it, politics is heavily involved in the rating process, with pressure for good credit ratings coming from both city hall and the financial community."

How great is the danger of default?

Altogether there is about $150 billion worth of municipal bonds outstanding. How much of this is in danger of default? Since World War II the risk has been considered very small. From 1940 to 1975 about 500 defaults were reported in municipal bonds, a very small percentage of the 150,000 issues now in existence. But in the Great Depression of the 1930s the indebtedness of state and local governments in default is reported to have amounted to about 15 percent of the total municipal debt outstanding at the time.

As far as municipal securities were concerned, this was the worst financial decade in the nation's history. No less than 4,770 cities, towns, counties, school districts, and other local government units defaulted on their debts. They included Detroit and President Ford's home town, Grand Rapids, Michigan.

This was probably about two thirds of all the municipal defaults in all of American history. From the 1840s—which is about as far back as accurate records extend—until this time, there have been 6,195 defaults by local governments. The South appears to have been by far the most feckless region, with more than 2,100. The most financially reliable has been Puritanical New England, with less than 20. Perhaps you should give New Hampshire preference over New Orleans in selecting your municipal bonds. But then perhaps not. Most of the Southern defaults were perpetrated by carpetbagger regimes after the Civil War.

In any event, once again we are back to the Great Depression as our yardstick of financial disaster. Let us assume that a rerun of this calamity is the worst that can possibly happen. Almost all of the municipalities paid their creditors every cent of principal and interest due to them by the early 1940s. So what it would boil down to is a 15% chance of having your money tied up for 10 to 15 years before you can get your hands on it again—a not inconsiderable risk in these inflationary times.

How to insure your municipal bonds against default

You can eliminate this risk entirely through an insurance

policy which guarantees your municipal bonds against default. MGIC Indemnity Corporation, the company offering the insurance, says that "premiums have been computed to afford it reserves sufficient to meet its obligations under economic circumstances as serious as those that occurred in the Depression of the 1930s. Besides establishing reserves to meet normal anticipated losses, the company must set aside into a contingency reserve 50% of its premiums as earned for a period of at least 20 years to enable it to pay claims under catastrophic economic conditions.

"This new portfolio protection," says the insurer, "guarantees to owners of municipal bonds prompt payment of principal and interest when due, should a municipality fail to fulfill its obligations to its bondholders." The protection is not cancellable by the insurance company. However, while it guarantees the payment of interest and principal when due, it does not of course guarantee the market value of the bonds. This kind of insurance is also available, however, and we shall get to it farther ahead.

"Any amount of eligible bonds totaling $50,000 par value or more can be insured," says MGIC. "The bondholder is afforded the privilege of automatic annual policy renewal at the same premium rate as long as the portfolio continues to meet the size and diversity requirements of the insurer, regardless of whether investment ratings on the bonds in the portfolio are changed or removed, or the bonds default."

If you have bonds of three or more issuers, MGIC requires that their average quality must be as good or better than the Standard & Poor's BBB rating or Moody's Baa rating. If you have only one issue, it must be rated A+ or better by Standard & Poor's or A-1 by Moody.

The insurance of a $100,000 portfolio of three or more bonds could cost you $143, that is about $1.43 a year on each $1,000 bond. In the event of a default, you send in your unpaid bonds or coupons and get a check from the insurance company within 30 days. Further details may be obtained from the MGIC Indemnity Corporation, Municipal Bond Insurance Department, MGIC Plaza, Milwaukee, Wisconsin 53201.

If the $50,000 minimum insurable portfolio is too high for you, another possibility is the Tax Exempt Municipal Trust sponsored by Shearson Hayden Stone Inc., 767 Fifth Avenue, New York 10022. The Trust has a portfolio of bonds insured against default by MGIC, and is divided into units that were worth about $1,000 at the time of issue in 1975. Interest is paid monthly.

Also insured against default by MGIC is the First Trust of Insured Municipal Bonds, sponsored by Van Kampen Wauterlek & Brown Inc., 300 W. Washington Street, Chicago, Ill. 60606. It was issued with 4½% sales charge, and a minimum purchase of $5,000.

Some municipal bonds come with their own insurance against default, provided directly to the issuer by at least two companies in the business. One is American Municipal Bond Assurance Co. (AMBAC), and the other is Municipal Bond Insurance Association (MBIA). Issues insured by MBIA (more than 140 of them in early 1976) are given the highest AAA rating by Standard & Poor's, those insured by AMBAC are rated one notch lower, at AA. Moody's does not upgrade insured municipal bonds because it says it is not in the business of rating insurance companies.

Bank certificates of deposit, floating rate certificates, and notes

Bank certificates of deposit, issued by some big commercial banks, pay more than savings accounts—as much as 12% in 1974—but they are for the well-heeled investor. The minimum legal investment in a CD is $100,000, and some banks prefer to deal in $1 million lots. Only the first $40,000 is covered by FDIC insurance. A CD is a short-term investment maturing in 30, 60 or 90 days or more—rarely in six months to one year. You have to approach a bank directly to invest in a CD.

Floating rate notes were pioneered by Citicorp. (holding company of the First National City Bank of New York) in 1974, and they have now been issued by about a dozen major commercial banks. The Citicorp notes are a way of getting high interest rates in the short-term money market. They pay the going Treasury bill rate plus 1%, and they are accessible to the small investor, as they come in $1,000 denominations. The interest rate paid by Citicorp notes is adjusted every six months, and is set 1% above the prevailing rate for three-month Treasury bills. The notes expire in June 1989, but they carry optional maturities every six months all the way up to that date. What this means is that you are assured of redeeming your notes at 100 cents on the dollar every 180 days—a significant advantage over a conventional bond without this feature. The Citicorp notes thus "should be considered as six-month obligations and can be an attractive investment for the odd-lot buyer who wants to deal on the money market," says William McCullough of Merrill Lynch.

The floating rate notes issued by other banks vary in their details and interest rates. Some have six-month optional maturities, others do not. The latter, adds McCullough, "are an interesting investment for a small investor who wants to speculate on the movement of money market rates. But they are not suitable for an investor who needs an assured fixed level of income."

Some of the floating rate notes are listed below.

> Alabama Bancorporation (final maturity 1999)
> Chase Manhattan (final maturity 1999)
> Citicorp. (final maturity 1989)
> First Security Corp. (final maturity 1999)
> Mellon National Bank (final maturity 1989)

All these floating rate notes are rated AAA by Fitch's investor service, and have optional maturities every six months. They are all quoted on the New York Stock Exchange.

One floating rate note without optional maturities is that of the New York Bank for Savings, maturing in 1981. It yields either the current three-month Treasury bill rate plus 1¼%, or 10%, whichever is higher. It is rated AAA by Fitch.

In 1975 Chase Manhattan Bank and First National City Bank of New York started offering certificates of deposit with floating interest rates. The advantage was that you could get a better yield than on Treasury bills and avoid the trouble and inconvenience of constantly cashing in and repurchasing these short-term investments every few months. The Chase Manhattan floating-rate CD, for example, offered a yield 1¼% above the current three-month Treasury bill yield, with the rate readjusted monthly. Buyers of Chase Manhattan CDs could choose maturities of two to ten years and thus get the prevailing Treasury bill rate plus 1¼% throughout that period. Chase Manhattan offered non-negotiable certificates, while the First National City Bank's floating-rate CDs were negotiable instruments yielding 1% more than the bank's current certificate of deposit rate, with the rate being updated every 90 days.

Bankers acceptances

Bankers acceptances can be bought directly from a bank or through a dealer. The minimum lot is $25,000, but they are more suited to financial institutions than individual investors as the usual amount is $100,000 or more.

Acceptances usually mature in nine months or less. Like Treasury bills, they are bought at a discount and redeemed at face value. The issuing bank guarantees payment at maturity.

Acceptances are among the highest yielding investments. In 1974, interest rates went up to 12.5% on a six-month acceptance. The acceptance is a negotiable time draft drawn to finance a foreign trade deal or other business transaction that is "accepted" by a bank from the firm involved in the deal. The bank charges the firm 1½% to put its bank guarantee of payment on the document, so acceptances can be a horribly expensive way of financing trade deals. But they are apparently indispensable—there are more than $18 billion worth outstanding in the United States.

Corporate bonds

If the mushrooming government debt gives you nervous fits, the nation's corporate debt should be an eye-opener, too. In 1975 American corporations owed nearly twice as much money as the federal government, federal agencies, state governments, and local governments combined. United States corporations owed $1.25 trillion, while the government debt was $642 billion. And what is more, corporate debt was growing at a faster rate than the government debt or the debt of individual citizens. It had doubled in just six years, from $631 billion in early 1969.

"The burden of supporting this mounting debt load has been intensified," says Kidder Peabody economist Sam Nakagama, "because it occurred during a period of escalating interest rates.

Gross interest payments by non-financial corporations climbed from $12.2 billion in 1965 to $41.6 billion by 1973." In 1974 the figure appears to have topped $50 billion. Nakagama points out that "until the mid-1960s American corporations had been largely self-sufficient" in financing themselves, and he finds their growing debt load worrisome—particularly so because their indebtedness has been growing sharply in proportion to their equity capital.

This general picture is the first thing to keep in mind when you buy the bonds of any American corporation. Such a corporate borrowing spree is a strong warning to buy only the bonds of the strongest and most credit-worthy companies.

Corporate bonds are rated in the same way as municipal bonds. Standard & Poor's ranking system is identical—AAA, AA, A, BBB, BB, B—until it comes down to outright junk, classified CCC, CC and C. The latest ratings are available in Standard & Poor's monthly *Bond Guide*. To be safe, it would be advisable not to go below A-rated bonds, or perhaps even AA.

In view of the constant danger of inflation flaring up in the decades ahead, the shorter the maturity, the safer you are against being paid off in progressively more worthless dollars. Maturity five years ahead would be around the outer limit of prudence as far as inflation is concerned. "Call protection" is also important. This is a promise made by some issuing companies not to call in and pay off the bonds for at least five years. This assures the initial investor of receiving his yield for a specific period of time.

Private enterprise corporations may be more productive for the national economy than the federal government or local governments, but as investments their bonds have weaknesses. For one thing, the United States government can print more money as needed to pay off its creditors, and local governments can raise taxes to meet their obligations. Corporations can do neither. For another thing, government and municipal bonds are tax-exempt, while corporate bonds are not.

Another drawback for the small investor buying just a few bonds, or perhaps even one bond at a time, is that the bond market is set up for the big financial institutions. Ninety-five per cent of the people in the bond market are making million-dollar deals, and the competition is sharp among dealers for this kind of business, with brokers offering razor-thin spreads. When you come into this market with a $5,000 order, you are likely to find that the bond quoted at 90 in the newspaper will cost you 95 if you are buying and fetch you only 85 if you are selling. The brokerage commission on bond trading may be small compared with common stocks, but the price spread can be murderous for the small investor.

Bond funds

One way to avoid this problem is to buy the shares of a bond fund quoted on the New York Stock Exchange. You would thus pay the normal buying or selling commission for stocks and buy a diversified portfolio of bonds in one package without being scalped by the bond dealers. Bond funds quoted on the NYSE include the following:

American General Bond	John Hancock Income Securities
Bunker Hill Income Sec.	John Hancock Investors
CNA Income Shares	Massachusetts Mutual Inc. Invest.
Current Income Shares	Montgomery Street Inc. Sec.
Drexel Bond	Mutual of Omaha Int. Shares
Excelsior Income Shares	Pacific American Income
Fort Dearborn Income Sec.	Standard & Poor's Intercapital
Hatteras Income Sec.	St. Paul Securities
INA Income Sec.	State Mutual Securities
Independence Square Inc. Sec.	USLIFE Income Fund

These are closed-end funds, and they tend to sell either at a premium or a discount from their net asset value. You will find them listed weekly in *Barron's* magazine in a table headed Closed End Funds, which gives the latest price and the premium or discount. The disadvantages of these funds are that some are not really as safe as they might appear because they can leverage their operations by borrowing. Others churn their portfolios with great vigor, incurring high operating expenses. The average fund charges a $\frac{1}{2}\%$ annual management fee and has operating expenses of $\frac{1}{2}$ to $\frac{3}{4}\%$ a year, which reduces the effective yield by 1 to $1\frac{1}{4}\%$.

There are also open end mutual funds available, but the usual $8\frac{1}{2}\%$ sales charge could take up the entire first year's interest income or more. One no-load fund is Fidelity Thrift Trust, which specializes in corporate and United States government obligations maturing in less than seven years.

Convertible bonds

Convertible bonds were all the rage in the late 1960s. About $12 billion worth were issued in the three years up to 1969. They were apparently a sure thing, with the safety and assured income of a bond, plus the capital appreciation potential of the common stock into which they were convertible.

The combination was seemingly foolproof. It did not work out that way, however, after 1969, when interest rates soared and the stock market plunged. The convertibles had too low a yield to compete with higher interest rate bonds, and it was pointless to convert them into a stock that had dropped far below the stipulated conversion price. By the early 1970s less than a million dollars worth of new convertible bonds were coming on the market.

It is risky to invest heavily in a single convertible bond. One is betting heavily on the fortunes of an individual company. However, there are convertible bond funds available that spread the risk over perhaps 20 or 30 different companies. Such a fund might make a good investment when the stock market is in a strong uptrend and interest rates are low—an unlikely combination in a period of high inflation. This is something to consider when inflation is firmly under control and seems likely to remain so for some time. Funds specializing in convertible bonds include American General Convertible Securities, Bancroft Convertible Fund, Castle Convertible Fund and Chase Convertible Fund.

Preferred stock

Preferred stock pays dividends instead of interest, usually quarterly. Unlike a bond, it has no maturity, no fixed date on which you will get your investment back.

When you buy preferred stock, you rank between the bondholders and the common stock owners. If times are bad and the company goes into liquidation, the bondholders have first claim on the proceeds, then come the preferred stock holders, and the common stock owners get whatever scraps are left over, if any. In good times, the bondholders get their interest first, then the preferred stock holders get whatever fixed rate of interest they are entitled to, and any profit left over after that is available to pay dividends to the common stock owners.

If the company has a bad patch and is unable to pay dividends on its preferred stock one year, some preferred issues are entitled to be paid the skipped dividend in some later year. This is cumulative preferred stock. Other preferred issues have a right to share in the company's profits over and above their fixed interest rate when business is extraordinarily good. These are participating preferred stocks. Yet others give the owner the right to exchange his preferred stock for common shares at a predetermined price. These are convertible preferred.

Every preferred stock is thus highly individual, depending on the rights its owner enjoys. Even more fundamentally, its worth hangs on the quality of the company issuing it.

Standard & Poor's has a rating system that ranks preferred stock in seven categories: AAA (prime), AA (high grade), A (sound), BBB (medium grade), BB (lower grade), B (speculative), and C (nonpaying). The latest ratings may be obtained from Standard & Poor's monthly *Security Owner's Stock Guide*.

Commercial paper

This is where you get the highest yield in the short-term money market and for a good reason—commercial paper carries the highest risk. When you buy it you are acquiring an unsecured obligation of a finance company or some other corporation that promises to repay your money plus interest in a period ranging up to nine months. The only guarantee is the word of the borrowing corporation itself, so you had better be sure whom you are dealing with.

About 700 big companies regularly issue commercial paper, which is graded by the rating services. The rating gives you a general idea of the quality, but it is not infallible. Moody's has three rankings: Prime 1, Prime 2, and Prime 3 (lower ratings might as well be disregarded, as there is no market for them).

Standard & Poor's also has a three-tier classification: A-1, A-2, and A-3 (B, C, and D ratings exist but are not used). Fitch, too, uses three rankings: F-1, F-2 and F-3.

Do not let a high rating lull you into complacency. When Penn Central went bankrupt in 1970, the holders of $85 million worth of the railroad's commercial paper saw their money go down the drain. This paper held a Prime rating right up to the day that Penn Central filed its petition for bankruptcy.

The commercial paper market is a big one, and the average deal is not for the little guy. There is about $50 billion worth of commercial paper floating around in the American economy nowadays—despite the Penn Central fiasco—and the usual deal is for $100,000 to $1 million at a time.

Through some brokers, however, (Merrill Lynch is one) you can buy $25,000 worth of paper for a $25 fee. Some companies also offer their paper directly to the public. General Motors Acceptance Corporation sells paper in $25,000 lots. Chrysler Financial Corporation has even offered minimum denominations of $5,000. Other direct sellers of their own commercial paper include Ford Motor Credit, General Electric Credit, Sears Roebuck Acceptance, and CIT Financial.

Commercial paper has usually yielded around 1% more than the prevailing rate on Treasury bills, but in 1974 it went as high as 13%, the biggest yield since Civil War days.

Insurance against loss

Now that we have run through all these possibilities, from United States Savings Bonds down to commercial paper, there is still one crucial point to consider. This is the risk of selling at a loss.

With the exception of Savings Bonds and a savings account, all the other investments mentioned expose you to this risk. Even if you feel absolutely secure by holding the highest quality AAA bonds that are also insured against default, the bonds will fluctuate in price on the market and you may have to sell at a loss if you need your money back before the bond matures.

In some cases you can insure against this risk, too.

The insurance is provided by Harleysville Mutual Insurance Company, of Harleysville, Pennsylvania, to a number of mutual funds, which in turn guarantee that you will not have to sell your fund shares at less than you paid for them, within certain time limits.

Bond funds providing their investors this guarantee against loss include, at the present time, the Westminster Bond Fund, the Fund for Federal Securities, and Whitehall Money Market Trust in the Vanguard group of funds, as well as the National Bond Fund, and National Preferred Fund in the National Securities group. All these are load funds, however—in buying them you have to pay an 8.5% sales charge.

Harleysville Mutual is given the highest rating for insurance companies by *Best's Insurance Reports.* You can insure your mutual fund holding against loss for fixed periods of 10, 12½ or 15 years. The minimum insurable holding with any of these mutual funds is $3,000, and the yearly premium is 0.6% of the insured assets.

You will find more details on this type of insurance in the chapter on common stock investments, as the guarantee against loss is aimed mainly at investors who are nervous about the wild ups-and-downs of the stock market.

With all this insurance guaranteeing you 100 cents back on every dollar you invest, there is, however, still no insurance against inflation. Until somebody in the United States gets around to issuing bonds indexed to the cost of living, inflation will continue to eat the assets you invest in bonds and other securities denominated in paper dollars.

Money market funds

Pending the arrival of an inflation-indexed security, your best protection—and not a very effective one when the rate of inflation is accelerating—is to get the highest possible yield and to tie up your money for the shortest possible time. A special type of fund has been created in recent years to meet this need—the money market fund or liquid asset fund.

This is a specialized type of mutual fund that invests in some or all of the short-term paper listed in this chapter—Treasury bills, bankers' acceptances, commercial paper, certificates of deposit, and federal agency securities. The typical liquid asset fund has a portfolio of securities with an average maturity of less than one year—in some cases only 30 to 60 days—so your money is not tied up in long-term investments. You can also get your money back quickly when you want it, within 24 hours in some cases.

You might consider the money market fund a package deal of all the short-term investments mentioned in this chapter. It has two big advantages. Firstly, it relieves you of the fuss and bother of constantly reinvesting your money every few months. Secondly, it places within your reach such high-yielding investments as a bank's negotiable certificate of deposit, where the minimum investment is $100,000.

Some of these funds have a minimum initial investment of $1,000 or even less. They are a relatively recent invention—the pioneer in the field, Reserve Fund, was launched in 1971—but their growth has been phenomenal. From 1971 to 1976 the number of money market funds grew to more than 30, and their total assets mushroomed to over $3 billion. Their most spectacular growth was in 1974, a highly inflationary year in which they were able to provide investors with yields of 11%, 12%, or more.

The funds grew because they met a basic need. Until they were created, the high-yield money market instruments paid far more than any investment the small investor could make on his own, but the big ticket deals were out of the small man's reach.

In choosing your money market fund you should keep in mind that they vary considerably in safety. A fund with all its assets invested in commercial paper may yield more, but it will be considerably more risky than a fund that restricts itself exclusively to United States government securities. And you will find all sorts of gradations in between.

Some of the more conservative money market funds (at the time of writing, at least—fund policies and portfolios change and may be different when you read this book) are described below.

Fund for United States Government Securities, 421 Seventh Avenue, Pittsburgh, Pennsylvania 15219, invests exclusively in securities guaranteed by the United States government. The sales charge is 1½% and the minimum investment $250.

California Fund for Investment in United States Government Securities, 1616 W. Shaw Avenue, Fresno, California, is a no-load fund investing mainly in federal securities. Minimum investment is $100.

Capital Preservation Fund, 459 Hamilton Avenue, Palo Alto, California 94301, limits itself to investments maturing in six months or less, and concentrates heavily on Treasury bills. Minimum investment is $1,000.

One of the biggest funds in the business is Dreyfus Liquid Assets, 600 Madison Avenue, New York 10022, a no-load fund with assets of about $900 million, invested mainly in bank certificates of deposit at the time of this writing. Minimum investment is $2,500.

Another large fund is Reserve Fund, 1301 Avenue of the Americas, New York 10019, a no-load fund with assets of $500 million, split half-and-half between certificates of deposit and letters of credit.

The time to invest in money market funds is when the Federal Reserve starts clamping down on the money supply to contain an unusually virulent outburst of price rises. Double-digit inflation then is followed by double-digit interest rates, as in 1974, and short-term investments such as bankers' acceptances suddenly start yielding twice as much as bank savings accounts.

The next swing of the economic cycle is the logical outcome of the tight-money stage. The scarcity of money and credit cause a business contraction that knocks the stock market for a loop. And the attraction of high interest rates pulls even more money out of common stocks into higher-yielding fixed interest securities, aggravating the stock market decline even further.

The time to invest in common stocks comes when the government is getting the inflationary upsurge under control and starts relaxing the monetary squeeze. Double-digit inflation and double-digit interest rates then begin receding. The high interest rate you are collecting from your money market fund starts sinking down to the level of an ordinary bank savings account. The time has come to start thinking about common stocks.

8

Common stocks:
When the rate of inflation
drops below 8.5% a year

The stock market has become increasingly volatile, in both directions. In this respect, it has been making the wild and woolly years when pools and bear raids operated without benefit of regulation look like a cakewalk.

—The *Wall Street Journal*, in early 1975

The name of the game in the stock market is to anticipate the future. If you could predict the movement of stock prices correctly six times out of ten, you would be assured of getting rich. It is as simple as that.

Unfortunately, the state of the fortune-teller's art has not progressed much since the reign of King Croesus of Lydia, who consulted the oracle at Delphi about his chances if he went on the warpath. "If you make war," said the oracle, "you will destroy a great empire." Off to war went Croesus—and the empire he destroyed was his own.

Judging by results, the writers of market letters, investment advisors, financial analysts, and other modern-day readers of omens in the stock market are to be treated as skeptically as the

Delphic oracle. About all that can be said with any certainty about the stock market—as J.P. Morgan stated many years ago—is that prices will fluctuate. That is just about where the stock market is at right now, and when it comes down to individual stocks, the fluctuations have been so wide, sudden, and erratic in recent years that it is a question whether a follower of the "Prudent Man" rule has any business nowadays buying shares in any company on Wall Street.

In one week in 1972, Levitz Furniture, the darling of Wall Street analysts up to that time, plunged from $59½ to $35 a share. Nearly half your money gone in seven days. One big mutual fund alone lost $24 million on Levitz stock. Levitz was a company with a dazzling record of unbroken sales and profit growth for the previous eight years—until the Securities and Exchange Commission questioned the financial data Levitz accountants were giving investors. Then the growth stock bubble burst.

One day in February 1974, Simplicity Pattern, another favorite of the growth stock cult, with a 14-year record of constant profit increases, plummeted from $32 to $20. A third of your money gone in 24 hours. A month later the stock was down to $15½. More than half your money gone in one month. And what heinous sin had this belle of Wall Street committed to become such a financial pariah? Management had estimated that quarterly profits would drop six cents, from 26 to 20 cents a share. In the ups and downs of the clothing business this may seem like a small thing. But to an officially anointed growth stock, any kind of earnings drop is the sin against the holy ghost.

Even Avon Products, a door-to-door supplier of women's beauty aids and the high priestess of the growth stock cult, fell from grace. But here the faithful fought harder to retain their faith and refused to let the Avon lady plunge to her death in a single day. It took Avon from the spring of 1973 to mid 1974 to drop from $140 to $18⅝ a share. More than 85% of your money gone in a little more than a year. And what had Avon done wrong? To begin with, a venial sin—the rate of earnings *growth* was allowed to decline. Profits were ahead six cents a share in the first quarter, up another four cents in the second, and then a mere two cents higher in the third. After that came the really unforgivable trespass—Avon, a certified blue-ribbon stock, showed an actual *decline* in earnings.

Is it really a prudent, or even rational decision to risk the loss of more than 80% of your capital on a bet that a company will enjoy larger and larger earnings to the end of time without a single quarterly dip in the rate of growth? And what will be the share's decline if, may the gods forbid, the company ever suffers a *loss*?

Perhaps never in the history of investing has there been a growth stock like IBM. It has grown and grown to the point where it makes something like three-quarters of the computers in the entire world. You could have bought this stock in a burst of euphoria at a high of $365½ in 1973, and sold it to meet a pressing financial need at a low of $150½ in 1974. More than half your money gone in a year in a stock that is rated A+ by Standard & Poor's—the highest corporate accolade, given to less than 60 aristocrats among American public corporations.

The growth cult has its points, but as Teuton sages observed long ago in some sacred grove of the Black Forest, the trees, folks, do not grow to the sky. And another kind of growth, that of the financial institutions trading in the stock market, has vastly increased the dangers for the individual investor. These giants have squeezed out the little guy to such an extent that it is questionable whether the market any longer performs its traditional function of pricing stocks in an orderly way through a continual flow of thousands of orders to buy or sell.

There are days when block trades of 10,000 shares or more hit the market by the hundreds, as the big institutions throw millions of dollars around at a time, with a violently disruptive effect on the prices of individual stocks. The institutions dominate the market. About 60% of the shares traded nowadays on the New York Stock Exchange are bought or sold by them. If you reckon it in the dollar volume of transactions, the figure rises to nearly 70% according to the Exchange. Small individual investors are left with only 30% of the market, and they run a considerable risk of being trampled underfoot by the financial behemoths.

Mutual funds are the first big institutions that come to mind in the stock market, and they do have considerable market clout. They own about $36 billion worth of stocks, and they trade heavily. Insurance companies are big, too, probably much bigger than the mutual funds, although there seems to be no accurate appraisal of their total common stock holdings.

But the superheavyweights of the stock market are the banks. Bank trust departments are estimated to manage about $360 billion worth of stocks—ten times more than the mutual funds. One bank alone, Morgan Guaranty Trust Company, controls stock market assets equal to somewhere between one-half and two-thirds of all the stocks owned by all United States mutual funds. This one bank plus the next two in size have more clout on the stock exchange trading floor than 500 mutual funds.

This awesome concentration of financial power is by no means a tightly-knit conspiracy or cabal of a handful of tycoons and family fortunes. The banks manage pension plans and profit-sharing programs for thousands of big companies and handle the wills and trusts of wealthy individuals. Altogether, their funds probably serve about 30 million employees, pensioners, and other people. Nevertheless, the fact remains that in these few banking institutions is concentrated control of a large proportion of the country's wealth.

What chance do you have when you match wits with the leviathans of the stock market? How does your 100-share order stack up against Morgan Guaranty's 10,000-share order to sell, reinforced by Chase Manhattan's 10,000-share sale, and perhaps First National City Bank's 20,000-share sale on a day when the bank trading officers see a 30-cent-per-share decline in the quarterly profits of the XYZ Corporation on the Dow Jones ticker? A decline that you don't see at all because you don't have access to a ticker and may or may not catch in the next day's newspaper, if, indeed, the item gets printed and you are not too busy to read it?

Do you have access to a computer to evaluate your stocks before you buy or sell? The big banks do. Do you employ a battery of financial analysts? The big banks do. A typical big bank operation goes like this: its computer constantly scans about 2,000 different stocks and spits out the names of about 200 that are doing especially well in sales, profits, or return on capital. The bank's two dozen analysts get to work on these 200, interview the management, study industry reports, surveys, trends, and projections, check the competing companies in the field, make further computer analyses, and narrow the field down to perhaps 20 stocks. By this time they know each company's prospects perhaps better than the top brass of the company itself.

The analysts' recommendations are rechecked by the bank's chief economist, who sees how they square with his prognosis for the United States economy as a whole. Finally, the whole package is set before the bank's investment officers, who make the ultimate decision to buy, sell, or hold. And then the 10,000 share orders start reeling off, perhaps swamping the XYZ Corporation with a 30% decline the day after you decided, by the seat of your pants, that XYZ is a good buy.

If you are getting the impression by this time that your 100-share order is something like a juicy little piece of plankton in an ocean of voracious whales, this would not be entirely accurate. Indeed, it would not be accurate at all. The banks are not all that good at swallowing little investors alive. In fact they usually do rather poorly. A number of recent studies have shown that bank trust departments have not even been able to match the performance of stock market averages, such as Standard & Poor's index of 500 stocks.

Take the case of the Continental Illinois National Bank of Chicago, which has the tenth largest bank trust department in the United States, with more than $7 billion in assets. According to the *Wall Street Journal,* "Continental's decision (in late 1974) to stay mostly with growth stocks cost it dearly. Its showcase $100 million pooled stock fund for pension funds dropped 40% through September 30, while the Standard & Poor's 500 stock average dropped only 32.7%."

There is a self-defeating quality in bigness. Just try to unload all your stock in Getty Oil Co. when your name is Jean Paul Getty and you own 65% of the shares outstanding. Just see what that does to the price. Some of the banks are so big that it is not worth their while to invest less than $10 million in a single company. They are also leery of owning more than 5% of any company's stock because of the wild price swings they would cause against their own interest by buying or selling in such large amounts. This limits them to a universe of perhaps 1,000 stocks that have a market valuation of $200 million or more. The big banks in many cases are locked into many of their investments by the sheer size of their holdings, and this lack of freedom to maneuver may in the end head them onto the same trail as the dinosaur.

If the stock market is dropping and you are so big that you cannot sell without making the decline even worse, you are doomed to sit still and watch your holdings shrink in value day after day. If you are a big bank and the decline goes on for months, the paper losses run into billions of dollars. How would you like to lose $9 billion in the stock market? You would still have to shed another $600 million more to match the amount that Morgan Guaranty dropped in two years in the bear market of 1972 to 1974. The total assets held by the bank as trustee or adviser to its clients shrank $9.6 billion, from $27.4 billion at the end of 1972 to $17.8 billion at the end of 1974.

One may be reasonably certain that if there had been any way to prevent a $9.6 billion shrinkage in 24 months, the big banks would have found it. Evidently, for all their sophisticated computers and investment analysts, this particular philosopher's stone has not yet been found. Croesus, were he a modern bank trust officer with a bullish oracle to egg him on, would probably not do much better today.

The biggest loss in Morgan Guaranty's financial empire was taken by the bank's employee-benefit funds, which declined from $14.1 billion in 1973 to $10.6 billion in 1974. If your company's profit-sharing or pension plan was somewhere in this dwindling pile of goodies, it could be that the analogy of the whales and the plankton may not seem so apt. Perhaps a more appropriate comparison would be to someone who finds himself trapped in a department store with a bunch of blind elephants. It would be invidious to single out Morgan Guaranty in the pension fund game, however. According to a study by Dreher, Rogers and Associates, a consulting firm, the equity portfolios managed by 188 banks and insurance companies for a large number of corporate pension funds lagged behind the market averages in recent years. On the average, these pension funds managed a mere 2.3% annual rate of return in the 1966-76 decade, compared with 2.7% for the Dow Jones average of 30 industrial stocks and 3.3% for Standard & Poor's average of 500 stocks.

You probably have no control over your company's pension plan and its investments, so there is nothing to be done about that. But if you invest your surplus cash in mutual funds, this is a financial institution over which you have veto power at least. You can sell out if your fund is not performing up to expectations.

So what can you expect from a mutual fund? Through diversification it should protect you against sudden deathly plunges of individual stocks. But do not pitch your expectations too high. The funds have not done much better than the big banks. According to studies by the Stanford Business School, the Wharton School of Finance, and the University of Rochester, mutual funds have just about matched the market indexes.

Despite all their vaunted claims of "professional management" of your portfolio, they might just as well have fired their highly paid analysts and bought their stocks at random. The results would have been the same.

Professor Michael C. Jensen of the University of Rochester found, in a 1969 study, that the funds actually do worse than the market once you compare the riskiness of their portfolios with that of the market as a whole. He found further that the funds underperform the market because of their management fees and brokerage costs, which in the 1945-64 period that he studied came to 0.9% yearly. What Jensen did not find was any solid evidence that any mutual fund can outperform the market on the basis of skill. While some funds did get better results than the market in general over a long period, their portfolios carried greater risks, and in any case there were no more of these overperformers than you would anticipate from the laws of probability.

If anything, the situation has perhaps worsened since Jensen's study, because the funds have been turning over 30% of their portfolios yearly since the performance-cult craze of the late 1960s, compared with only 20% previously, and this has added to the funds' brokerage costs.

You can check all this for yourself if you buy *Barron's* magazine and look up a table titled Lipper Mutual Fund Investment Performance Averages. This table exhibits the investment results obtained by 537 mutual funds, including 297 growth funds, 107 growth and income funds, 22 balanced funds, 107 income funds, and 4 bank and insurance funds. It compares them with the Dow Jones 30 industrial average, Standard & Poor's 500 stock index, the New York Stock Exchange index of all its listed stocks, and the American Stock Exchange average of all Amex stocks. The comparison is weighted in favor of the funds because their figures include reinvested dividends and capital gains (stock market averages exclude dividend reinvestment). Even so, the mutual funds of all types usually come out behind some of the market indexes every week, and sometimes underperform them all. If you assume, charitably, that they manage to keep level, a typical mutual fund investor would still be behind because of the usual 8½% mutual fund sales charge.

Evidently—comparing the big financial institutions with the average market performance, and even with the results of the small individual investor—bigger does not necessarily mean better. The essential reason for this is that—for the big bank, the mutual fund, and the small investor alike—the future remains The Great Unknown.

At first sight it might seem that a stock's price is a sober evaluation of a company's assets, productiveness, prospects, and of the efficiency of its management. One subconsciously assumes that the appraisal is made by cost-conscious accountants and shrewd analysts with slide rules, and that the consensus of all these judicious opinions is summarized in the price you see listed in the stock columns of your daily newspaper.

But to a large extent these prices are mere reflections of an imaginary universe of fears that may never come to pass and hopes that may never be fulfilled. Those prices that are figured so precisely to eighths of a point are something like mirages of things that never happened and probably never will happen. The only tangible evidence of this phantom world is, in fact, the stock's price.

Which is one way of saying that investors try to anticipate the future when they buy a stock. Rearmament and the prospect of a fat government defense contract pushes Lockheed stock higher because the company will presumably sell more planes to the Air Force. The fear of an Arab oil embargo and a gasoline shortage drives Ramada Inns stock lower because fewer motorists will patronize its motels. But in the end perhaps neither of these events will occur. For a while the stock prices acted as though they had occurred, and soon—when the adjustment to reality is made—the stock prices will reflect other imaginary hopes and fears.

Accountants may be accurate to the penny in reckoning past gains and losses, but in predicting coming political, governmental, or economic events you might just as well rely on a voodoo expert. There are no slide rules to measure the future, and the future is where the game is at in the stock market.

The unpredictability of what is to come is ruefully recognized by the financial giants themselves. Here is king-pin Morgan Guaranty looking back on 1975 in December of that year: "The past year has provided still another sobering reminder of the limited ability of anyone to peer confidently into the economic future. With the benefit of hindsight, it seems remarkable that the collective myopia of economists, policymakers, and businessmen could have been as pronounced as it was. The dominant outlook judgment for 1975 failed to warn of the debacle that lay ahead."

And in December 1974, Morgan Guaranty said: "The year now drawing to a close, surely no candidate for the economic Hall of Fame, has been doubly depressing because it did not even remotely resemble anyone's preconceptions. Some pessimists anticipated the extent of inflation, and some the decline of real output. But none saw the combination that in fact emerged. The majority of forecasters embraced a fairly bright view for 1974. Why have the events of 1974 departed so radically from the course charted?" This was the year that the Dow Jones average plunged to 577.60.

Maybe, you will say, 1974 and 1975 were exceptionally bad years for the economic soothsayers. Here is what came to pass in 1973, according to Morgan Guaranty: "What actually happened in 1973 bore little resemblance to what had been anticipated. The optimism of forecasters that inflationary pressures would remain reasonably moderate proved to have been totally unfounded. No matter what measure is used, 1973 was sheer disaster from the standpoint of price performance." Coming from a bank that dropped $9.6 billion in the stock market in 1973-74, that appears to be a fairly reasonable evaluation of what actually occurred and what was supposed to have happened according to the economists.

Indeed, if economic forecasters are still in business, it could be due largely to the fact that practically nobody goes to the trouble of looking up year-old newspapers to see whether last year's predictions turned out to be correct. Here is how the government's economic experts did in a thirteen-year period starting in 1963, according to Geoffrey H. Moore, Vice President of the National Bureau of Economic Research: "In four years the forecasts of a rising or falling inflation rate were correct, in four they were wrong, and in five the results were ambiguous. One could do as well, and with less ambiguity, by tossing a coin."

All of which is worth keeping in mind when sorting through the current crop of predictions at the time you read this book. If the forecasts have one thing in common from one year to the next, it is a tendency to violate the ancient Teutonic rule against trees growing to the sky. That is, they project current trends into the future as if they would continue forever. The earnings of growth companies will go on growing until doomsday. Japan was flooding the world with a rising tide of exports in the 1960s, therefore Japan will take over world trade, and perhaps the world, too. The Arab oil producers quadrupled the price of oil in the early 1970s and started piling up such a heap of cash that they would dominate the world's financial markets within twenty years, according to one batch of predictions—to say nothing of their buying up all of Japan on the side.

So, if it is not necessarily true that growth stocks will go on growing forever; if individual stock prices gyrate so wildly that they can halve your investment in a week; if the big bank trust departments can't beat the market averages; if mutual funds can't do any better and probably will do worse in the long run; if your own economic forecasts and stock market predictions are unlikely to beat those of the professionals, then what can you do about investing in the stock market that is anything better than a gamble or speculation on the future?

Insurance policies against stock market losses

In certain circumstances you can take out an insurance policy against selling your stocks at a loss. This type of insurance is sold by the Prudential Insurance Company of America to the buyers of its Prudential Gibraltar Fund who invest through a systematic investment plan.

Prudential gives you the option of making sure through this voluntary policy that at the end of a ten-year period you will get back whatever amount you have invested in the fund, plus the sales and custodial charges. The coverage costs 0.4% of your investment annually, and the minimum insurable investment is $1,000. What this means is that if you invest $10,000 in the fund and ten years later stock market prices have slumped to such an extent that your holdings are worth only $6,000, the insurance policy will make up the $4,000 difference. You will thus always get back 100 cents on the dollar, provided you hold your shares for ten years, no matter how the stock market sinks in that time.

Another two dozen funds offer similar optional insurance against loss, provided by Harleysville Mutual Insurance Co., of Harleysville, Pennsylvania. The Harleysville company is small, but it has an A+ policyholders' rating from *Best's Insurance Reports* and a financial rating of AAAAA, both of which are the highest ratings awarded to property and casualty insurance companies by Best's.

Harleysville, a company founded in 1917 by members of the puritanical Mennonite religious sect, does not deal directly with the public. It insures the fund distributor, who in turn offers the insurance to the buyers of the fund's shares. Funds offering the Harleysville insurance-against-loss plan as an option at the time of this writing include the following (the list seems to be growing fairly rapidly as the idea catches on among investors burned in the disastrous 1974 bear market):

> Alpha Fund
> Colonial Fund Group
> > Convertible Senior Securities Fund
> > Equities Fund
> > Growth Shares Fund

Income Fund
Ventures Fund
Delaware Group
    Decatur Income Group
    Delaware Fund
    Delta Trend Fund
    Delchester Bond Fund
National Securities & Research Group
    Fairfield Fund
    National Stock Fund
    National Growth Fund
Provident Fund for Income
Wellington Group
    Explorer Fund
    Fund for Federal Securities
    Ivest Fund
    W.L. Morgan Growth Fund
    Trustee's Equities Fund
    Wellesley Income Fund
    Wellington Fund
    Westminster Bond Fund
    Windsor Fund

This is how the plan works. When you buy your mutual fund shares you apply for the Harleysville insurance coverage. This provides you with an insured guarantee that on a specific date in the future—you may choose a term of 10, 12½, or 15 years—your holdings in the account will be worth in redemption value at least your original dollar investment, plus all other costs associated with the program. This means that on the valuation date, 10 to 15 years ahead, you must get back what you paid for the shares, plus the sales commission, the insurance premium, and the charge for administering the insurance program.

The premium amounts to 6% of the total investment and over a ten-year period would thus come to 0.6% a year. Administrative fees are 0.2% yearly, with a $12 yearly maximum. These costs are automatically deducted from the dividends and capital gains on your fund shares, so they are relatively painless to pay.

Suppose you buy $10,000 worth of fund shares in 1977. Your total premiums over ten years will be $600, or $60 a year, and the fees will total $120 ($12 a year). Total insurance cost $720. Total amount insured $10,720. When the valuation date comes round in 1987, let us suppose the worst—the stock market has crashed and your shares are worth only $4,000 on the market. You will collect the $6,720 difference from the insurance company. What is more, you do not have to sell your shares. You can hang onto them, and if they go up in value later on, the profit is all yours, in addition to the insurance payment.

Now let us make a more cheerful assumption about the future. In 1979 the stock market rises spectacularly and your $10,000 investment has grown to $30,000. You can lock in this profit by cancelling your old $10,000 policy and buying a new one that will guarantee you repayment of $30,000 in 1989. (In this case the insurance clock is set back to zero and you start a new ten-year insurance period.)

Some of the fund groups mentioned above allow you to switch from one fund to another within the group at a nominal charge, letting you take your insurance with you. The minimum investment you can insure under the Harleysville plan is $3,000, and the plan itself has been cleared by the authorities of nearly 40 states.

The insured mutual fund account gives you effective protection against loss in the stock market, but it has its limitations. Under the Harleysville plan you must agree to leave your shares in the custody of the administrator of the plan, and you also must agree to the automatic reinvestment of dividends and capital gains. If you want current income, this plan is not for you. If you should have to sell your shares before the 10, 12½, or 15 year term is up, you are not covered against loss and you will also forfeit your insurance premiums. So if you are an in-and-out trader or are likely to need your money back prematurely, this is not for you either.

A surprising number of investors apparently think the plan is not for them or are unaware of its existence. The couple of dozen mutual funds offering the coverage have combined assets of about $4 billion. In 1975 Harleysville reported a total of only $4.3 million in assets insured under its program. Apparently mutual fund buyers have not yet caught on to an idea that could have given them much peace of mind in the 1973-74 bear market, when the Dow Jones industrial average dropped from 1,051.70 to 577.60. The Fairfield fund and others were offering the insurance as far back as 1971.

The logical time to insure your mutual fund holdings against loss is when the stock market is hitting an all-time high. You then lock in all your profits. You must also keep in mind that your insurance will only pay off when ten years are up.

The question is what to do the rest of the time to protect yourself against the big risks of loss that common stocks entail.

Mathematics and the stock market

If you have the time and inclination for a do-it-yourself approach and are willing to take the risk of sudden, irrational plunges in individual stocks, here is one possible solution. Let's assume that our performance in the crystal ball department is unlikely to be better than any of the experts' dismal results.

Conceding that the future is unpredictable, mathematical rules are not. If you buy ten stocks at $50 each, your total investment is $500. Suppose you sell seven of them at a $10 loss each. Your total loss is $70. Suppose you sell the other three at a $40 profit each. Your total gain is $120. In other words, you have been wrong seven times out of ten, but you still come out $50 ahead on your $500 investment. This is the rationale of an old adage much quoted by stock market professionals: cut your losses short, let your profits run.

Simple though it seems, this is an extraordinarily difficult rule to follow. The natural human tendency is to let losses run, because to sell at a loss would be an admission of error. One hangs on to a losing stock and hopes against hope that the price will go up again. To sell at a profit comes easier—it is a confirmation that one was right. One tends to cash in and boast, "I made 30% on my XYZ stock"—which is all set for a 300% advance.

One old-timer who played the stock market strictly by the mathematical rules was Cyrus Q. Hatch, and he did extraordinarily well at it over a period of nearly 70 years. Hatch inherited $100,000 in 1871, when he was 21 years old. He died a multimillionaire in 1940. Deciding to put his $100,000 into the stock market, Hatch soon realized that nobody can predict when the market is going to top out or hit bottom. Nobody rings a bell when the market is turning, he observed.

The system he evolved was the next best thing, he thought, and it involved no predictions whatever. All it required was regular stock-taking and automatic buying or selling if prices were high or low. Hatch's basic system was simple. He bought a selection of common shares that represented a fair cross-section of the entire market, and under each stock he placed a stop-loss selling order if the price dropped by ten percent. He was thus sold out automatically whenever his losses hit more than ten percent. Every month he calculated the value of his holdings at the latest market prices. If prices were rising he stayed in the market, raising his stop-loss limits accordingly. When the value of his entire portfolio declined 10 percent, he sold out everything. He then stayed out of the market until it had hit a bottom, only buying back when prices had risen 10 percent from their lows.

His losses were thus limited to 10% each time, and this kept him out of a lot of trouble whenever the market plunged heavily. Hatch emerged unscathed in 1929, for example, by being sold out automatically before the stock market decline lurched down into the Great Depression. His gains were whatever the percentage difference was between the stock price low plus ten percent and the stock price high minus 10 percent. His system thus tended to do especially well in periods of great stock market volatility, when his gains could really roller-coaster upward on a rising market. And volatility is where the game is at in today's stock market, as we have noted.

The Hatch system was not infallible. Obviously, by its very nature, it cannot take optimum advantage of market swings. And it does not work at all when the upward swings are 10% or less. But it worked well enough for Cyrus Q. to parlay his hundred grand into several million dollars. During Hatch's long career the stock market as a whole made two dozen turns as defined by his system, and fifteen of them were winners—more than enough to stay ahead of the game when you cut your losses short and let your profits run.

A number of more sophisticated versions of the Hatch system

have been devised, such as going for the more volatile stocks, or reducing the stop-loss margins to 5%, both of which result in much more in-and-out trading, if action is what you want. By going for the swingers, however, you may wind up with a grab-bag of cats and dogs in your portfolio, and in this book we are stressing the safest and best of everything.

High quality stocks

The quality of common stocks cannot be measured in the same way as bonds, which are rated according to the safety of interest and principal they provide. But the common stocks of different companies are obviously different, and the differences "are well worth measuring and comparing" says Standard & Poor's, which has a seven-point scale for ranking several thousand stocks. The scale is as follows:

A+   (Highest)
A   (High)
A−   (Above average)
B+   (Average)
B   (Below average)
B−   (Low)
C   (Lowest)

Standard & Poor's rankings indicate the relative stability and growth of earnings and dividends. The best companies have a more consistent record of growth in earnings per share and dividend payments.

If you limit yourself to the very best, those in the A+ class, you will cut down on possible investment choices from several thousand companies to 50 or so top-ranking firms. They provide a pretty good cross-section of the market and include at the time of writing:

Company	Specialty
Air Products & Chemicals	industrial gases, chemicals
American Home Products	drugs, cosmetics, foods
American Hospital Supply	hospital and laboratory supplies
American Tel. & Tel.	biggest U.S. telephone company

ARA Services	vending and food services
Baxter Laboratories	medical care products, enzymes
Beatrice Foods	dairy and grocery products, candy
Becton, Dickinson	medical, surgical, laboratory supplies
Black & Decker Mfg.	portable electric tools
Bristol-Myers	toiletries and drugs
Carnation Co.	dairy and food products
Coca Cola Co.	world distributor of syrup and juices
Colgate-Palmolive	soap, toiletries, drugs, cosmetics
DEKALB Ag. Research	hybrid seeds, poultry, oil
Eastman Kodak	photographic equipment
Emerson Electric	electronic products
Emery Air Freight	air freight forwarding
Exxon Corp.	world's biggest oil company
Ford Motor Co. of Canada	leading Canadian auto maker
General Electric	largest U.S. maker of electric equipment
Genuine Parts	distributes auto parts
Gulf Oil	major U.S. international oil company
Heinz (H.J.)	processor and packer of food products
International Business Machines	world's biggest computer maker
Kellogg Co.	ready-to-eat cereals
Kresge (S.S.)	discount and variety stores
Mallinckrodt Inc.	chemicals and pharmaceuticals
Malone & Hyde	wholesale and retail groceries
Marsh & McLennan	insurance brokerage agency
Mercantile Stores	department stores
Mobil Oil	worldwide oil company
Moore Corp. Ltd.	business forms
Philip Morris	cigarettes, brewery, razors
Procter & Gamble	soap, food manufacturer

Revco	discount drug stores
Reynolds (R. J.) Industries	cigarettes, food, container freight
Richardson-Merrill	ethical drugs
Roadway Express	major freight motor carrier
Rohm & Haas	chemical products manufacturer
Schering-Plough	drugs, toiletries, cosmetics
Schlumberger Ltd.	oil industry services
Searle (G.D.)	drugs, health care equipment
Sears, Roebuck & Co.	biggest general merchandise retailer
Shell Oil	major oil company
Squibb Corp.	drugs, cosmetics, food, candy
Standard Brands	food products
Standard Oil of California	major oil company
Standard Oil of Indiana	midwest oil refinery
Sterling Drug	proprietary drugs
Tampax Inc.	tampons
Texaco Inc.	U.S. international oil company
Texas Utilities	electric utility holding company
Warner-Lambert	drugs, cosmetics, candy, gum
Xerox Corp.	copying machines, photo paper

The rankings are not unchangeable of course. Standard & Poor's modifies them whenever a company's performance improves or worsens significantly. Avon, for example, which used to be ranked A+, is now down to an A ranking. You can keep track of the latest classifications, as well as earnings, dividends, stock prices, and other data on thousands of companies by subscribing to Standard & Poor's *Security Stock Owner's Guide* (345 Hudson Street, New York 10014). This is a monthly publication, and a yearly subscription costs $40. Let's get this straight, though. Standard & Poor's is only telling you which ones are the good ones. It is not telling you to buy them or sell them at any particular time, because "a high graded stock may at times be so overpriced as to justify its sale; while a low score stock may be attractively priced for purchase."

One indication, and not an infallible one, of the right time to buy or sell each stock is the mathematical formula that made money for Cyrus Q. Hatch. It did so quite simply by stacking the mathematical odds in his favor and abandoning all attempts at predicting the future. Investors who have used the system say it works especially well in bad times—no doubt because it practically guarantees a maximum 10% loss. The gains in good times are variable, depending on the strength of the bull market above the first 10% rise. The fact seems to be that few investors have the strength of purpose to stick with the system through thick and thin. It is only human to be influenced by the general gloom and despair at the bottom of a bear market and to be carried away with enthusiasm around the top of a bull market, when there is not an economic cloud in sight and brokers are pushing growth stocks on you that are guaranteed to grow forever. Most people are repelled, too, by the system's absolute renunciation of predictions about the future.

There is evidently a natural human tendency to gaze into the crystal ball, to foresee the unforseeable. If you are stricken by this temptation, here are some predictions that have had a better than average record in the past. Since they involve the actions of politicians, there is some psychological basis for their success, and ever more so as the government gets an ever tighter grip on manipulating the economy. The first prophecy is this: stock prices rise in the third year of any new President's four-year term of office. The stock market rose in 1947-48, 1951-52, 1955-56, 1969-60, 1963-64, 1967-68, and 1971-72. The reason is probably not far to seek. Presidential elections are decided in great measure by the state of the economy at the time of the presidential campaign. So the man in the White House quite naturally turns his attention, as the time approaches, to stimulating economic growth, and this in turn perks up the stock market. Once the election is over, the new man in Washington, whoever he may be, has to take the unpleasant measures required to control the inflation set off by his own or his predecessor's pump-priming activities. And this economy-squeezing act also puts a tight squeeze on the stock market.

Whether in the third year of the presidential cycle or in any other year, the symptoms to watch are the same. When the return on United States Treasury Bills is dropping away below the yield on long-term corporate bonds, a big stock market advance has usually followed. The low return on Treasury bills means the government is following an easy money policy, which means companies find it easier to borrow money to expand operations, which means business picks up, which pushes stock prices higher. And at the same time the low yield on Treasury bills and other fixed interest securities lures investors into the stock market, thus reinforcing the bull market in common stocks.

Whenever the yield of fixed income securities improves significantly as compared with common stocks, investors leave the stock market. The same reasons are now working in reverse. The government is tightening the screws on the credit system, interest rates are soaring, companies find it hard to borrow money, business operations are contracting, and the poor business outlook is showing up in the prices of stocks. Investors in ordinary shares are tempted by the higher yields available in Treasury bills and depart with their money.

One last prophecy, which has come true in 31 of the last 43 years: if stock prices rise in January, they will end the year higher, too; if they fall in January they will be lower at the end of the year than they were at the beginning. If there is a rational explanation why January should be the bellwether month in about three years out of four, the author is unaware of it. Should you want to bet on it, the results have varied widely in the past. A good year to test it out would have been 1933, when the Dow Jones average rose 3% in January and ended the year with a gain of 64%. But if you had been encouraged by this to repeat the experiment in 1934 you would have been sadly disappointed—stock prices rose 7% in January but by December 31 the advance had been pared to only 4%.

Can you beat inflation with common stocks?

We have left for last the crucial question in our inflationary times: can you beat inflation by investing in common stocks? In the short run the answer seems to be no. Most investors have recognized the danger to their stock investments from inflation, and they now react smartly to a sudden inflationary flareup, as the following news item illustrates:

New York, July 22, 1975—Stock prices fell sharply today following the report of a surge in consumer prices last month.

As the stock market opened, the Labor Department reported that consumer price inflation in June jumped at an annual rate of 9.6%, twice the rate in May. The June spurt comes after a gradual cooling of consumer price inflation during the first five months of the year.

Those first five months of 1975, incidentally, witnessed one of the strongest stock market advances on record, which carried the Dow Jones industrial average from 577 to 850.

For years common stocks were sold to millions of investors as "a hedge against inflation," but recent bouts of double-digit inflation while stocks were sinking to twelve-year lows show that the stock market tends to do best when inflation is under control and well down into the one-digit area. One of the main reasons for this is that the measures the government has to take to get inflation under control—such as restricting credit and reducing the money supply—are bad for business. They cause an economic slowdown, cut into profits, and make stock prices slump. You are thus left with an investment that declines daily while the price of everything else around you is soaring. Such was the experience in 1973-74 of millions of people who had put their trust in common stocks to give them an extra income or provide for their retirement. When you take the double-whammy of a bear market and double-digit inflation into account, investors in common stocks were probably hit just as badly in the 1973-74 debacle as they were in the 1929-33 disaster. At least in the 1930s they didn't have inflation to accentuate their losses.

The critical question nowadays is whether the return you can expect from common stocks is greater than the rate of inflation. If it is not, it is obviously a waste of time and money to invest in stocks.

Perhaps the most thorough investigation ever made of the return on common stocks over the long run was published in 1964 by the University of Chicago. The study, made by professors Lawrence Fisher and James H. Lorie, covered all the common stocks listed on the New York Stock Exchange—about

1,700 of them—over a period of 35 years, starting in 1926 and ending in 1960. The study answers the question of how much gain or loss an investor might have made if he had bought all these stocks at 22 different dates and held them for varying lengths of time from 1926 to 1960. It takes into account the commission rates then in force and the taxes the investor would have had to pay on dividends and capital gains.

Over the entire 35-year period, the rates of return (including dividends reinvested and compounded annually) came to 9.01% for tax-exempt institutions. For investors paying taxes on a $10,-000 yearly income the return was 8.2%, and for those making $25,000 yearly it was 6.84%.

The worst period was the four-year span from 1929 to 1933, when all three types of investor showed yearly losses of just over 48%. The best periods were 1926-1929 and 1932-40, when the yearly return for all investors fluctuated in the 20-21% range.

As the authors of the study noted: "The period from 1926 to 1960 is a long span, with booms and depressions—prime examples of each—and war and peace. The periods beginning in September 1929 were included to indicate the experience of those who invested at the height of the stock market boom of the 1920s. The periods beginning in June 1932 were included to show the results of investing at the nadir of the country's worst depression."

For half of the 22 periods studied the rates of return were above 10%, and for two-thirds they exceeded 6%.

How do the results of investing in common stocks compare with other investments in the same period? Savings banks throughout the 35-year period never went above 6% a year, and for most of the 1926-60 period, savings accounts earned less than 4%. Yields on mortgages ranged from 4% to 6% and averaged around 5% a year. Municipal bonds and United States government bonds ranged from -7% to +7%, and averaged 4%. Corporate bonds produced returns running from -6% to +15% a year. During most of the period, corporate bonds yielded 5% to 8% a year. Common stocks, in a word, provided a better return on average than the alternatives.

Fisher and Lorie concluded: "The fact that many persons

chose investments with a substantially lower rate of return than that available on common stocks suggests the essentially conservative nature of those investors, and the extent of their concern about the possible risk of loss inherent in common stocks. And yet their experience with mortgage foreclosures during the 1930s and the substantial rate of default on bonds during the same period shows that even such 'conservative' investments carry considerable risks."

An updating of the 1926-60 study indicates that from 1926 to 1974 the annual return on common stocks was down to 8.5% a year. The comparison is worse than it looks, because from 1960 to 1974 the rate of inflation soared from around 2% to above 12% a year. Investors thus not only got a lower return, they were also being paid in dollars that shrank from 100 cents in 1960 to 54.5 cents in 1974. It thus seems a vain hope to anticipate a higher rate of return on common stocks when the inflation rate rises. The reverse seems to be true.

The rising tide of inflation did not submerge common stocks only, however. Savings accounts, bonds, and Treasury bills were also falling behind inflation or at best barely keeping even at times. A $10,000 investment in all New York Stock Exchange stocks in 1960 would have been worth $19,500 by December 1974. Since the dollar had declined in value to 54.5 cents in that period, the investment would be worth just about the original $10,000 in real terms. In these same 14 years a $10,000 savings account would have "grown" to $19,200, with considerably less risk than in common stocks. A typical portfolio of high-quality corporate bonds would have been left far behind by inflation from 1960 to 1974, lagging at $13,100 in December 1974.

In the long run, over the nearly five decades of the entire 1926 to 1974 period, common stocks were still ahead of bonds, which showed an average yearly yield of 3.6%. They were also far ahead of Treasury bills, which had an average yearly yield of 2.2%, just about level with the average yearly rate of inflation in those 48 years.

The essential point to keep in mind is that, as inflation accelerated in the 1970s, the return on common stocks was beginning to lag behind the rate of inflation. Let us assume that the 8.5% average return on common stocks in the 1926-74 period is a reasonable expectation for the future. What is the point of making such an investment when the rate of inflation is above 8.5%? If the yearly inflation rate is 12.5%, your 8.5% illusory "growth" is transformed into a real loss.

As a rule of thumb, one might say that common stocks begin to make sense as an investment when the rate of inflation starts to drop below 8.5% a year. With an inflation rate of 4%, you could figure you have a reasonable chance of making 4.5% a year on your common stocks.

To sum it all up: avoid certain losses, by investing in common stocks only when the inflation rate stays below 8.5% a year—the lower the better. Spread your risks, by buying a mutual fund, and cut down your trading costs by making it a no-load fund. Reduce the risk of loss by using the Hatch system—buying when the market is 10% above its most recent low point. Lock in your profits by using the Hatch system of selling out when the market is 10% down from its most recent high. Or, if you are willing to stay in the market at least ten years, insure your mutual fund holdings against loss when the market is near an all-time high.

The big dangers: Reverse yields and inflation

In this book we are concerned above all with safety, and it is obvious that common stocks offer less of safety than fixed interest securities. Stock prices and dividends depend on profits, which can fluctuate wildly from year to year or even be wiped out altogether. Nobody can guarantee that you will be able to cash in your common stocks at a certain date at a fixed price, as is the case with a bond. Traditionally, stock prices were required to yield more than bonds so as to compensate for the extra risk involved. But in recent years it has been the other way around.

In 1949 common stocks were returning 6% while high-grade corporate bonds yielded only 3% and United States government bonds a mere 2%. This yield-spread turned into reverse as a result of the growth stock cult of the 1950s and 1960s. By May 1975 common stocks were yielding 4.1%—less than half the 8.9% yield on high-grade corporate bonds. Even two-year Treasury notes at 6.6% were yielding more than common stocks.

The reverse-yield pattern is a lingering residue of the cult of growth stocks, which were supposed to outperform fixed-interest securities in the long run by plowing profits back into the business, thus making the stock price rise in value. Beware of this reasoning. It may work in the case of some outstanding companies, but their price fully discounts this anyway. There is another danger that hangs over the stock market: should the market return one day to its normal, traditional pattern in which bonds yield more than stocks, the Dow Jones industrial average may well halve in value to reflect this fact.

And then there is the whole inflationary environment in which we live. The Dow Jones average of 30 industrial stocks first reached the 1,000 mark in February 1966. It went over 1,000 again in February 1976—but this was by no means the same thing. The first time around, the United States consumer price index stood at 96—ten years later it had climbed to 167. The dollar, as well as the average share of common stock, had lost 43% of its purchasing power in this decade. In 1976 the Dow Jones average would have to hit 1,750 to surpass in purchasing power the 1,000 mark of 1966. Remember August 15, 1971. On that date the dollar became a totally unbacked paper currency, and ever since then the sky is the limit for the supply of paper money. It is a whole new ball game now. The painstaking studies of stock market results were mostly made when the dollar was anchored in one way or another to a fixed value of gold. There is no anchor now, no theoretical limit to the dollar's debasement. One simply cannot look ten years ahead now and count on inflation staying below 8.5% a year throughout that period. As long as the return on common stocks remains at 8.5% a year, one is forced to take a short-term view of the stock market.

9

Foreign fixed interest investments:
When the rate of inflation
in the United States is higher
than it is abroad

It is the end of the year, and you are figuring out how you stand
financially. You have had a good 12 months in the stock market,
and your shares have appreciated by about 15%. Your insured
savings account is yielding 5%. Judging by recent neighbors'
sales, your house has gone up 10% in value over the year. Over
all, you estimate that your net worth has risen from $100,000 on
January 1 to $120,000 on December 31.

Not bad at all, you say to yourself complacently. Even with a
10% inflation rate you have managed to come out ahead and
end the year a satisfactory 10% richer than you were at the
beginning. Throughout the United States thousands of people
are making these mental calculations in dollars and cents as
another New Year's Eve approaches, lulling themselves with
the comfortable feeling that they are getting richer and richer.

Do the same figuring in terms other than dollars and cents,
however, and you may sometimes be in for a chastening experience. The Swiss franc, let us say, has risen from 25 to 35
American cents—as it did in 1973-74. On January 1 you had
$100,000, which was worth 400,000 francs. On Dec. 31 you had

$120,000—now worth only 343,000 francs. In terms of the Swiss franc, you are ending the year with a loss of 57,000 francs. On January 1 gold was worth, say, $120 an ounce, and by December 31 it is up to $180 an ounce. Translated into dollars, your $100,-000 was the equivalent of 833 ounces of gold on January 1, and your $120,000 on December 31 has shrunk to only 666 ounces. Calculated in gold, your fortune shows a loss of 167 gold ounces.

Everyone tends to think and plan exclusively in the currency of the country where he lives and works. It is only natural. But the habit can make one blind to the losses one suffers when the dollar, or whatever the local currency is, goes down against other currencies and gold. These mental blinders also prevent one from seeing the profits that can be made by taking into account other standards of value. It is a salutary exercise to make this comparison at least once a year, particularly with Swiss francs and gold as the standards of comparison. If the results show that you are falling behind by holding all your assets in dollars, you may want to investigate ways of investing at least some of your assets in monetary units that could bring you greater profits than the dollar. You are then ready to explore the foreign fields of Euroland.

Eurocurrencies

You may not find Euroland on any map, but it is a financial power with all the economic clout of a second West Germany. This is where Eurocurrencies circulate—Euromarks, Eurofrancs, and, above all, Eurodollars—$250 billion worth altogether in 1976, which is the equivalent of everything the West German economy produces in one year.

You, too, can be part of the Eurocurrency economy, buying and selling money and securities in what is one of the most open and unrestricted financial markets in the world. When you send $500 abroad and deposit it in a Swiss bank account, you have just added $500 to the Euromarket economy. Your $500 are now Eurodollars—American dollars held outside the United States. In the same way, Euromarks are German marks held outside Germany. You could turn your Eurodollars into Euromarks by converting them into marks and holding them in the same Swiss bank. If the Swiss government forbade you to deposit dollars in Switzerland, as it does from time to time, you could turn them into Eurofrancs by converting your dollars into Swiss francs and depositing them in a bank in Austria.

There are thousands of big-time operators moving money like this all the time—American multinational corporations, international oil companies, American and foreign banks, foreign governments, individuals like you and me, and even the central banks of Communist nations. The Arab oil-producing nations alone have billions of dollars on the line, moving their funds from country to country in search of the most secure currency and the best available interest rates. In 1974, according to the Bank of International Settlements in Basel, Switzerland, the Arab states invested $21 billion in the Eurocurrency market.

The fact is, however, that nobody really knows exactly how big the Eurodollar market is because there is no central authority over it. This huge mass of money sloshes back and forth like a tidal wave between one nation and another. It can move with astonishing speed. Billions of dollars may be telexed from country to country in a matter of hours. On March 1, 1973, during the dollar devaluation crisis, panic-stricken holders of depreciating American dollars converted $2.7 billion worth of greenbacks into German marks, and within hours the flood of unwanted dollars forced German central bank officials to slam the door shut temporarily by closing down the official exchange.

According to a Morgan Guaranty Trust Company survey made in mid-1975, the net total of Eurocurrencies held in the banks of major European countries, the Bahamas, Canada, Japan and Singapore amounted to about $210 billion. About 75% of this was held in expatriate dollars and the remaining 25% in other currencies deposited outside their native countries. The Eurocurrency market has been doubling in as little as two years—in March 1973 it was estimated to total around $100 billion—and it is still mushrooming.

And this is still not the whole story. Once in Euroland, your $500 in a Swiss bank account may go to a French bank, which lends it to a French businessman, who buys goods with it in Italy. Whenever a deposit is passed from one overseas bank to another, a new Eurodollar obligation is created, and Eurodollars multiply out of thin air. The original dollar sent out of the United States may thus become $3 in the Eurodollar market. Taking this into account, Morgan Guaranty estimated that the gross Eurocurrency total amounted to a staggering $365 billion—about a quarter of what the entire American economy produces in a year.

It is obvious that this huge heap of paper money is potentially the biggest engine of worldwide inflation ever invented. When the United States Treasury and the United States Federal Reserve try to clamp down on inflation by restricting the American money supply, they are doing so under the constant threat of an avalanche of uncontrollable Eurodollars. The German authorities were hit by this avalanche in 1973. The only way they could take in the onrushing Eurodollars without the exchange value of the mark rising through the roof and damaging German export trade was to print more marks, which would fuel inflation in Germany—an unacceptable result for a fiscally conservative government. After slamming the exchange shut, the German authorities faced up to the dilemma by just letting the mark rise in value.

At this point the world monetary system set up at Bretton Woods, New Hampshire, in 1944, based on a fixed value for the dollar and gold, reached final collapse. For nearly three decades the United States dollar had been fixed at an unchanging $35 per troy ounce of gold, while the German mark and all other currencies had a fixed exchange rate to the dollar from which they were not allowed to deviate more than 2% up or down. From this time forward, currencies were "floating"—they could rise or fall as far as supply and demand would take them, which proved to be a considerable distance.

Your stake in the Eurocurrency market

And this is where we start figuring what the modern, unrestricted Eurocurrency market means to us personally and how we can profit by it. The German mark was worth 26.5 United States cents in August 1972. By August 1973 it had risen to 42 cents. If you had owned German marks instead of dollars in this period you would have been ahead about 50% in one year. To put it more brutally, by owning dollars and not owning marks you lost 50% of your capital and purchasing power in 12 months.

The Swiss franc is an even more dramatic example of your possible gain or loss. From May 1971 to January 1975 the franc rose 68.9% in value against the American dollar and rose an average 47.2% against 20 major currencies in that four-year period. It soared 74.4% against the Italian lira, 73.6% against the British pound, 34.1% against the French franc, 38.4% against the Japanese yen, and even had a 10% rise against the West German mark. The mark and the Swiss franc were known as the "strong" currencies in this period.

It is obvious that before you even think of how to invest your money, the first thing is to decide which currency to hold it in. By putting your funds into a strong currency, you could conceivably come out 60% or 70% ahead in a few years, while you could lose that much by holding a weak currency. This is before even deciding whether to invest in a savings account, a bond, or some other security.

Your first problem is to find the strong currencies, which may not necessarily always be the mark or the Swiss franc. One way is to compare interest rates in the Eurocurrency market. Here is an Associated Press dispatch, for example, which gives you the pertinent information:

> London, May 22, 1975 (AP)—Three-month French Eurofrancs were offered Thursday at 8.5%, compared with 6.13% for Eurodollars, 5% for Euromarks and 4% for Euro-swiss francs.
>
> Eurosterling rates have consistently remained higher than any of those currencies, with the three-month rate at 11.5% Thursday.

Evidently, the currency with the lowest interest rate is the strongest—at this time the Swiss franc, followed by the German mark, and the American dollar. Before being tempted by that juicy 11.5% return available in Eurosterling, you might as well know that inflation was raging at somewhere between 20% and 30% a year in Great Britain at the time.

Another way to check on the relative strength of different currencies is to glance at the trading figures in foreign currency futures on the International Monetary Market in Chicago. The figures are published daily by the *Wall Street Journal* and other major newspapers. This market deals in foreign currencies for delivery about a year into the future. The quotations thus represent what speculators and businessmen involved in foreign trade think is going to be the relative value of each currency a few months or a year ahead. The currencies that are quoted at higher and higher exchange rates into the more distant future months are the strong currencies. Those that dip lower and lower from the current exchange rate down to the farthest-off delivery are the weak currencies. The trading figures bear rechecking every once in a while—the market is constantly altering its appraisal of future prospects and may signal you ahead of time that a strong currency is weakening.

Having chosen the strongest currency, the next problem is to choose the safest and most profitable investment in it. You have a large number of options available. You could open a Swiss franc savings account with a Swiss bank or in some other currency in a bank abroad. You could buy bonds denominated in francs, marks, pounds, yen, or another foreign currency. You could invest in a foreign bond fund, which spreads your money over a portfolio of bonds denominated in several currencies. You could buy multiple currency bonds, which give you the choice of which currency you prefer when the time comes to collect your interest and principal. There are other possibilities, such as SDR bonds, Mexican *financiera* investments, Swiss franc life insurance policies and annuities. Let us now examine these alternatives in detail.

Swiss bank accounts

The Swiss franc is a paper currency like any other paper currency in the world today. You cannot go to the Swiss Treasury and demand a fixed amount of gold for your francs. In this sense it is no different from the American dollar, which is also inconvertible into gold at any officially specified price. But the franc has commanded much more trust in recent years than the dollar and most other currencies because, with gold at around $160 an ounce, the Swiss government has enough bullion in its vaults to cover 74% of the Swiss paper money supply. It is required by law to have at least 40% gold backing for all banknotes in circulation. While the Swiss franc is backed 74% by gold, the United States paper dollar has only 16 cents worth of gold in the United States Treasury vaults when gold is at $160 an ounce.

A strong gold backing is a common characteristic of strong currencies, even when they are not convertible into gold at any particular fixed rate. A study by Hoenig & Strock Inc. of Boston shows that in the 1970-74 period the Dutch government held gold equivalent to 64% of the country's paper money supply. The Dutch guilder gained 36% against the American dollar in this period. The Austrian government's gold backing was 60% of the money supply. The Austrian schilling gained 41%. West German gold was 38% of the money supply. The German mark gained 41% against the dollar. These four countries had the world's highest percentage of gold backing for their paper currencies, and they also had the strongest currencies in the foreign exchange markets. Evidently there was a psychological link with gold, even though these countries were not formally on the gold standard.

Switzerland is not only a financially conservative country, with one of the lowest inflation rates in the world; it is also a symbol of neutrality, with such a resolute aversion to the political disputes of the modern world that it will not even join the United Nations or the International Monetary Fund. It is small wonder that worried investors around the globe consider this country the safest haven for their money. In peace or war, come revolution or inflation elsewhere in the world, Switzerland has been ready to welcome foreign money—provided it is not absolutely swamped—and to protect it with the renowned Swiss banking secrecy laws.

No Swiss bank will reveal anything about any of its customers to any foreign authority except when compelled to do so by a Swiss court order proving criminal activities by the client. Any Swiss banking official who violates the secrecy laws is liable to a stiff jail term. Swiss banks are usually so discreet that they send their mail abroad in envelopes with no return address, so as not to embarrass customers in countries that do not allow their citizens to keep money abroad.

All this has given Swiss bank accounts an aura of mystery and illegality that is not deserved. There is nothing illegal about opening a bank account in Switzerland. The only requirement in the United States is that the Internal Revenue Service wants you to report your foreign bank accounts in the same way that you report your United States income from interest and dividends. Whether you do this or not is no concern of the Swiss bank, which is obliged only to follow the laws and regulations of Switzerland. Swiss laws, incidentally, do not consider tax evasion to be a crime.

There are several hundred Swiss banks to choose from. The three largest are: Union Bank of Switzerland, Bahnhofstrasse 45, 8021 Zurich; Swiss Bank Corporation, Paradeplatz 6, Zurich; and Swiss Credit Bank, Paradeplatz 8, 8021 Zurich. A smaller bank that is oriented towards English-speaking customers is the Foreign Commerce Bank, Bellaristrasse 82, 8038 Zurich.

These banks answer your letters in English, issue you checkbooks printed in English, and send you bank statements in English. All you have to do to open an account is write for the application forms, fill them out and mail them, giving your United States bank as a reference and getting your American bank officer to certify your signature. You can open a checking account or various kinds of savings accounts, which usually pay 3% to 6% yearly interest, depending on how long you keep your money on deposit. The net interest rates should be reduced by about one-third because there is a 30% Swiss withholding tax on the interest paid to depositors not resident in Switzerland. You can claim this Swiss tax as a credit against your United States income tax. The minimum initial deposit required might be anything from $500 to $1,000, depending on the bank. The Foreign Commerce Bank requires at least $15,000.

From time to time the influx of foreign money seeking safety in Switzerland grows to such a flood that the Swiss government has to step in to stem the inrushing tide. At the time of this writing, for example, new bank deposits by non-residents of Switzerland were charged a punitive tax of 10% a quarter (40% a year!) in order to keep foreign money out. However, this only applied to deposits of more than 100,000 francs (about $40,000); if you had less than that to send to Switzerland you were not affected. Regulations change of course, and at the time you read this book the temporary punitive tax may not be in effect.

If it has not been lifted, and you have more than $40,000 available for conversion into Swiss francs, there is a way around the regulation. You can open a Swiss franc account with a bank in Austria, where there are no restrictions on Swiss franc holdings by foreigners and no withholding taxes on interest or dividends. One such bank is the Bankhaus Deak, Rathausstrasse 20, A-1010, Vienna, Austria.

If you prefer to keep your money in German marks, you can have a German mark account in a Swiss bank. You would thus avoid any punitive charges applied to foreign-owned bank accounts in Germany whenever the German government wants to keep out money from abroad. You would also be unaffected by any Swiss government measures against Swiss franc accounts held by foreigners. You can hold a United States dollar account in a Swiss bank too. Eurodollar accounts like this may earn you from ¼% to 1¼% more than similar deposits made in the United States banking system.

Foreign bonds

You can also use your Swiss or other foreign bank to buy bonds for you and perhaps get a higher interest rate than a savings account provides. The variety of possible investments here is bewildering. Eurocurrency-land is flooded with bonds of every size, shape, color, maturity, and description, denominated in all West European currencies, Japanese yen, American, Canadian, and Australian dollars, and even exotic issues such as Kuwaiti dinars and Saudi riyals. The quality of these bonds varies all the way from highly speculative to the highest accolades that American bond-rating services can bestow. They are issued by the Swiss, German, Norwegian, and other governments, Canadian provinces, American corporations, French private and state corporations, British municipal authorities, Italian highway boards, the European Coal and Steel Community, and issuers as far afield as the governments of New Zealand and Papua-New Guinea, as well as some Communist governments of Eastern Europe.

In this book we are stressing safety, and we shall concentrate on the top quality bonds.

First of all, you have bonds issued by the Bank for International Reconstruction and Development, otherwise known as the World Bank. Most of the globe's non-Communist nations are members of the bank, which has its headquarters in Washington, D.C. and has been headed in recent years by former United States Secretary of Defense Robert McNamara. The World Bank has issued bonds in American and Canadian dollars, Italian liras, Japanese yen, German marks, Swiss francs, French francs, Venezuelan bolivars, Kuwaiti dinars, Saudi Arabian riyals, Dutch guilders, and Swedish crowns. The bank's bonds denominated in United States dollars are rated AAA by Moody's, a leading American bond-rating service. This is the highest possible rating, also given to United States Treasury Bonds and other obligations backed by the full faith and credit of the United States government. Bonds with this rating, according to Moody's, are "judged to be of the best quality. They carry the smallest degree of investment risk and are generally referred to as 'gilt-edge.'" It seems reasonable to suppose that bonds issued by the World Bank in other currencies are of equally high standing.

Two sister organizations of the World Bank with bond issues in various currencies are the Inter-American Development Bank and the Asian Development Bank, whose dollar bonds are also rated AAA by Moody's. The Asian Bank has issued bonds in ten currencies, including the Austrian schilling and the Belgian and Luxembourg franc, for a total value of more than $600 million.

If you build up a portfolio of bonds of these three banks (which are issued in certificates of $1,000, $500 or even less in some cases) choosing the three or four strongest currencies, you will be in a strong position to minimize your losses through exchange depreciation. World Bank bonds are exempt from the Swiss withholding tax on interest. They were also exempt from the now-defunct United States Interest Equalization tax on foreign securities. This tax has been abolished, but the exemption is nice to know about if it should ever be reinstated.

Also of the highest quality are Swiss franc bonds issued by the Swiss Federal government. There are literally hundreds of other foreign currency bonds on the market, and scores of them are worth considering, but there is no room to mention them all here. As many of them are issued by national governments, however, it does seem worthwhile pointing out which countries are head over heels in debt already and which others might be better credit risks, to judge by their smaller national debts.

Uncle Sam is the world's biggest borrower, with outstanding government debt amounting to $3,002 for every man, woman, and child in the country. Israel is in second place with $2,981 in government debt per capita—and much lower per capita income than the United States to pay for it. Then come New Zealand, $1,949; Belgium, $1,924; Australia, $1,852; Great Britain, $1,636; Sweden, $1,371; Canada, $1,351; Norway, $1,334; and Ireland, $1,067.

On a considerably lower level of government debt are Holland with $722 per capita; Italy, $595; South Africa, $468; Argentina, $436; Austria, $377; France, $357; Japan, $345; West Germany, $339; and Switzerland $315 per capita.

The above figures are from *Pick's Currency Year Book*. The book's publisher, Franz Pick, an outspoken pessimist, has this to say: "The fact that government bonds can still be sold in this era of chronic currency decay is the baffling enigma of modern institutional and individual gullibility. These certificates of guaranteed confiscation, denominated in paper currencies of constantly shrinking purchasing power, are the most unethical instruments of government finance. Never in modern history has any one of these bonds been redeemed with money that had the same purchasing power as the units with which these debt certificates were acquired. The bitter lessons of devaluation will not be learned by bondholders. In the wave of devaluations, full and partial, de facto and de jure, which swept the currency world following the American dollar debacles of August 1971 and February 1973, none of the monetary administrations involved considered the plight of the unprotected bondholder. No compensation was given to patriotic owners of government bonds, whose purchasing power was cut through these fraudulent state bankruptcies. The nature of every government to reduce its 'real' debt will not be altered. The bigger the debt, the greater the pressure to shrink it by dubious methods, such as promoting inflation."

As we noted earlier in this book, it is suicidal to invest for a 4% return, no matter how "safe" the investment, when the inflation rate is 12%. All the investments in this chapter can be considered acceptable only when the return is at least a few percentage points above the rate of inflation, and this holds true even for the strongest currency available. Even if your return does beat the inflation rate by a reasonable margin, it still does not make sense to buy bonds that mature in 20 or 30 years' time. Inflation will almost certainly erupt into higher rates in some years of those two or three decades, wiping out whatever small gain you managed to make in the years of low inflation. As the *New York Journal of Commerce* observed in its Eurobond column, "Bankers continue to swerve away from any financing of more than five years in length, except in exceptional circumstances."

Playing it safe means shortening the term of investment even further. Five years of 5% inflation is 25% gone. Five years of 10% inflation means a 50% loss. Inflation at the British rate of 20% or more in 1974 to 1976 would practically wipe you out in five years.

Foreign bond funds

Buying bonds with short maturities means a frequent turnover of investments that may involve you in more decisions, more homework, and more constant attention than you have time for. In this case one possible solution is a fund specializing in an international portfolio of bonds that will handle all these problems for you.

One such fund is Rorento, Postbus 973, Rotterdam, Holland. This fund was started in July 1974 and its portfolio was worth about $55 million in late 1975. Rorento's investment policy is directed at fixed-interest investments, with a special accent on strong currencies. It is watched over by a supervisory board of top European bankers, industrialists, and economists. Board members have included two heads of the International Monetary Fund, Johannes Witteveen and Pierre-Paul Schweitzer.

Rorento says its policy is to "take advantage of international differences in the rate of interest. The assets may be spread over a number of currencies. In doing so, yield and currency risk will be weighed against each other." Early in 1975 the fund was invested mainly in Dutch and German government bonds. Later in the year it was 60% invested in top-grade Dutch bonds, with the remainder mostly in French franc and American dollar bonds.

Rorento also plays the difference between long-term and short-term interest rates, noting that "long-term bonds are far more sensitive to changes in interest rates than short-dated bonds. When interest rates are going up, it is generally advisable to opt for a short average life of the whole portfolio. When interest rates are following a downward trend, a long average portfolio life is advisable" because then long-term bonds tend to rise much more sharply than short-term bonds. In its first year of life Rorento guessed right. Interest rates fell and more than 70% of its bonds were in maturities of over 10 years. This enabled the fund to make a 15% capital gain in Dutch guilders (29.9% in American dollars) plus a 6% interest yield, a comfortable margin over the Dutch and American inflation rates in that period (about 12% inflation in the United States). By late 1975 Rorento had switched in favor of short-term bonds, with 40% of its portfolio in maturities of less than five years. As the fund observed in its annual report: "The days are long past when the private investor could sleep easily over bonds," buying them and then forgetting them.

Rorento shares are quoted on the Amsterdam stock exchange, where the brokerage commission is about 1% to buy and 1% to sell. You can also open a Rorento share account in Geneva, Switzerland, which functions much like a bank account. For a small fee you can also insure your Geneva share account against capital loss.

Another fund with an international bond portfolio is Bondinvest, sold by the Union Bank of Switzerland, Bahnhofstrasse 45, Zurich, Switzerland.

A third is Foco International Bond Fund, sold by the Foreign Commerce Bank, Bellariastrasse 82, 8022 Zurich, Switzerland. The sales charge is 4% and there is also a redemption commission of ½%. The fund's management fee is ¼% a year.

Multiple currency bonds

So far we have considered investments in a single foreign

currency—a Swiss franc savings account or perhaps a World Bank bond denominated in German marks. We have also considered a portfolio of World Bank bonds in various different currencies as a way of hedging your bets in the foreign exchange market. Bond funds such as Rorento and Bondinvest would spread your risks in the same way.

The problem is that—the future being unforeseeable—neither you nor the fund managers nor anybody else can be absolutely sure which currency is going to rise in value against the others in the months and years ahead. Even so, in recent years there has been an almost foolproof way of coming out with the most valuable currency, whichever one it may turn out to be. The answer is the multiple currency or Lombard bond, which guarantees to pay you off—both interest and principal—in whichever currency has the highest value at the time you are collecting your money. If the American dollar goes up, you collect in dollars. If the British pound rises, you collect in pounds. In this way you are able to dump all your risk of loss through depreciating currencies onto the issuer of the bonds. Whatever happens on the exchange markets, you come out ahead.

These securities were mostly issued some years ago, before the Bretton Woods monetary system broke down, when the world's major currencies were not allowed to deviate more than 2% against each other. The issuers did not foresee a situation in which the Swiss franc would rise 60% or more against the American dollar and other currencies, and they are probably wishing they had never thought of multiple currency bonds, which in present circumstances must seem to them like giving money away free.

Not surprisingly, this kind of bond is seldom issued nowadays. But there are still a number of issues on the market, that were floated in the 1960s and do not mature in some cases until the 1980s. In recent years other types of bonds have been offered that also give you a choice of different currencies. These are European Unit of Account and European Currency Unit Bonds. They are complicated and not as good as the earlier multiple currency Lombard bonds, but they do offer protection against the ups and downs of the foreign exchange market. And the very latest invention is the Special Drawing Rights (SDR) bond, which is valued in a cocktail of different currencies.

The multiple currency bond is not as well known as it should be—perhaps because the issuers made a big mistake in issuing it, perhaps also because the most recent types are so complicated that few people understand them at all well. But they serve a useful purpose.

Earlier in this book I mentioned what inflation did to my father in Argentina. This was a country in which the cost of living rose 30,587% from 1950 to 1973, according to official government statistics. Common stocks, preferred stocks, and conventional bonds payable in Argentine pesos were simply swallowed alive in this inflationary vortex. Fortunately, during his last years in a nursing home my father got some good advice on how to beat a 30,000% inflation. One was to buy a bond which the Argentine government had rashly indexed to the price of gold. It has been retired and is not likely to be reissued, so we shall give no details of it here. But those who bought it did exceedingly well when the price of gold shot up from $35 to $120 an ounce.

Another was an Argentine government multicurrency bond. It had a coupon of only 6½%, but the bondholder could collect his interest and principal in Belgian, French, or Swiss francs, British pounds, Dutch guilders, German marks, Italian liras, or United States dollars. All you had to do was look up the going exchange rates 30 days before your interest was due, select the most valuable currency at the time and demand payment in that money. By buying this bond you dumped all your foreign exchange risks onto the Argentine government. However much the dollar or pound sterling went down, no matter what disasters befell the Argentine peso, you were guaranteed possession of the strongest currency at all times.

These bonds were issued in 1961 and they matured in 1973. Listed on the Frankfurt stock exchange in Germany, they were traded over the counter in Europe, as are most foreign bonds. They enabled my father to keep this part of his capital intact during several years of wild Argentine inflation. He was also protected against the devaluations of the pound and the dollar in that period by collecting his interest and principal in German marks and Swiss francs.

You might say that the government bonds of an inflation-ridden South American country are not of the same investment quality as United States government bonds, and this is indeed a valid objection. But what did the full faith and credit of the United States government do for its bondholders when the dollar was devalued 7.89% in 1971, when it was devalued another 10% in 1973, and when it dropped another 10% in free market trading in 1974—all this in a quarter century in which the dollar lost half its purchasing power within the United States? As Franz Pick says, those bonds were certificates of guaranteed confiscation.

An essential consideration in buying any bond is safety against default, and all noncommunist nations (even some Communist states lately) are very touchy about their reputations in this respect. Any suspicion of possible non-repayment will dry up the country's sources of foreign credit. Argentina has had more than the average share of internal political problems and revolutions, as well as inflation and economic mismanagement. But in more than 160 years of national life it has only failed to meet its obligations on a foreign bond issue once—in 1891, when payments on an 1886 issue were delayed two years. Like many other nations, it is well aware of the importance of a good credit rating if it wants to continue raising money abroad.

This is a factor to keep in mind when looking at the following list of some multiple currency bonds that are still on the market. The list is by no means exhaustive—there are many others. In some cases an alternative currency may have risen so much against the others that it might seem there is not much point in buying the bond. The ideal time to buy this type of bond is, of course, at the time of issue, before the alternative currencies offered have had time to diverge significantly.

The Rural and Industries Bank of Western Australia 6½% of 1972, due Aug. 15, 1987. Guaranteed by the government of Western Australia. Payable at the bondholder's option in Australian dollars, in U.S. dollars (converted at the prevailing rate of exchange on the second business day before the due date), or in West German marks at 3.7831 marks per Australian dollar. Fourteen days' notice are required for payment in marks. The bonds are issued in certificates with a face value of 1,000 Australian dollars.

Petrofina S.A. (a major Belgian oil company) 7½% of 1957, due Sept. 10, 1977. Principal and interest payable in U.S. dollars, or, at the bondholder's option, in Belgian francs at 50.35 francs per dollar, Swiss francs at 4.285, Dutch guilders at 3.83 to the dollar, or in Canadian dollars at current buying rates. Notice of 15 days required for currencies other than the U.S. dollar. Bonds are issued in $10,000, $1,000 and $100 denominations.

City of Copenhagen 6¼% of 1972, due Sept. 1, 1987. Bonds with a face value of 2,000 Danish crowns, payable in crowns, or in German marks at 0.458 marks per crown. Notice of 21 days required for payment in marks.

Republic of Finland 6¼% of 1964, due Sept. 1, 1979. Bearer bonds issued by the Finnish government in denominations of 200, 500, 1000 and 5000 German marks. By giving 30 days notice bondholders may receive principal and interest in U.S. dollars at $1 per 4 marks.

I.C.I. International Finance Ltd. 8% of 1971, due Aug. 1, 1986. Bonds of 500 pounds face value, guaranteed by Imperial Chemical Industries (the biggest chemical company in Great Britain). Payable in British pounds, or in German marks at 8.3647 marks per pound.

Ireland 7% of 1966, due March 1, 1981. Bonds of 100 and 500 pounds, payable also in German marks at 11.24 marks per pound if the holder gives 14 days notice.

New Zealand 6¾% of 1967, due March 14, 1982. Bonds of 90 pounds (1,000 German marks) and 450 pounds (5,000 marks), payable in marks at 11.11 marks per pound on 14 days notice.

New Zealand 7½% of 1968, due Feb. 5, 1978. Bonds of 100 pounds (963 German marks) and 500 pounds (4,815 marks), payable in marks at 9.63 marks per pound on 14 days notice.

Norwegian State and Municipal Power Consortium 7¼% of 1968, due March 1, 1983. Coupon bonds of 100 and 500 British pounds, payable also in German marks at 9.65 marks per pound on 14 days notice.

If you prefer to deal with American corporations rather than any of these foreign governments, municipalities and companies, here are multiple currency bonds issued by two big U.S. firms:

Mobil Oil Holdings S.A. 5¾% of 1965, due June 15, 1980.

Coupon bonds of 100 and 5000 British pounds, guaranteed by the Mobil Oil Company, payable also in German marks at 11.17 marks per pound on 14 days notice.

U.S. Rubber Uniroyal Holdings 6% of 1965, due July 31, 1980. Coupon bonds of 100 and 500 British pounds, guaranteed by Uniroyal Inc., payable also in German marks at 11.18 marks per pound on 21 days notice.

European Unit of Account bonds

European Unit of Account bonds are a slightly different variation of the multiple currency bonds dealt with above. Each bond issue may be payable in anything from six to seventeen European currencies, of which you may choose any one to suit your own convenience.

However, their terms are more favorable to the issuer—and less favorable to you the bondholder—because the exchange rates are fixed and cannot be raised upward. If the mark is revalued, for example, you will still be paid at the old lower rate.

Even so, according to John Fountain of White, Weld & Co., a specialist in this field, the EUA bond "offers the creditor limited but nevertheless valuable protection against devaluation."

An additional advantage is that the EUA bond offers a wider choice of currencies than most of the multiple currency bonds we mentioned above. You will be able to choose among six or more currencies to be paid off in instead of only two or three.

The European Unit of Account is based on a standard of 0.88867088 grams of fine gold. The significance of this curious decimal figure is that it is exactly 1/35th of a troy ounce—the equivalent of one U.S. dollar when the dollar was officially valued at $35 an ounce. This is only the basic standard, however. Units of Account are not payable in either gold or dollars. The first issues were payable in some or all of these seventeen currencies at the following exchange rates:

26 Austrian schillings	625.001 Italian liras
50 Belgian francs	50 Luxembourg francs
6.907 Danish crowns	3.620 Dutch guilders
4.937 French francs	7.143 Norwegian crowns
4 German marks	28.749 Portuguese escudos

0.357 British pounds   5.173 Swedish crowns
30 Greek drachmas   4.373 Swiss francs
43 Icelandic crowns   9 Turkish pounds
0.357 Irish pounds

As new issues came along, the exchange rates have been changed and the number of currencies reduced.

When you buy a EUA bond, the big advantage is that if any of these currencies is devalued, you can choose to be paid in another that has maintained its value.

It seems surprising that multiple currency bonds and EUA bonds have not become more popular in a world of wildly fluctuating exchange rates since 1971. One reason, says Mr. Fountain, may be the complexity of the EUA bond. "Even people in the business don't always understand it, and the ordinary investor is baffled."

However, when your U.S. dollar holdings in American stocks, bonds, or savings accounts can lose as much as 60% of their value as compared with other currencies, it seems well worth the effort to seek some protection abroad.

The usual EUA bond provides that the bondholder may pick the currency with the highest value, notifying the trustee or paying agent well in advance of the payment date. Actually, however, it is the duty of the chief fiscal agent to pick the most favorable currency, and most bondholders rely on this.

Here are some of the EUA bonds currently on the market (it is not a complete list—there are many others):

Commonwealth of Australia EUA 8% of 1971,
    due Aug. 1, 1986
Kingdom of Denmark EUA 8% of 1971, due June 25, 1986
European Coal and Steel Community EUA 5¾% of 1966,
    due Feb. 1, 1986
Province of Manitoba EUA 7% of 1969, due June 17, 1989
Province of Manitoba EUA 9% of 1970, due March 16, 1982
Norges Kommunalbank EUA 7¾% of 1971, due
    March 15, 1986, guaranteed by the Kingdom of Norway
North of Scotland Hydro-Electric Board EUA 8% of 1969,
    due Dec. 10, 1984, guaranteed by
    Her Majesty's Treasury

Société Nationale des Chemins de Fer Français EUA 7¾%
of 1971, due March 25, 1986, guaranteed
unconditionally by the government of France
Republic of South Africa EUA 8¾% of 1970,
due Dec. 30, 1982

You should be careful about any EUA bonds that may be issued in 1975 or later years. In April 1975 the European Community finance ministers decided to redefine the European
Unit of Account, basing its value on a basket of nine currencies
of the European Common Market member countries. Bonds issued from 1975 onward will reflect this fact.

European Currency Unit bonds

Another variation is the European Currency Unit, which is
more similar to the EUA bond than the Lombard multiple currency type of security.

One example of the European Currency Unit bond is the
Federative Republic of Brazil 8% issue of 1972, due March 1,
1984. It was issued in certificates of 1,000 European Currency
Units each. The Unit was defined in the prospectus as being
equal to 3.2225 German marks, 44.8159 Belgian or Luxembourg
francs, 5.1157 French francs, or 3.2447 Dutch guilders.

Other issues of this type are:

Ente Nazionale per l'Energia Elettrica (ENEL) 7¼% of
1971, due May 1, 1986 (certificates of 1,000 European
Currency Units, guaranteed by the
government of Italy)
European Coal and Steel Community 8% of 1970,
due Dec. 15, 1985
Republic of South Africa 8% of 1971, due April 1, 1986

As with EUA issues, the bondholder may give advance notice
of which currency he wants, or simply let the paying agent decide in his best interests.

Special Drawing Rights (SDR) bonds

The very latest invention in the multicurrency bond business
is an issue denominated in Special Drawing Rights (SDRs). The

pioneering issue was made in May, 1975, by Alusuisse, a big Swiss aluminum company, and it was snapped up by eager investors. It was soon followed by SDR bonds of the Swedish Investment Bank and other big institutions.

Maturing in five years, the Alusuisse SDR bond carries a 9¼% coupon and the interest is payable exclusively in U.S. dollars at the prevailing exchange rate against SDRs.

The SDR is a sort of worldwide unit of account created by the International Monetary Fund, comprising a basket of the world's 16 most important currencies, including the U.S., Australian, and Canadian dollars, the Japanese yen, the South African rand, as well as the major European currencies. An important exception is the Swiss franc. Switzerland has always refused to join the IMF. The world's most respectable paper currency is thus not a part of the SDR.

Each currency included in the SDR is weighted according to its relative importance in the world economy. Thus the U.S. dollar represents about one-third of each SDR and the German mark about 10% of the SDR basket of currencies. At the time of writing, the SDR is worth $1.14579, but its value is recalculated daily by the IMF.

By purchasing the Alusuisse SDR bond you would in fact be buying the weighted average depreciation rate of these 16 major currencies. You would not be able to pick this currency or that to suit your own convenience, as you could do with Lombard, EUA, or European Currency Unit bonds.

If you are an American investing dollars and the U.S. inflation rate turns out to be higher than the worldwide average, the dollar will go down in value and you will come out ahead with your SDR bonds. If the U.S. dollar holds its exchange value higher than most of the other 15 currencies, you will lose out by holding SDR bonds.

The SDR bond is in fact a second step down in the quality of the protection against currency devaluations provided to you the bondholder, just as the European Unit of Account and European Currency Unit bonds were a first step down from the original multiple currency bonds.

Alusuisse, for example, is almost sure to do better than the buyers of its SDR bonds, because the Swiss franc, on current form, is almost sure to depreciate less than the 16 SDR currencies. And the firm will pay off its debt in the average of these depreciated currencies.

How to go about it

Many of the foreign bonds mentioned in this chapter have not been registered with the United States Securities and Exchange Commission and could not originally be offered or sold to United States citizens or residents. (Canadian or European readers of this book are of course not affected by American regulations if they do not live in the United States.) United States brokers will usually deal in such securities after a waiting period, which may be up to one year.

Those bonds that have been registered with the SEC (mainly bonds denominated in United States dollars) may be bought from American brokers right from the day of issue. One brokerage house specializing in this kind of security is White, Weld Inc., 1 Liberty Plaza, 91 Liberty Street, New York 10003, with offices in London and elsewhere abroad. Another firm is Merrill Lynch, with head offices at 1 Liberty Plaza, 165 Broadway, New York 10006, and many branch offices throughout the United States and abroad.

All brokers have a certain minimum below which new business is not profitable to them. White, Weld, for instance, deals mostly with institutions and other brokers in the field of Eurobonds, and trades are usually in lots of $50,000 and up. At Merrill Lynch, which prides itself on serving millions of little investors, the minimum is more like $1,000.

There are also reputable banks and dealers outside the United States with whom you can correspond in English, particularly in Great Britain, Holland and Switzerland. These banks and brokers may scrupulously observe the laws and regulations of their own countries, but they would go out of their minds if they tried to keep up with the constantly changing laws of all the foreign countries where their foreign clients reside, including the United States. Consequently, if a customer of a Swiss bank with an account in Switzerland, whether he is resident in the United States, Albania, or China, wants to buy any of the bonds mentioned in this chapter, the Swiss bank will buy it for him, provided it can do so under Swiss law.

You should realize, of course, that the SEC is trying to protect American investors from foreign shysters by requiring registration of foreign securities, just as it tries to shield them from the homebred sharpies by demanding registration of American securities. Anyone who buys unregistered foreign securities is therefore well advised to seek the best possible guarantees in whichever country he lives. It is a matter of applying one's common sense. A bond issued by the French state railroad system and guaranteed unconditionally by the government of France, for example, is not exactly a fly-by-night operation.

The Big Three banks of Switzerland are paradoxically (like Merrill Lynch, the biggest United States securities dealer) the ones most likely to welcome smaller accounts. They are: the Swiss Bank Corporation, 6 Paradeplatz, Zurich; Union Bank of Switzerland, 45 Bahnhofstrasse, Zurich; and the Swiss Credit Bank, Paradeplatz 8, Zurich. An investor with $15,000 or more to invest might try the Foreign Commerce Bank, Bellariastrasse 82, Zurich, which is smaller and claims it gives more personal attention to a somewhat wealthier clientele.

In England, to mention two among many, you have Barclays Bank Ltd., 54 Lombard Street, London EC3, and Lloyds Bank Ltd., 71 Lombard Street, London EC3. The essential thing to remember in England is to insist that the bank open an *external sterling* account for you. You will then be able to move your funds freely in and out of Great Britain. Ordinary accounts, such as British residents have, are subject to all kinds of exchange controls. If you wish to deal direct with a British broker you may write to the Secretary, the Stock Exchange, London EC2N1HP, indicating the size your investment transactions might be, and he will submit a list of a few firms, without recommendations.

Among Dutch banks that are also brokers there are Pierson, Heldring & Pierson, 214 Herengracht, Amsterdam; the Amsterdam-Rotterdam Bank, 595 Herengracht, Amsterdam; and the Algemene Bank Nederland, 32 Vijzelstraat, Amsterdam.

Mexican accounts

One way of investing abroad that gains in popularity, particularly when the Swiss financial authorities slam the door against incoming foreign money, is the Mexican bank account. This is quite a different kettle of fish, however. You invest in Mexico to get higher interest—at times twice what you can get from an American bank savings account. You do not invest in Mexico with any great expectation that the peso is going to rise in value against the United States dollar as the Swiss franc has done.

The peso has been worth eight United States cents since 1954. One reason for its rock-like stability for a quarter of a century is that the Mexican economy is closely tied to that of the United States. More than half of all Mexican imports and exports cross the American border, and American tourists pour one billion dollars into Mexico every year. The Mexicans hold up the value of the peso, but it simply does not make sense for them to scare off Yankee tourists by raising the exchange rate.

Mexican banks do not have government insurance such as depositors in United States banks get from the FDIC, but they are safe. Since 1925 there has never been any report of any depositor losing principal or interest in any authorized Mexican banking institution. The Mexican Central Bank has always stepped in to help a bank in financial difficulties or to take it over if necessary. You should deal directly with a big, reputable Mexican bank and avoid any American intermediaries. Investors have lost money in a couple of cases in recent years by yielding to the blandishments of United States-based "investment houses" of dubious repute who took their money and reinvested it in some shaky Mexican credit unions (not banks), which is illegal in Mexico. The Mexican authorities, besides, have no control over shady operators in the United States.

You have the choice of a number of first-class Mexican banks to deal with, one of which is Nacional Financiera, Isabel la Catolica 51, Mexico 1, D.F. This is Mexico's official national development bank. It is owned 51% by the Mexican government and 49% by private investors. It has assets in excess of $3 billion and it finances many of the country's industrial firms. Nacional Financiera offers easily marketable Titulos Financieros, which were yielding 8.75% after Mexican taxes at the time of this writing: three-month fixed term deposits with a net yield of 9.5% (11% if you invested more than $8,000); six-month fixed-term deposits yielding 10% (11.5% on an investment of more than $8,000); and fixed-term deposits of twelve, eighteen, or twenty-four months with a net yield of 10.5% to 12%, depending on whether your investment is more than $2,000 or more than $4,000. All these rates were for investments in Mexican pesos. The bank also offered United States dollar certificates for fixed term deposits of three, six, twelve, eighteen, or twenty-four months, with net yields ranging from 8.5% to 9.5% after Mexican taxes. United States Treasury Bills and American bank savings accounts were yielding 5% to 6% at this time.

As money market conditions change in the United States, sometimes the biggest financial houses on Wall Street find it convenient to send their idle funds to Mexico on these terms. The peso is freely convertible into foreign currencies and there are no restrictions on taking money out of Mexico.

It is true that you run a risk of the peso being devalued against the dollar while your money is in Mexico. You can protect yourself against this possibility—if it worries you and your investment is $80,000 or more—by selling a peso futures contract on the International Monetary Market in Chicago for a period of six months, a year, or whatever is the term of your peso deposit in Mexico. Each peso futures contract is for the equivalent of about $80,000 and requires a margin of $2,000 or so. Major brokerage houses such as Merrill Lynch can handle your orders in the futures market. Whatever you may lose on your investment in Mexico through a depreciation of the peso you will then make back in Chicago. If you have less than $80,000 on the line and are a chronic worrier, the answer is to make a dollar investment in a Mexican bank and settle for a slightly lower yield. The Mexican bank will then have to worry about any foreign exchange fluctuations, as it is obligated to repay you in dollars.

Just as in the case of Swiss banks, a faint air of illegality clings to Mexican bank accounts. Americans have reportedly deposited more than a billion dollars in the banks of Baja California alone, and much of this is allegedly tainted money from criminal sources and tax evaders. In fact, Mexico has no reciprocal taxation treaty with the United States and will not ·cooperate with American investigators from the Treasury or the

F.B.I. The Mexican Banking Commission forbids any disclosure on Mexican bank accounts. How much of this money is actually on the wrong side of the law is impossible to discover. It seems reasonable to suppose, however, that most of it is the capital of ordinary citizens who don't see why they should be held to a 5% interest on their side of the border when they can quite legally make 10% on the other.

Other investments abroad: Insurance, annuities

To a large extent, the investments for your later years and for the welfare of your family when you are gone are completely beyond your control. If you are an American, they are also tied irrevocably to the somewhat shaky fortunes of the U.S. dollar.

Your U.S. Social Security benefits, for example, will be paid in dollars. Any life insurance or annuities you have in the United States will also be paid in dollars. If you work for a big American corporation, your pension will come in dollars and any money in the pension fund will be invested in dollar securities. You have no control over any of these investments, and in the case of Social Security benefits you cannot even choose your beneficiaries—it is all ordained by law.

As executives of American firms in Germany and Switzerland have found, to say nothing of pensioners in Austria or even Social Security beneficiaries living in Poland and other countries, when the exchange rate of the dollar goes down 40%, your standard of living abroad goes down 40%, too.

So if you plan to live abroad during your working life or after your retirement, it makes sense to diversify your sources of income into other strong currencies. And even if you plan to live your life out entirely in the United States, it would do you no harm to have an extra source of income that may rise substantially when converted into dollars in the years ahead.

The safest and most conservative currency in which to hedge against the possible debasement of your compulsory financial commitments to the U.S. dollar is undoubtedly the Swiss franc. As a resolutely neutral nation, Switzerland is unlikely to be involved in any wars, and with its record of fiscal responsibility it is likely to have the lowest inflation rate in the world in the years ahead.

In planning your own supplementary income to make up for

any devaluation of your Social Security benefits, insurance, annuities, or company pension, you might therefore consider the services of a Swiss insurance company.

The biggest insurance firm in Switzerland is the Swiss Life Insurance and Pension Company, P.O. Box 740, 8022 Zurich, Switzerland. Founded more than 100 years ago, it has more than 1.7 million policies in force. This company is not licensed for business by state insurance authorities in the United States or Canada. You have to deal with it in Switzerland, where all insurance agreements are subject to Swiss law. Under current regulations, life insurance policies on persons residing outside Switzerland do not have to be reported to the Swiss tax authorities.

From Swiss Life Insurance you can buy Swiss franc policies that are basically similar to the policies offered by American insurance companies in dollars: level term, endowment, joint life, whole life, and so on. The company will also sell you annuities of various kinds, guaranteeing you, or you and your spouse, a fixed income for life in Swiss francs.

Another, smaller, firm is the Geneva Life Insurance Company, P.O. Box 248, 8035 Zurich. You can deal with both companies through Assurex S.A., Obstgartenstrasse 7, 8035 Zurich, a consulting firm specially set up to explain in American-style English the complexities of insurance in a foreign land under foreign laws.

In buying insurance coverage and annuities in Switzerland, you will be protected against dollar devaluations, but you will not be protected by U.S. insurance authorities. You will be protected only by the laws of Switzerland. Each of the 50 U.S. states has its own insurance department, and it is this maze of differing state regulations that apparently keeps many Swiss insurance companies from registering for business within the United States. They don't know how to handle 50 regulatory authorities or whether it would even be worth the effort. There would not be much point in competing with American insurance companies in their own territory if they were only allowed to offer insurance policies and annuities in U.S. dollars. Their whole selling point is that they provide coverage in Swiss francs.

10

Foreign stocks:
How to maximize profits, stability, and safety
with a global portfolio of common stocks

Investing in foreign stocks can be highly rewarding—at times
two or three times as profitable as investing in the United States
stock market, even more profitable if you are lucky. Here are
some figures to prove the point.

Over the ten-year period to June 30, 1975, the average United
States mutual fund gained 58.53%, including reinvested
dividends and capital gains, according to a study of 545
American investment companies made by Lipper Analytical
Services. Considering the risk of loss involved, it is not a particularly brilliant result. A 5.853% savings account would have
achieved the same at simple interest and with practically no
risk. One should not assume that one would necessarily have
made that much in mutual funds—the average covers a wild
disparity of results in individual funds. Half a dozen ended the
decade with a 30% *loss*. The top ten funds gained 150% or more.
The results of the actual fund you invested in could have been
anything from outstanding to plain awful.

But the really significant point we want to make here is that
the top two funds out of the 545 studied by Lipper did not invest

in American stocks. International Investors, which invested mainly in South African gold mines, wound up the ten years with a 481% gain. Templeton Growth Fund, with a portfolio of international stocks, gained 331%. The nearest fund totally invested in American companies was Rowe Price New Horizons, in the number three spot, which was up 232%. This fund, specializing in small American growth companies, at one time in the early 1970s was such a hot investment that it had to impose a $25,000 minimum initial investment in order to slow down the avalanche of incoming money. And yet this star of the United States stock-picking contest performed only two-thirds to one-half as well as the two funds that picked and chose among foreign stocks.

As we noted in a previous chapter, the results you get in the United States stock market all depend on the period you happen to invest in. The timing of your investment can mean the difference between a 48% yearly loss and a 21% yearly gain. Exactly the same sort of thing happens in foreign stock markets. If you pick a different ten-year period, you may well find United States stocks and mutual funds outperforming foreign stocks and funds.

Even so, it is obvious that putting some of your assets into foreign stocks will give you a powerful counterbalance to the ups and downs of Wall Street. In some years it could put you far ahead of the stick-at-home investor; in others it could hold up one end of your investments while the other sinks into a bear market. Consider it as a way of making extra money or as a defensive strategy—either way it can make sense.

How to do it

There are several possible ways of investing in foreign stocks. Here is a brief rundown of the alternatives before we study the advantages and drawbacks of each one in detail.

Firstly, if the thought of venturing into overseas stock markets is alarming, you can be a stay-at-home and put your money into the stock of American multinational companies quoted on the New York Stock Exchange. American multinationals have billions of dollars invested in foreign countries around the world, and a portfolio of their shares would give you a diversified stake in their worldwide operations.

Secondly, you can buy the stocks of about 400 foreign companies whose shares are listed on United States stock exchanges. This means going one step further into foreign investment fields, but you are still dealing with your usual United States stockbroker and are involved in no further complications than you are when buying American stocks.

Thirdly, you can put your money into investment trusts quoted on United States stock exchanges that specialize in buying shares of foreign companies in such countries as Japan, South Africa, Israel, or Canada. You can also buy American-based mutual funds that concentrate on foreign shares. In both cases a lot of your work is done for you—the funds or investment trusts provide you with a ready-made portfolio and relieve you of the burden of selecting individual foreign stocks yourself. All your purchases and sales are still transacted entirely in the United States.

Fourthly, for countries such as Switzerland or Germany, where there is no United States-based trust available, it is possible to buy foreign-based mutual funds that invest in shares of these two countries. There are similar funds available for Great Britain, France, Italy, Spain, and Australia. In this case you are taking one step further into foreign lands—you will be dealing directly with a dealer or bank overseas.

Fifthly, you can buy individual stocks yourself directly through a stockbroker in Paris, London, Frankfurt, Zurich, or other markets. But here you run into a number of drawbacks, such as differing local customs, languages, and regulations. It really only makes sense if you are actually living in the foreign country in which you are investing.

And finally, what is the easiest and simplest investment of all—a mutual fund or investment trust with a worldwide portfolio of stocks in a package.

Investing in United States multinationals

The multinational corporation bestrides the modern world, ranging across national frontiers in search of profits. Its multi-billion dollar operations exceed the gross production of many nations. President Salvador Allende of Chile complained on one occasion to the United Nations that one such multinational, "a gigantic corporation whose capital is bigger than the national budgets of several Latin American countries put together, launched a sinister plan to prevent me from acceding to the presidency."

Allende, who was later assassinated in a rightist revolution, was a Marxist, and the company he denounced—International Telephone & Telegraph—was American, as are perhaps half the world's great multinational corporations. But they are not an exclusively capitalist phenomenon. The communist world too is breeding globe-girdling enterprises with tentacles that extend ever deeper into the economies of the West and the Third World. Soyuzneftexport of Russia runs chains of gas stations in Belgium, Great Britain, and Finland. Skoda of Czechoslovakia has assembly plants in Mexico, India, Iran, and Turkey, and sells machinery throughout Western Europe. Auto Tractor of Romania even teamed up with the Canadian province of Saskatchewan to invade the United States tractor market.

The multinational company may well be the wave of the future. Behind all the multinationals, East and West, is the irresistible impulse of modern technology, thrusting them through national and ideological barriers. Commerzbank, one of the largest commercial banks in West Germany, keeps the books of its New York branch on its computer in Frankfurt, transmitting data by satellite hundreds of miles above the earth.

As in so much else, the American economy leads the world in the development of the multinational corporation. American companies have direct investments abroad estimated at about $110 billion. There are more than a dozen United States corporations with annual sales of more than $1 billion each outside the United States, and there are three dozen more with foreign sales of over $100 million a year. These companies are to a large extent insulated from the ups and downs of the American economy. Their operations are so widely based that they are in fact almost impervious to a slump in any individual country.

Take the case of Emerson Electric Corporation, a relatively small United States multinational. This is what the company had to say about its worldwide strategy in 1974, as the American economy was hit by its worst recession in 40 years: "The wide dispersion of Emerson operating subsidiaries, as well as the absence of total dependence on any one product line or foreign market, provide protection against economic cycles in individual countries. Each of Emerson's 60 foreign operating units serves a limited geographic sector of the world, and each contributes only a small portion of the total international sales volume. Outside of Canada, no single country contributes more than 10% of the company's total sales. By concentrating efforts on the development of a great number of rapidly growing small units, the company has been able to achieve strong growth rates." The policy evidently pays off—Emerson gets an A+ ranking from Standard & Poor's.

Indeed, the Standard & Poor's rankings of common stocks provide a powerful confirmation that a worldwide spread of operations gives a company a strong base for consistent growth of profits year after year. In a previous chapter we noted that only 55 absolutely top-notch firms get an A+ ranking from Standard & Poor's among thousands of American corporations. Let us now note a significant fact. No less than 35 of these 55 aristocrats among United States corporations have a substantial part of their operations, investments, and profits outside the United States. Such an overwhelming preponderance of multinationals is evidently not just a matter of random chance.

Standard & Poor's, let us recall, makes its rankings on the basis of "the relative stability and growth of earnings and dividends"—a process that has ended up with multinationals monopolizing two-thirds of the top ranking.

So in making your choice of multinationals for possible investment, consult the following top-quality selection list:

35 American corporations with significant operations abroad ranked A+ by Standard & Poor's

American Home Products	Heinz	Searle
American Hospital Supply	IBM	Sears, Roebuck
Beatrice Foods	Kellogg	Shell Oil
Black & Decker	Kresge	Squibb
Bristol-Myers	Marsh & McLennan	Standard Brands
Coca Cola	Mobil Oil	Standard Oil California
Colgate-Palmolive	Procter & Gamble	Standard Oil Indiana
Eastman Kodak	R.J. Reynolds	Sterling Drug
Emerson Electric	Richardson Merrill	Texaco
Exxon	Rohm & Haas	Warner-Lambert
General Electric	Schering Plough	Xerox
Gulf Oil	Schlumberger	

Many of these companies do not give shareholders detailed reports on their foreign operations. There is a widespread tendency to make generalized statements about progress overseas rather than to give facts and figures. But profits from foreign operations can in some cases outweigh the profits made at home. Coca Cola, for example, made 44% of its sales outside the United States in 1974, and no less than 63% of its profits came from abroad. In the same year, Squibb's foreign earnings were 42% of total earnings; the foreign sales and earnings of Standard Brands were 28% and 29% of the total; IBM's foreign operations contributed $5.9 billion in sales and $920 million in earnings; and Sterling Drug's foreign sales were 41% of the company's total sales.

The foreign sales of some of the oil companies were above the $10 billion mark: Gulf Oil $10.6 billion; Standard Oil of California $11.7 billion. The foreign *earnings* of Exxon were $1.9 billion, those of Texaco $1.1 billion.

While a portfolio of these shares will give you a diversified stake in the entire world economy, all the American multinationals share a common flaw. They are quoted on the New York Stock Exchange, and they are all subject to the ups and downs of the United States stock market. A bear market such as the drastic plunge of 1974 will carry all these shares down, too. They may insulate you from the effects of an American recession, but they will not necessarily protect you from the vagaries of the United States stock market.

So the logical next step is to seek out foreign companies whose shares are traded primarily in stock markets abroad—the stock exchanges of London, Paris, Tokyo, Frankfurt, Zurich, Milan, or other financial centers.

Foreign stocks

The essential advantage in buying the shares of foreign-based companies is that the stock markets of the world usually rise and fall quite independently of each other. To take a year at random, consider 1972, when the Dow Jones average of 30 industrials gained about 11% in the United States. In that same year the index of South African gold-mining stocks soared 100%; the Japanese stock market price level almost doubled;

and Canadian stocks were up around 20%. Any of these markets would have been a better bet than the United States stock market. On the other hand, American stocks would have been better than British stocks, which only rose 6%, or Italian shares, where the average gain was only 8%. An international portfolio of 50 of the world's biggest companies would have gained 37% in 1972, as measured by the Amro-Pierson 50 index.

There are years, of course, when United States stocks outperform all foreign stock markets. But they have not been too frequent lately. In the sixteen years from 1958 to 1974 the New York Stock Exchange index of all its listed stocks advanced 109% (about 4.7% a year compounded). This was a better record than the stocks of Italy, Great Britain, and France. But the stock indexes of Canada, Holland, Australia, Switzerland, Sweden, Germany, Japan, South Africa, and Spain all did better. Switzerland showed a gain of 373% over those 16 years, Germany 431%, while, at the top of the heap, Japanese stocks advanced 725% and South African gold-mining stocks rose 810%.

These figures (all converted into American dollars for the sake of uniformity) are taken from Capital International Perspective, a stock market information service headquartered in Geneva, Switzerland.

It is obvious that the United States stock market, where the Dow Jones industrial average is capable of plunging from 1051 in 1973 to 577 in 1974 is a high-risk basket in which to put all your eggs. So is any other individual stock market around the world. Scientific studies show that this risk can be significantly reduced by diversifying investments around the world. A recent academic study by Professor Bruno Solnik of Stanford University indicates that a portfolio of stocks chosen from seven European countries and the United States had about half the variability of return of a well-diversified but exclusively American portfolio. With the volatility of his stocks cut down by one-half, the conservative investor can sleep easier at nights—about as well, shall we say, as if the Dow Jones dropped only 50 points for you while it plunged 100 points for fellow-Americans who were fully invested in the United States.

Professional money managers who have to sweat it out in the

actual hurly-burly of the market place tend to be rather disdainful of the ivory tower theses of academia, but their results appear to confirm the academic conclusions.

Here, for example, is Landon Thomas of the Fiduciary Trust Company of New York. Mr. Thomas is executive vice president of the firm's international department, which manages about $350 million worth of stock and bond investments outside North America. While expressing skepticism on theoretical investments by "students who were never actually in the market," Thomas said Fiduciary Trust's portfolio of foreign stocks has shown superior results to its holding in United States stocks over a ten-year period. In the ten years to January 1, 1976—a dismal decade for the American and some other stock markets—Fiduciary Trust's aggregate institutional portfolio of United States common stocks showed a 3.7% annual gain compared with a 9.7% yearly gain for its portfolio of foreign common stocks. The Trust was thus able to boost its yearly return on its entire worldwide portfolio of common stocks to 5.5% a year compounded annually—a significant improvement over the 3.7% which the United States stock market alone would have provided in this period.

Fiduciary Trust manages investments for pension funds and other big institutions. It also deals with individual investors but is not interested in small accounts. If you have at least $500,000 to invest in a worldwide portfolio, the address is 2 World Trade Center, New York 10048.

Do not let these big figures scare you. All you really need to invest in foreign stocks is a few hundred dollars or so and a phone call to your plain old United States stockbroker.

How to invest in foreign stocks in the United States

About 400 foreign corporations have their shares quoted on United States stock markets. Thirty-four are listed on the New York Stock Exchange, another seventy on the American Stock Exchange, and the remainder are quoted over the counter.

Since the New York Stock Exchange imposes the most stringent financial and reporting requirements on its listed companies, the most conservative course would be to start with foreign stocks listed on the NYSE. These 34 stocks include 17 Canadian companies, as well as corporations based in South Africa, the Philippines, Great Britain, Holland, Panama, and Japan.

Foreign Stocks Listed on the New York Stock Exchange

Alcan Aluminum Ltd. (Canada)—aluminum producer
ASA Ltd. (South Africa)—investment trust of South African shares
Benguet Consolidated Inc. (Philippines)—mining
British Petroleum Co. (Britain)—petroleum holding company
Campbell Red Lake Mines Ltd. (Canada)—gold mining
Canada Southern Railway Co. (Canada)—railroad
Canadian Pacific Ltd. (Canada)—railroad
Carling O'Keefe Ltd. (Canada)—breweries
Deltec International Ltd. (Britain)—foods, commodities
Distillers Corp.-Seagrams Ltd. (Canada)—distilleries
Dome Mines Ltd. (Canada)—petroleum and gold mining
EMI Ltd. (Britain)—electronics, record, entertainment
Genstar Ltd. (Canada)—building
Hudson Bay Mining Co. (Canada)—mining
Intercontinental Diversified Corp. (Panama)—homesites, casinos
International Nickel Co. (Canada)—mining
Japan Fund (Japan)—investment trust of Japanese shares
KLM Royal Dutch Airlines (Holland)—airline
Massey-Ferguson Ltd. (Canada)—agricultural machines
Matsushita Electric Industrial Co. (Japan)—electronic products
McIntyre Mines Ltd. (Canada)—mining
Norlin Corp. (Panama)—holding company, musical instruments, beverages
Northern & Central Gas Corp. (Canada)—public utility
Northgate Exploration Ltd. (Canada)—mining
Pacific Petroleums Ltd. (Canada)—petroleum and natural gas
Plessey Co. Ltd. (Britain)—electronic equipment
Royal Dutch Petroleum Co. (Holland)—petroleum
Schlumberger N.V. (Holland)—petroleum services
Shell Transport and Trading Co. (Britain)—petroleum
Sony Corp. (Japan)—radios, recorders, television sets
Unilever Ltd. (Britain)—foods, commodities
Unilever N.V. (Holland)—foods, commodities
Walker (Hiram)-Gooderham & Worts Ltd. (Canada)—distilleries
Westcoast Transmission Co. Ltd. (Canada)—natural gas distributor

If you extend your selection to the American Stock Exchange, where the companies listed are generally smaller than on the

NYSE, you will add another three countries to your possible choice of foreign stocks—Israel, the Bahamas, and Mexico. The shares of 50 Canadian companies are traded on the Amex, as well as a score of corporations from other countries.

Canadian companies on the American Stock Exchange

The Canadian companies listed on the Amex offer interesting possibilities of worldwide diversification. Asamera Oil Co., for example, is heavily involved in oil exploration in Indonesia, although it is a Canadian firm. Brascan has a big stake in Brazilian industry as well as Canadian properties. Most of the Canadian companies on the Amex currently are a run-of-the-mill bunch, with a B+ to B ranking (average to below average) or lower from Standard & Poor's. They are mostly petroleum and mining outfits. Some outstanding issues are: Ford Motor Co. of Canada (A+), Gulf Oil Canada Ltd. (A), Hudson's Bay Oil & Gas Co. (A-), Imperial Oil Ltd. (A), and Union Gas Co. of Canada Ltd. (A-).

Other Foreign Stocks on the American Stock Exchange

Alliance Tire and Rubber Co. (Israel)
American Israeli Paper Mills (Israel)
Anglo Company Ltd. (Bahamas)
Atlas Consolidated Mining (Philippines)
British American Tobacco Co. (Britain)
Courtaulds Ltd. (Britain)—synthetic fibers
Dunlop Holdings (Britain)—synthetic fibers
Etz Lavud Ltd. (Israel)—wood products
Imperial Chemical Industries (Britain)—biggest British chemical co.
Imperial Tobacco Group Ltd. (Britain)
Marinduque Mining (Philippines)
O'okiep Copper Co. (South Africa)
Philippine Long Distance Telephone Co. (Philippines)
San Carlos Milling Co. (Philippines)—sugar
Sumitomo Chemical Co. (Japan)
Syntex Corporation (Panama)—pharmaceuticals
Tubos de Acero de Mexico (Mexico)—steel
Woolworth & Co. (Britain)—retail trade

Foreign stocks on the United States over-the-counter market

The over-the-counter market is a sort of grab-bag where you

can buy or sell any stock not listed on a regular exchange. Rather than a formal centralized market located at a specific place, like the NYSE or the Amex, it is a countrywide network of securities dealers linked up by a computerized quotation system. Something like 8,000 stocks are traded on the OTC market, some of them very small issues of limited regional appeal to investors.

This does not mean, however, that the 300 or so foreign stocks available on the OTC market are necessarily all cats and dogs. This market includes a few foreign stocks of companies that are really big, and one or two that are of the highest investment quality. It also gives you access to the stocks of a few more countries, among them Germany, Italy, Australia, and Sweden, enabling you to round out a truly worldwide portfolio. In the OTC market, for example, you can buy the shares of A.G. Bayer, a leading German chemical and pharmaceutical company; Fiat, the big Italian auto manufacturer; and Broken Hill Proprietary Co., a leading Australian industrial concern, as well as L.M. Ericsson, a Swedish manufacturer of telephone equipment. Moore Corp. Ltd., a Canadian producer of business forms quoted over-the-counter, is accorded an A+ ranking by Standard & Poor's.

Other foreign companies quoted over-the-counter in the United States include:

Anglo-American Corp. of South Africa, holding company, mining
Anglo-American Gold Investments Co., a trust of South African gold mines
Bank Leumi le-Israel, Israeli bank
Beecham Group Ltd. (Britain) pharmaceuticals
Blyvooruitzicht Gold Mining Co. (South Africa)
Bowater Paper Corp. (Britain)
Buffelsfontein Gold Mining Co. (South Africa)
Burmah Oil Co., (Britain) petroleum
Canon Inc. (Japan) photographic equipment
DeBeers Consolidated Mines (South Africa) diamond mining
Dresdener Bank, leading West German bank
Free State Geduld Mines (South Africa) gold mining
Fuji Photo Film (Japan)
Glaxo Holdings (Britain) drugs, food
Hitachi Ltd. (Japan) industrial machinery
Honda Motor Co. (Japan)

IDB Bankholding Ltd., Israeli bank
Japan Air Lines
Kansai Electric Power Co. (Japan)
Kirin Brewery (Japan)
Mitsui & Co. (Japan) trading company
Nissan Motors Co. (Japan)
Philips Gloeilampenfabrieken (Holland) lamps and electric
    equipment
Potgietersrust Platinums Ltd. (South Africa)
President Brand Gold Mining Co. (South Africa)
Rank Organization Ltd. (Britain) leisure-time industry
Telefonos de Mexico S.A.
Tokio Marine & Fire Insurance
Toyota Motor Co. (Japan)
Union Corp. Ltd. (South Africa) gold mining
Western Deep Levels (South Africa) gold mining

Most of the shares we have mentioned above are American Depositary Receipts (ADRs), which are issued by a few big New York banks, notably Morgan Guaranty, First National City Bank, Irving Trust Company, Chase Manhattan Bank, and Chemical Bank. The ADR is a certificate in which the issuing bank guarantees that it is holding the foreign company's shares abroad. The ADR is then traded in lieu of the shares in the United States. Each ADR may represent as many as 100 shares. The reason for this is that in many foreign stock markets, particularly Japan's, it is quite common for the bluest of blue chips to be quoted at less than $1 a share. The ADR thus brings the price more into line with the normal American price level for common shares.

Information

A major problem with investing in these foreign securities is getting reliable, up-to-date information about the company in which you have invested your money. Foreign companies usually do not disclose anywhere near as much information as United States corporations do, and this is especially aggravated for American shareholders who own ADRs. Once you wander farther afield than the New York Stock Exchange or the American Stock Exchange, where reporting requirements are more strictly enforced, you may find yourself getting next to nothing in the way of data on your company's progress. You can remedy this in part by asking the American bank which issues the ADR to make sure that you get the latest company reports.

There are other sources of information that you have to pay for. Standard & Poor's, 345 Hudson Street, New York 10014, publishes a periodical, *International Stock Report Service*, covering about 75 foreign stocks. Capital International S.A., 15 Rue du Cendrier, 1201 Geneva, Switzerland (partly owned by the Chase Manhattan Corp.) provides monthly and quarterly data and charts on 1,100 foreign stocks and 16 national stock markets. A trial quarterly subscription costs $35.

United States mutual funds and investment trusts that specialize in foreign shares

If you are too busy or have no inclination to spend time on keeping abreast with individual foreign stocks, the solution for you is the investment trust or mutual fund, which selects the stocks and manages the portfolio for you.

There are four countries—Canada, South Africa, Japan, and Israel—whose stocks you can buy neatly packaged in this way through United States-based funds and trusts:

Canada: Canadian Fund Inc., Calvin Bullock Ltd., 1 Wall Street, New York 10005, is a United States-incorporated mutual fund with a predominantly Canadian portfolio of shares. The sales charge is 8.5%.

South Africa: ASA Ltd., a South African corporation listed on the New York Stock Exchange, holds about two dozen South African issues in its portfolio, mainly gold mines. The rising price of gold gave its price a spectacular upward ride in the early 1970s. This is a closed-end fund, and ASA shares frequently sell at a substantial premium over the breakup value of the portfolio it holds. This premium is a sort of barometer of the public interest in gold and widens when the price of bullion is rising. When the gold price slumps, ASA shares may even sell at a discount from net asset value. The current premium or discount may be checked in a column headed "Closed End Funds" in *Barron's* magazine.

Two South African investment companies with confusingly similar names are traded over-the-counter in the United States.

One is Anglo-American Corp., a $2.4 billion giant that is one of the world's biggest precious metals mining finance houses. It also dominates the world diamond market through its control of DeBeers, the world's greatest diamond producer. Anglo-American has investments in real estate, coal, and other interests in South Africa as well as gold and diamonds. Anglo-American Corp. is about 50% invested in gold mining. The big difference between it and Anglo-American Gold Investment, a company with about $1.5 billion in assets, is that the latter is almost 100% invested in gold mining, with major holdings in South Africa's leading mines. This is the world's largest concentration of gold mining assets. Unlike ASA Ltd., the price of Anglo-American Gold Investment does not swing so wildly to a big premium or discount over its net assets.

International Investors Ltd., 420 Lexington Avenue, New York 10017, is a United States mutual fund heavily invested in gold mining companies, most of which are South African. The sales charge is 8.75%.

Japan: The Japan Fund Inc., an investment trust quoted on the New York Stock Exchange, is the only American fund devoted exclusively to investment in Japanese securities. From its launching in 1962 to mid-1975, a $10,000 investment in Japan Fund would have grown to more than $85,000, closely paralleling the rise in the Tokyo stock index. Like ASA Ltd., Japan Fund frequently sells at a wide premium or discount from net asset value.

Israel: Israel Development Corp., a closed end trust quoted on the American Stock Exchange, provides a package of Israeli stocks. Its latest report is available from 30 East 42 Street, New York 10017.

Foreign mutual funds and investment trusts

There are also many trusts and funds headquartered in foreign countries. If you invest in these you will add ten countries to the list open to you—Australia, France, Germany, Great Britain, Ireland, Italy, Mexico, New Zealand, Spain, and Switzerland. The funds listed below all send you their reports and statements in English and correspond with you in English. In most cases you open an account with a bank in the foreign country concerned, which handles the transactions and holds your shares in safe custody.

Australia: Delfin Australian Inc., Delfin Investment Services, 16 O'Connell Street, Sydney 2000, Australia, has a portfolio of about a hundred Australian companies and aims to provide long-term capital growth. Besides many other Australian-based funds, there are also four British mutual funds that specialize in Australian shares. The largest of these is Unicorn Australia Trust, Barclays Unicorn Ltd., 252 Romford Road, London E7. The British-based trusts have two advantages—they carry a 5% sales charge as compared with the usual 8% in Australia, and they are quoted daily in the *Financial Times of London*, which is more readily available in the United States than most Australian newspapers.

France: Francit, a Swiss-based fund with investments in about 40 French companies, is run by the Union Bank of Switzerland, Bahnhofstrasse 45, Zurich, Switzerland, and is set up to deal with English-speaking investors. There are many French-based trusts, with about $5 billion under management, but they are mostly oriented to the French-speaking investor. If you have a working knowledge of French, further information on these French funds may be obtained from the investment companies association, Association des Sociétés et Fonds Francais d'Investissement, 1 Rue d'Astorg, Paris 8.

Germany: German funds are of the open-end type, similar to American mutual funds, which redeem their shares at net asset value. Their total investments come to about $6 billion. One of the biggest firms in the field is the Deutsche Investment Trust, 6 Frankfurt-am-Main, Biebergasse 6-10, West Germany. Two of its funds are Concentra, which has a portfolio of about 60 companies covering most areas of the German economy, and Thesaurus, which is more growth-oriented, with all dividends plowed back into the fund. If you know enough German, other funds oriented to German-speaking investors will be open to you. Details on these may be obtained from the German investment trust association, Bundesverband Deutscher Investment Gesellschaften, Eschenheimer Anlage 26, Frankfurt.

At times the German government takes action to stem an inrush of foreign money into the strong German mark and temporarily bans foreign investments in German stocks and bonds. Such bans may be circumvented by investing in Germac, a mutual fund of German shares run by the Union Bank in Switzerland.

Great Britain: The British have about 300 closed-end investment trusts quoted mostly on the London Stock Exchange, and 350 unit trusts, which are similar to American mutual funds. Information on these is available from the Association of Investment Trust Companies, 7 Angel Court, Throgmorton Street, London EC2, and from the Association of Unit Trust Managers, 306 Salisbury House, Finsbury Circus, London EC2. Many of the British trusts specialize in American, European, Australian, Far Eastern, Japanese, and worldwide stocks. Others specialize in specific investment areas, such as commodities, raw materials, financial services and real estate companies.

The biggest British unit trust is Save & Prosper Investment Trust Units, 4 Great St. Helen's, London EC3. This mutual fund offers an enormous spread of investments by investing in about 100 British investment trusts, which in turn run their own portfolios of individual stocks. The minimum investment in this fund is about $120 and the sales charge is 5% (the usual charge for most British funds). The Trust has assets of about $200 million and 117,000 shareholders.

The second largest is M & G General Trust Fund, Three Quays, Tower Hill, London EC3. This mutual fund has a portfolio of about 100 British industrial and commercial stocks, including a large proportion of British blue chips. The minimum initial purchase is about $150 and the sales charge is 2½%.

Ireland: National Shamrock Unit Fund, Slater Walker Trust Management Ltd., 45 Gresham Street, London EC2, England, is a small mutual fund with a good cross section of British and Irish shares in about 50 different companies.

Italy: There are a dozen-and-a-half mutual funds of Italian shares, but due to an Italian legal technicality they are all registered abroad, mostly in Luxembourg. One of these is Interitalia, Cadit S.A., 14 Rue Aldringer, Luxembourg, which has a broad Italian portfolio as well as a wide international selection of securities. ITAC, a mutual fund run by the Union Bank of Switzerland, Bahnhofstrasse 45, Zurich, Switzerland, concentrates on a narrower selection of stocks, exclusively in Italian companies.

Mexico: The Mexico City Stock Exchange is a small affair but it supports three mutual funds, at least one of which, Fondo de Inversiones Rentables Mexicanas (FIRME), Paseo de la Reforma 213, Mexico 5, D.F., is set up to deal with English-speaking investors. It holds a portfolio worth about $20 million spread over about 50 Mexican companies.

New Zealand: Mutual funds in New Zealand, hampered by a small local stock market, tend to spread their investments out into Australia as well. This policy is followed by Dominion Unit Trust, P.O. Box 1486, Auckland, New Zealand, and First New Zealand Unit Trust, 296 Lambton Quay, Wellington, New Zealand.

Spain: There are more than a dozen Spanish mutual funds, but they are oriented mainly to the Spanish-speaking investor. An exception is ESPAC, a Swiss-based fund of Spanish shares run by the Union Bank of Switzerland, which sends you its reports and statements in English.

Switzerland: Swissvalor, run by the Swiss Bank Corporation, 6 Paradeplatz, Zurich, has a portfolio of about 100 Swiss companies. Fonsa, sold by the Union Bank of Switzerland, 45 Bahnhofstrasse, Zurich, spreads its portfolio over about 70 Swiss companies.

Canada and Israel, which, as we noted earlier, are represented by United States-based funds and trusts, also have their own home-based outfits. Canadian funds are too numerous to list here. *The Financial Post Survey of Investment Funds,* MacLean Hunter Publishing Co., 481 University Avenue, Toronto, Ontario, provides a comprehensive listing, with many details on each fund. The funds known in Canada as "trust company investment funds" are no-load funds. They include Canada Permanent Investors, Canada Trust, Guaranty Trust, Montreal Trust, Royal Trust, and others.

Home-grown Israeli investment trusts include Bank Leumi Investment Company Ltd. and Discount Bank Investment Corporation. Both are quoted on the Tel Aviv stock exchange, but orders may be placed in the United States through Leumi Securities Corporation, 18 East 48 Street, New York 10017.

Seapac Fund, 11 Rue de la Corraterie, Geneva, Switzerland, holds a portfolio of companies based in the nations of Southeast Asia.

Foreign regulations and taxes

Most of the foreign-based funds mentioned above relieve you of the need to learn the ins and outs of overseas stock markets, each of which has different regulations, business methods, and customs from United States stock markets. All you have to do is send the check for the amount you are investing and the shares will be bought, dividends will be credited to your account, and you will receive quarterly or half-yearly reports in English. The funds will also deduct automatically any local taxes that are due. The income taxes you pay back at home are of course your own affair. It is your responsibility and not the fund's to report your foreign income to the United States Internal Revenue Service. In countries with which the United States has double taxation agreements, you can credit your foreign taxes against your American taxes.

The only major worry you may have is to get your money back home when you want it, but this is not usually a problem. Most countries are eager to encourage investors from abroad and do not usually hinder the repatriation of capital by fund investors. Britain, for example, has strict exchange controls for its own citizens, but as a foreign investor you can open an external sterling account with a British bank that allows you to move your money in and out of the United Kingdom as you please. The bank will buy and sell your fund shares and keep them in safe custody.

When investing in Australia, you are required to get official approval from the Exchange Control Authority when sending your money for investment and again when bringing it back home. But this is currently only a formality that your local Australian bank or broker will obtain for you in 24 hours. Other countries, such as Switzerland and Germany, impose no restrictions whatever on the return of your money to the United States. They do occasionally prevent you from investing from time to time, whenever they want to keep out a flood of unwanted dollars.

Investing in foreign stock markets on your own

You may think you can do better on your own in foreign stock markets than a United States-based or foreign-based fund would do for you. Perhaps so, but the practical difficulties are many. Your buy and sell orders, if sent by airmail, may take ten days to execute and confirm. Only a handful of United States brokers accept orders for foreign stock exchanges, and they will relay your order to a foreign broker anyway, thus doubling your brokerage charges. The business methods and requirements of some foreign stock markets may also be baffling to an American.

Investing directly in foreign stock markets yourself only makes sense when you actually live abroad in that particular country and have a working knowledge of its language and business practices. In this event you will find a wealth of information in *How to Buy Foreign Securities*, by Rainer Esslen, Columbia Publishing Co., Frenchtown, New Jersey 08825. This book contains data on brokers, securities, stock exchanges, financial publications, and other essential details for more than twenty different countries, from Great Britain to Singapore.

The ultimate worldwide investment

And finally there is the lazy man's way to build up a worldwide portfolio of stocks. It requires little more effort and thought on your part than writing checks whenever you have money to invest. This is the mutual fund or investment trust with an international portfolio of stocks, which fits into a single package all your financial commitments to the world's stock markets.

Two such funds in the United States are Templeton Growth Fund and Scudder International Fund. Both have consistently stood at or near the top of the performance rankings of United States mutual funds in recent years.

Templeton Growth Fund, headquartered at 110 Yonge Street, Toronto, Ontario, Canada, with United States sales head-quarters at 50 North Franklin Turnpike, Hohokus, New Jersey 07423, has an international portfolio valued at more than $18 million as this was written. A $10,000 investment in this fund in 1954 had grown to $83,000 in 1975, including reinvested capital gains. Total dividends in this period came to an additional

$6,800. The fund has a sales charge of 8.75%, and the minimum investment is $500.

Scudder International Fund, 10 Post Office Square, Boston, Massachusetts 02109, is a no-load fund. In 1975 it was invested in about 40 companies in 13 different countries and had assets of about $18 million. The minimum initial investment is $1,000. This fund is a good complement to your portfolio of American stocks, as its policy is not to invest in United States companies (other worldwide funds mentioned here usually include a sizable stake in American companies).

Funds with a global portfolio that are headquartered abroad include:

Intervalor, run by the Swiss Bank Corporation, 6 Paradeplatz, Zurich. Has investments in the blue chips of twelve countries, with the United States and Switzerland most prominently represented.

Globinvest, sold by the Union Bank of Switzerland, Bahnhofstrasse 45, Zurich, has a worldwide portfolio of stocks.

S & P Ebor Universal Growth Fund, 4 Great St. Helen's, London EC3, is one of the largest British funds, with a worldwide portfolio worth about $25 million at the time of writing and spread over 10 countries.

But the giant in the field of worldwide investing is Dutch-based *Robeco,* the largest investment trust outside the United States, with assets of about $1.4 billion. This enormous pool of capital is spread over about 300 companies in 17 different countries. In 1975 about 32% was invested in the United States and Canada, 44% in European countries, 12% in Japan, and the remaining 12% in other areas or cash. Started in 1929 as an investment club by a dozen wealthy investors in Rotterdam, Robeco has grown until it is the world's first truly international investment trust, with its shares listed on nineteen different stock exchanges and its shareholders spread around the world.

True to its origin as an investment club, Robeco cuts expenses by running itself, without any salesmen or outside management firm (the typical United States fund charges a 0.5% annual management fee as well as the customary 8.5% sales charge). Robeco is a unique hybrid among investment companies—it is listed on exchanges like a closed-end United States investment trust, but redeems its shares at net asset value like an American mutual fund. It thus avoids two disadvantages—the premium or discount usually found in closed-end funds and the sales commission charged by most mutual funds.

If you are going to boil down your worldwide stock portfolio, including American stocks, into one investment, Robeco is the undoubted leader in the field. Its home address is 25 Heer Bokelweg, Rotterdam, P.O. Box 973, Holland. Robeco also offers a shareholders account, which is virtually a current account, expressed in shares and fractions of shares. You can use this as a sort of bank account since money can be deposited or withdrawn at any time. Through the shareholder's account, Robeco also offers the option of life insurance against stock market risks. The insurance provides that in the event of the holder's death his heirs will be paid whatever amounts were invested in the fund plus 10% interest a year compounded annually. As far as the shareholder's estate is concerned, therefore, the investment is guaranteed to appreciate at a 10% yearly clip, regardless of what happens to prices on the world's stock markets. Robeco also offers what it calls inflation insurance: you set a specific savings target, and in the event of your death your heirs receive this predetermined amount—whether or not you managed to invest it all—plus 6% yearly interest compounded, to compensate for inflation. The premium varies according to the investor's age and country of residence. A 40-year-old investor living in Switzerland would pay 3.84 Swiss francs annually for every 1,000 francs insured. Further details on the shareholder account and the two optional insurance policies may be obtained from Robeco, 12 Quai General Guisan, Geneva 3, Switzerland.

An insurance policy against stock market declines and inflation is no small matter in today's world. As we noted in an earlier chapter, some American mutual funds now offer insurance against declines in the United States stock market. Robeco appears to be the only fund which will insure you against worldwide stock market declines. And Robeco's insurance policy against inflation appears to be unique among all stock funds, in the United States or abroad.

Timing is all

As in the United States stock market, timing is one of the most important factors in foreign stock exchanges. If you had plunged into the New York stock market at the height of the great boom in 1929 and sold out at the depths of the Depression in 1932, your losses would have been horrendous. Conversely, an investment in 1932, when American stock prices were scraping bottom, was likely to have been profitable in just about any subsequent year that you decided to sell out. The problem is how to identify the market's bottoms when buying and tops when selling.

This is what a stock market index is for. It tells you in cold, unemotional figures whether the market is near an all-time low, around an all-time high, or somewhere in between. The most commonly used American indexes are the Dow Jones average of 30 industrial stocks and the New York Stock Exchange index of all the exchange's listed stocks.

The Dow Jones hit a high of 381.17 on September 3, 1929, and plunged to a low of 41.22 on July 8, 1932. If you had invested in the component stocks, your portfolio would have shrunk from $38,117 to $4,122 in this period.

Each foreign stock market has its own index, and the figures for most markets show periods of volatility comparable with the 1929-32 debacle in the United States. To take an extreme example, the Hong Kong market index rose from 100 in 1964 to 1,775 in March, 1973, and then collapsed to 290 in May, 1974. In other words, you could have run a $1,000 investment up to $17,750 in nine years and then seen it shrink back to $2,900 in 14 months.

When buying foreign stocks—or American stocks for that matter—a common-sense plan would be to buy when the local stock market index is low and sell when it is high. It is an easy matter to keep track of foreign stock market indexes. All you have to do is buy *Barron's* magazine, a weekly sold on most United States newsstands. On one of its back pages, *Barron's* runs a table every week that shows the current year's high and low figures for foreign stock exchanges. The only problem with the table is that a typical stock market boom and bust cycle may take ten years or more to run its course.

Table 3 is the *Barron's* table for the 13-year-period 1962-1975:

Table 3
Foreign stock indexes

	High	Low
Australia	663.48	256.89
Austria	3,661	1,743
Belgium	157.50	93.50
Canada	238.26	105.77
France	113.9	50.28
Italy	11,014	4,100
Japan	5,359.74	1,020.49
Netherlands	177.30	66.00
Switzerland	460.1	160.3
United Kingdom	543.6	146.00
U.K. Kaffirs	424.30	43.50
West Germany	920.5	493.7

The U.K. Kaffirs index is an average of the South African gold mining issues quoted on the London Stock Exchange.

You can easily update this table yourself by buying *Barron's* around January 1 each year and filling in the previous year's high and low figures. (The index for French stocks is a tricky exception, however. The December 31 figure is reduced to 100 each year and becomes the base for the following year. Making a homogeneous year-to-year series thus involves a mathematical calculation.)

A cosmopolitan investor with a really global overview of stock market investments would consider the United States stock market simply as one among many where he might profitably put his money. If you want to act on this basis see Table 4.

Table 4
American stock indexes for 1962-1975

	High	Low
New York Stock Exchange Index	65.48	28.20
Dow Jones 30 Industrials	1051.70	535.76

If you are able to obtain the *Financial Times of London* (it is available in New York and some other major United States cities), you will be able to keep track there of the stock indexes of Montreal, Johannesburg, Hong Kong, Singapore, Denmark, and Sweden, in addition to the countries covered by *Barron's*.

Foreign currency fluctuations

There is one crucial difference between investing in the United States and investing outside the country—abroad you are investing in a foreign currency that may rise or fall against the American dollar. This introduces another variable into your calculations: if the foreign exchange value of the dollar goes up, your foreign investments will correspondingly go down. In recent years it has been nearly all downhill for the dollar. Almost any major foreign currency would have benefited the American who invested abroad, in many cases by a startling amount.

From December 31, 1970 to June 1, 1975—a period of only four and a half years—the Australian dollar rose 21% in value against the United States dollar, the Japanese yen rose 24%, the Hong Kong dollar 29%, the Swedish crown 31%, the French franc 32%, and the Belgian franc 44%. The Dutch guilder soared 51%, the German mark 56%, and the Swiss franc appreciated no less than 73%, from 4.37 francs to 2.51 francs per dollar. The British pound was the odd man out—it went down 3% against the American currency. All you had to do in this period was open a Swiss franc checking account or simply buy Swiss banknotes to make a 73% gain in less than five years.

To turn this concept around, if you had invested in Swiss stocks on December 31, 1970, the Swiss stock market could have suffered a disastrous collapse—comparable to the precipitous 1974 decline in the New York stock market—and you would still have broken even after converting your Swiss investments back into dollars.

When the rise in value of a foreign country's currency is added to the advance of its stock market, the gain is compounded for an American investor. To take one example: the Tokyo stock market advanced 100% from 1971 to 1973, but for an American investor in Japanese stocks the rising value of the Japanese yen would have turned this into a 160% gain for the three-year period. Over a ten-year span, from 1964 to 1973, the Japanese stock owner would have been ahead 230%, while the American investor in Japanese stocks would have gained 320% after converting his money back into dollars. Similarly, Dutch investors in Heineken, the big Netherlands brewery, made a 92% gain in 1971-74, while Americans gained 156% in the same stock in the same three-year period. In the 1964-73 decade the Dutch stockholder of Heineken profited by 800%, while his American counterpart was ahead 1,060% because of the advancing value of the guilder against the dollar.

This means it is just as important to pick the right currency to invest in as it is to select the right foreign stocks. The ideal candidate is the currency of a country that has a strong grip on inflation and no balance of payments deficits, whose government is not running head over heels into deficit financing, and whose monetary system has solid backing in gold. All this is reflected in the Chicago Monetary Market, where deliveries of major foreign currencies are quoted about a year into the future. If the German mark is quoted at a hefty premium for delivery a year hence, the market is telling you that it has confidence in the German economy and its monetary system. It is not really necessary to research thoroughly the reasons for this—a big German trade surplus, a firm government policy against inflation, or whatever. All you have to know is that the currency is considered sound by the money market at large. And if at the same time the German stock market index is near a low point, you have good odds of a double gain: a stock market advance boosted further by a rise in the value of the German currency.

11

If the worst comes:
The ultimate calamities—
war and defeat

The world faces a grave risk of the breakdown of a generation of economic peace. The international economic order which provided a postwar generation of economic peace has collapsed and we do not know what will take its place. There is a risk that governments could lose control of events—as they did politically in 1914 and economically in 1929-32—with unpredictable and possibly disastrous results for the world economy and world politics. Military peace could prove elusive in the absence of a restoration of economic peace.

—The Ford Foundation, October 1973, on announcing a 1 million dollar appropriation for a major research effort to "help resolve the ongoing crisis in world economic relations."

Every word so far in this book is based on one unspoken assumption: that there will be no major war, that is, a global conflict involving the United States, the Soviet Union, China, and other major powers. If worst comes to worst and there is such a war, then everything you may have read in the recent spate of doomsday books becomes valid.

You then have to think in terms of the ultimate, basic realities. Cities with their power supplies bombed out—no heat, no light, no public transport. Homes with waterpipes poisoned by nuclear contamination. Hospitals overflowing with patients dying of radiation burns. Bodies lying uncollected in the streets. Contagious diseases spreading uncontrollably. Food distribution disrupted, law and order breaking down. Looters.

Is such a calamity probable? Most likely not. Is it absolutely inconceivable? Well, we had two world wars already in this century, and since then confrontations in Berlin, Cuba, and elsewhere seemed about to make World War III a reality. It appears that, however reluctantly, we should at least consider the unthinkable.

What are the government's plans to meet a war emergency? And what should our own plans be to survive the catastrophe if it ever comes?

Generals, it is said, are always preparing to fight the previous war, and thus are almost totally unprepared for the nature of new conflict. After the long trench warfare of World War I came the super-trench, the Maginot Line in France, which was easily bypassed by the German panzers in World War II. In World War III perhaps the tanks will be skewered by cheap hand-held rocket-launchers, as they were in the Arab-Israeli war of 1973.

However, let's leave that worry to the generals. Our main concern in this book is how the generals' plans are going to affect you if we are suddenly plunged into a nuclear war. First of all, even if war never comes, the military's plans are highly inflationary. The Pentagon requested nearly $105 billion for its defense budget in 1975 and expects to be asking Congress for nearly $150 billion by 1980. As long as the world remains a circle of armed camps, there is no realistic hope of avoiding yearly escalations in military budgets and the inflationary government deficits that pay for them. We discussed ways of defending your assets against inflation in other chapters of this book, but now the problem has come down purely and simply to the matter of physical survival.

Like most people, you may never have wondered what the government is going to do for you personally if war should ever come. Within the vast military establishment of the Pentagon you will find, if you look hard enough for it, the Defense Civil Preparedness Agency (DCPA), the Pentagon unit in charge of planning civil defense. It is a not unimportant function. Civil defense planners estimate that a timely evacuation of 70% of the population from the nation's big cities would enable 174 million Americans to survive an all-out nuclear attack. They calculate that only 109 million would stay alive if they remained where they were.

This agency, which thus apparently holds the lives of something like 65 million Americans in its hands, has a budget of $88 million for civil defense planning—about $1.35 a head. Out of three million persons in the military establishment, the agency employs a grand total of 650 people. But they do not do very much anyway. In a time of detente with the Soviet Union, anything the agency does to ensure the survival of the American civil population has a somewhat paranoid look about it. Public and Congressional interest in the agency is just about zero.

Still it is interesting to know what the agency's plans are if it should ever be needed. Current civil defense planning starts from the assumption that war will not come like a bolt from the blue. There will be a period of growing tension as trouble flares in some hot spot—say Berlin, Korea, or the Middle East. This may go on for weeks, giving you a fairly long warning as the headlines become larger and shriller.

At some point, as the situation heats up, the Soviets may start evacuating their cities. The Russians, incidentally, spend about one billion dollars a year on their counterpart of DCPA, according to American disarmament expert Paul Nitze. United States intelligence sources say the Russians would need about 72 hours to complete the evacuation. At this stage, American civil defense plans would presumably swing into action, and you could count on one, two, perhaps three days to get yourself and your family to a safe place, if you could find one.

Unless, of course, you had the foresight to live in a safe place before any crisis loomed over the horizon. There is, after all, a chance that war may come suddenly and without warning, even if civil defense measures do not take this into account.

The Kremlin does not broadcast its strategic plans to the

world, and you will not find any official Soviet list of American cities scheduled for nuclear bombing. But you can deduce what their plans are by studying American military plans for a possible nuclear war. Up to 1974, the Pentagon's reckoning was based on maintaining a force sufficient to absorb a surprise attack from the Russians and still have enough surviving power to inflict "unacceptable damage on the attacker." Defense Secretary Robert McNamara spelled this out more precisely: "unacceptable damage" to the Soviets would be the loss of 20% to 25% of their population (50 to 60 million people) and 50% of their industrial capacity. For this purpose the United States maintains a force of 8,500 nuclear warheads, which comes to about 40 atom bombs for each of the Soviet Union's 220 major urban areas. In 1974 the American military leaders enlarged this strategy to include also the assured destruction of the main Soviet military installations, such as underground missile silos, which required a more pinpoint accuracy than the indiscriminate levelling of big cities and large industrial areas.

On the other side, according to the International Peace Research Institute of Stockholm, which bases all its figures on official sources, the Soviet Union had (in 1975) 140 nuclear bombers, 42 nuclear submarines, and 1,540 land-based strategic missiles, capable altogether of launching 2,600 strategic nuclear warheads against the United States and other potential enemies.

Where would these projectiles be aimed? The American military assumes the Russian targets in America would closely parallel the American targets in the Soviet Union. In the event of war American civil defense planning calls for the evacuation of about 250 American metropolitan areas with more than 50,-000 inhabitants each, as well as about 150 other areas located near important military and industrial targets. It is conceivable, particularly in the event of a lightning Soviet attack launched without warning, that the bombing might be limited to military targets only and that mass civilian targets like New York City and Chicago could escape unscathed. But even then the toll would be high. The Department of Defense estimates that somewhere between 3.5 million and 22 million Americans would be killed in a Soviet attack against the intercontinental ballistic missile bases inside the United States. If the blitz were successful, it might then be unnecessary to bomb the cities. So one might consider that it is perhaps twice as dangerous to live near a military base as it is to live in a big American city.

The initial danger can be considerably reduced by living in a home with an approved fallout shelter. Many such homes were built in New York State due to the encouragement of former governor Nelson Rockefeller. President John F. Kennedy also told Congress in 1961 there was a need for fallout shelters, and about 835,000 homeowners built special shelters across the United States in the 1960s, according to DCPA estimates.

But why cower in a shelter or wait to the last minute for evacuation in an emergency? If you have the choice of living and working in a small town remote from the big cities and any military bases, take it now in preference to a city with a population of 50,000 or more. It may increase your chances of survival, not only if war comes but in the aftermath as well. When the basic structures of civilization break down, it is much easier to survive in an uncrowded rural area than in a congested urban zone where millions of people are milling around in desperation as mobs and looters clean out all the available food from the stores in the first few days.

If war does come, is it likely to be a long struggle lengthening into years like the two world wars, or will it be over in a matter of hours? Military experts are divided on this, with the American military planners tending to visualize a protracted months-long conflict, while the Russians appear to envisage a short, sharp clash.

These military disagreements need not affect one's personal planning too much. In either case the destruction will be so widespread, amid a wholesale disruption of economic production, that one should plan to survive on one's own resources for a period of say at least one year. Even a half-hour exchange of nuclear missiles followed by an immediate armistice would leave a country ravaged for many months. This means storing food for at least twelve months, as well as fuel, water, and, above all, medical supplies, which would be unavailable as hospitals and doctors were overwhelmed by millions of victims from the big cities.

The United States government has a small booklet titled *Disaster Diet* that suggests a minimum kit of non-perishable items to ensure a sufficient supply of nutritious food in case you are stranded for a period of days without power, heat, or refrigeration. It is intended for use in case of floods, hurricanes, and other natural disasters, but the circumstances are likely to be similar after a nuclear bombardment, only for a more prolonged period. (*Disaster Diet* may be obtained for 25 cents from the Superintendent of Documents, Government Printing Office, Washington DC 20402. Ask for folder NOAA/PA 73017).

Storing enough food for a year may be quite a project. In twelve months the average American consumes 116 pounds of beef, 285 eggs, 85 pounds of processed fruits and vegetables, 123 pounds of potatoes, 247 pounds of milk and cream, and 107 pounds of wheat flour.

Accumulating a year's intake of nourishment may also demand some detailed planning in order to ensure a balanced diet. There are firms that will do this for you, but the price you pay for their pre-packaged year's supply may be substantially more than you would pay yourself at your local supermarket. To take one example, Self-Sufficiency Projects, 1 Appletree Square, Minneapolis, Minnesota 55420, offers a package of twelve cases of assorted foods comprising half a dozen size-10 cans per case. The whole package of 72 cans fits in an average size closet, weighs 370 pounds, and is intended to provide a nutritionally balanced diet for one adult for one year or four adults for three months. The cost at the time of writing was $418. The firm claims the food, which is dehydrated so as to occupy less volume, will last for ten years when stored in a cool, dry place at a temperature of 40 to 60 degrees Fahrenheit. The package includes everything from ham to hamburger to apple and banana slices.

If you want to compare prices, other firms in the disaster survival business include Commodity Resources, 449 North 400 East, Kaysville, Utah 84037, and Federated Food Storage Co., 380 N. Broadway, Jericho, New York 11753.

A drinking water supply from your own well or storage tank would be essential if the local water supply system were knocked out. It might also be impossible to count on normal delivery of gas, oil, or electricity for heating, light, and cooking for weeks or months. *Energy for the Home,* a $5.95 book put out by Garden Way Publishing, Charlotte, Vermont 05445, provides details on getting heat and light for the home from solar energy, wind and water power, water-waste systems, and wood heating. It gives plans and cost estimates of windmills, solar air heaters, and other gadgets, as well as the names and addresses of manufacturers and of specialized periodicals that give further information on becoming self-sufficient in heat, light, and power.

For the real pessimists who foresee a total collapse of the economic order, including food distribution, such as occurred in Germany for a couple of years after both world wars, there is always the possibility of living off the land, even if local farms are not in production for a time. *Sturtevant's Edible Plants of the World* ($5.00, Dover Publications, 180 Varick Street, New York 10014) lists 2,897 species of plants, explains which parts of them are edible, and tells how to prepare them.

But even if one is reduced, like St. John the Baptist, to eating locusts and wild honey in a nuclear wilderness, there will always come a time when human society will reconstitute itself again. At such a time the technical ability to run a small farming operation might well make the difference between living on the starvation level or on a relatively full stomach. *Five Acres and Independence* by M.G. Gains (another Dover Publications book sold at $2.50) is a practical manual on how to coax a life of rude plenty from a small area of land. Originally published in 1935 by a recognized authority on farming, the book describes the techniques of running a small farm in the Depression days before DDT and other pesticides—circumstances which might well resemble post-World War III conditions. Other useful books in the same area are *Growing Vegetables in the Home Garden* and *Complete Guide to Home Canning, Preserving and Freezing,* which are United States Department of Agriculture bulletins reprinted by Dover Publications.

Financial planning

As in the choice of a safe place to live, your financial planning for a possible nuclear disaster should start long before the first shadows of war fall over the landscape. In the last few weeks it will probably be too late to take any action to keep your assets safe.

With the onset of war all sorts of draconian measures may be summarily imposed: emergency taxes, forced loans, capital levies, frozen dividends, even outright confiscation. By this time, with the nation at war, fervent patriots will revile any who attempt to make their private assets secure by evading the new impositions, and inflamed public opinion will demand exemplary punishment of offenders. The time to act is before disaster is at hand, when the world is at peace, when it is still easy, legal, and socially acceptable to do so. However, the available precautions are few.

The first is to keep some of your assets in a neutral nation. The safest and most financially responsible of these is Switzerland. In previous chapters we discussed the possible investments you could make through a Swiss bank: foreign stocks and bonds (risky in wartime), savings accounts (vulnerable to inflation even in Switzerland), and, best of all in times of catastrophe, gold and silver bullion and coins, held in safe custody by the bank. The Swiss understand these situations thoroughly and guard the assets well. Emperor Haile Selassie, having been forced to flee his country once by the Italian invasion of Ethiopia in the 1930s, held a numbered account in Switzerland. When he was deposed in 1974 the rebellious military government that held him prisoner forced him to sign over all his wealth but were met with a stone wall in Switzerland. The Swiss bankers could recognize a coerced signature when they saw one and demanded proof that it was made "under full freedom of decision."

However, assets held abroad are not necessarily beyond the reach of the United States tax collector. When World War II broke out the British government took over practically all the foreign investments of British citizens by decreeing a forced sale of these securities to the government. The only people who escaped this measure were those who had not reported their holdings to the British government in the first place. The only way you could avoid a similar confiscation by Uncle Sam would be by not reporting your foreign holdings on your income tax return as now required by the Internal Revenue Service and by dealing directly through the mail with a bank in Switzerland so that no record of any transaction is kept in the United States. A United States branch of the Swiss bank would obviously be no good for this purpose.

A second precaution against the coming of Armageddon that is in full compliance with present laws but might be declared illegal by emergency decrees in wartime is to store gold or silver coins or bullion oneself. For this purpose, the more anonymous the purchase and the fewer records kept the better. Gold was confiscated from American citizens even in peacetime by President Roosevelt in 1933, and it could quite plausibly happen again. Your gold holdings in a certificate type of investment such as Dreyfus Gold Deposits are a matter of record. So is the bullion you hold with a brokerage firm such as Merrill Lynch. A contract or a warehouse receipt from one of the gold or silver futures markets can easily be traced to you. The government could even uncover your purchases of coins from your local dealer if you pay by check. The most anonymous way to purchase is to buy from a reputable dealer and pay cash.

Storage is also a problem for gold-hoarders who anticipate the absolute worst. Bank vaults and safety deposit boxes could be closed if the banks are shut down at a time of financial panic—precisely when you need your gold the most. A safety deposit company might remain open during an enforced bank holiday, but could be sealed by government order as an emergency measure in wartime. In any event, depositors in both banks and safe depositories could be forced to reveal the contents of their boxes before they emptied them. All of these problems are avoided if you keep your gold in a safe at home, but then you have to worry about the possibility of burglary, theft, or fire. Over the ages, the cache of hidden coins has apparently been the most effective means of concealing wealth in times of troubles. Many of the ancient coins now in existence were probably preserved in secret hideaways by owners who were engulfed or swept away by invading forces. There is, of course, no way of knowing how many others returned to claim their wealth and start life anew once the disaster was over. If the idea of a hidden cache of wealth seems ridiculously unlikely to you, it does not seem so to the United States government, which has hidden $4 billion in new currency in a $7 million dugout at Pony Mountain near Culpeper, Virginia—just in case a nuclear attack wipes out the nation's currency.

Defeat

And finally, after the unthinkable there still remains the unspeakable: the possibility of a war that is lost. For millions of people in Vietnam, Cambodia, and Laos this is a raw, recent reality. For many, after years of weary struggle, the end came as swiftly as sudden death. Even Marshal Lon Nol, the anti-communist President of Cambodia, who was surely in a position to know what was coming, left his personal plans to the last minute. Only a few hours before the Communist forces took Cambodia, the National Bank in Phnom Penh sent an urgent telegram to a New York bank enquiring whether it had carried out an order to pay one million dollars to the Marshal. Lon Nol had already escaped abroad, but he was cutting his financial corners pretty closely and laying himself open to charges of unpatriotic corruption. Other leaders of Cambodia and South Vietnam were apparently too late in shipping wealth abroad. On April 30, 1975 the Swiss government banned imports and deposits of gold from both countries. There had been rumors that leading figures in the tumbling nations were shipping as much as $160 million to Switzerland.

For ordinary people, defeat was a shattering experience. Wild rumors ran through Saigon as the Communist forces closed in. Every woman would be forced to yield to ten victorious comrades, it was said. Vietnamese ladies offered themselves and $10,000 to any foreigner who would marry them—the only remaining way of getting out of the country. Army officers and leading bourgeois elements would be shot on the spot, some said. Drugstores were sold out of tranquilizers and sleeping pills—the easiest means of committing suicide. Houses, apartments, cars, and other possessions were sold at huge losses in the last days by people desperate to raise money to flee the country. The market was glutted with television sets, air-conditioners, and other appliances as merchants tried to liquidate their stock. For many of these assets there was no longer any market at all. Even gold plunged to half the world market price in those last few desperate days—it was heavier, bulkier, and more difficult to conceal than dollar bills. In the end about 130,000 Vietnamese made it out of the country to the United States. Most of these people were not destitute, according to Nicholas Deak, head of a leading gold and foreign exchange firm that set up shop in the refugee camps. Many arrived with French francs, Dutch guilders, and other currencies, as well as dollars and gold. Their South Vietnamese banknotes were of course worthless, but their gold was again salable at world price. "It shows once again that gold is the ultimate value, not paper money," said Deak.

The calamity of defeat has been suffered by millions around the world in this century. It was experienced twice in a generation by the German people. It was suffered with even more shattering effect by the Japanese, where a traditional, hierarchical society of feudal militarism under the millennial rule of a dynasty of god-emperors was abruptly handed over to General Douglas MacArthur, American-style capitalism, Coca-Cola machines, and pacifism enshrined in a United States-modelled constitution.

The culture shock would be not much different for Americans subjected to military conquest by a Marxist power. Traditional values would be turned upside down. Under the new order a college education might well depend on the ability to present a certificate of clean proletarian family origin. Education is a weapon in the class struggle that the Marxist state does not give freely to its class enemies. Military officers, government officials, and business executives would be compelled to take re-education courses. In some extreme cases, atrocities might occur, similar to the shooting by the Russians of 5,000 Polish army officers in Katyn forest during World War II because they were considered "unre-educable bourgeois elements."

The mental adjustment would be especially hard for the backbone of the American economic system, the entrepreneur. To see a business opportunity and to seize on it would no longer be a way of serving the community—it would be "exploiting human labor," "diverting state property to private ends" or would involve other "economic crimes." These trespasses are liable to be punished with extreme severity under a Soviet-style system. Such was the recent case of Mikhail Leviyev, manager of a specialty store in Moscow, sentenced to be shot by a firing squad for some of these "antisocial" activities, and also of Yuri Sosnovsky, head of a Soviet state furniture buying agency, shot by a firing squad for wheeling and dealing with a Swiss businessman.

For the recalcitrant there would always be the concentration camps, which, if the Soviet pattern is followed, might involve millions and be erected into a whole system of forced labor.

But for the population at large, life under socialism, even under the most benign conditions and without the ruthless regimentation of Russian and Chinese Marxism, would mean an existence steadily drabber, seedier, more squalid and more frustrating, as the state-controlled economy first stifled the competition of private enterprise and then eliminated it altogether.

In a free-market economy, competition and relative efficiency in the market place tend to ensure that the best producers succeed the most and are the best rewarded. Given a free choice, the public buys their products because they are of better quality or cheaper or both, thus eliminating the more inefficient competitors. The system is self-correcting. In a socialist economy, everything, from the smallest personal amenities to the most basic human freedoms, is encroached upon by the bureaucrats in charge of the nation's economic life.

Socialism means buying one government-issue of toothpaste, as in East Germany, because there is no other, rather than having one's choice of 150 brands, as in the United States. It means standing in line for four hours in a government-owned monopoly store to buy a blender or some other appliance that is usually off the market altogether, as in most countries of Eastern Europe. It means rudeness from the sales help, a stony indifference to complaints, and a refusal to make refunds or accept the return of shoddily made items because you have no place else to go anyway. Capitalist competition is a wonderful stimulus to politeness and good service.

Socialist control of the economy means waiting five years to get a government-controlled apartment, as in Sweden, or a government-owned council house, as in Britain. It means waiting for years for a telephone from the state-owned telephone company. (An aunt of mine in Buenos Aires once held a party to celebrate the installation of a phone she had ordered 24 years before.) It means paying bribes to minor officials to be placed at the top of the waiting list for a phone, a new car, an apartment, or a house. It means a sharp curtailment of your trips abroad, as the funds you are allowed to take out of the country are limited to a few hundred dollars, as in Britain. It may mean the end of foreign travel altogether without special government permission, as in the Soviet Union, Eastern Europe, and many other communist and socialist countries. It may mean in the end that you have to get a government permit to move to New York, San Francisco, or elsewhere in the United States itself, such as Soviet citizens now have to apply for in order to live in Moscow and other Soviet cities.

Indeed this is the logical end result of the centrally planned socialist economy. The central planners, a committee of bureaucrats and political infighters, are simply incapable of accommodating or even permitting a mobile population because they are unable to provide the housing when it is wanted where it is needed. Since it is unthinkable for ideological reasons to allow private businessmen to step in and handle the demand as people move from one area of the country to another, the bureaucratic socialist solution is to issue passports for travel within the nation as well as abroad.

Russian serfs under Czarism stood in about the same relationship to the noble landowners as Soviet citizens do to the Soviet bureaucrats today in the choice of where to live. Nor is this all. The Soviet state, which provides free education to certified proletarian students, cannot let those students emigrate until they have repaid the full cost of their education. There is a graduated scale of fees for each profession, the highest being for medical doctors.

Under systems of this type, where the state is all and the individual nothing, already ruthlessly imposed on half of mankind by Marxist one-party states in more than a dozen countries from Eastern Europe to the Far East, resistance has so far proved futile once the Marxist apparatus is clamped down. There has been no case to date of any nation throwing off an established Communist dictatorship. The repressive apparatus is simply too strong. The best that people have been able to hope for is that, as in Yugoslavia, the system will gradually evolve from within, restoring bit by bit, pragmatically and reluctantly under the thrust of economic realities, the free-market elements that make for a life of greater prosperity and freedom.

On a personal level, the imposition of such a Marxist system in the United States after a military defeat would mean waiting patiently for this slow evolution to take place, keeping in reserve for better times whatever assets one managed to put in a safe place—one's own home (if house ownership is still allowed); a cache of coins; perhaps even an unreported bank account in Switzerland, a nation that might be allowed to stand as a neutral haven even in a Marxist-dominated world.

Self-defeat

Unfortunately, much of this squalid existence under socialism need not be predicated on a Soviet military victory. As Nobel prize winner Alexander Solzhenitsyn has bitterly observed: "The Third World War has taken place and has ended in defeat. The powerful Western states, having emerged victorious from two previous world wars, in the course of these 30 years of peace . . . have totally ceded more countries and more peoples than have ever been ceded in any surrender in any war in human history."

Indeed, life under socialism is simply the logically forseeable conclusion of present trends within the American economy if they continue on their present course.

The railroad system, government-regulated over the years into a chronic depression, is already partly nationalized. The airlines are well on the way down the same road. The case of electric utilities and telephone companies is not too different—the government decides the rates they can charge, and politics makes them particularly vulnerable to inflation. When millions of customers scream about soaring utility rates, the political urge becomes irresistible to hold rates down. After a few years of this process, the income-starved industry is ripe for government takeover. The aerospace industry is almost completely dependent on government decisions about moon landings and weapons systems and the political maneuvers that go with those decisions. The Post Office has always been a socialized bastion as a government monopoly. Part of the health care industry is already under government control through Medicare and Medicaid, and the rest may soon follow if medicine is socialized completely through a comprehensive national health plan. In the rest of the economy, from trucking to farming to oil pipelines, there is scarcely an industry that is not subject to government regulation, subsidy, control, interference, or outright ownership. All of this enlarges the role of centralized, monopolistic, non-competitive, authoritarian government control of economic production and diminishes the role of the free market in which the people decide what they want and who is to produce it.

For millions of Americans socialism has already arrived, and for millions more it is soon coming. Many of the defenders of private initiative and enterprise are too compromised to offer any credible resistance. Such is the case of medical doctors, who made no objection to socialism when they accepted a state monopoly to practice medicine through the government licensing of physicians but who balk at the logical corollary—government authority to regulate their professional activities and income. There are even captains of private industry, teamed up with influential politicians, who advocate central government planning for the economy of a kind that is not too different from the central committee system that directs the Soviet economy. The Initiative Committee for National Economic Planning spearheads this campaign, and its arguments are embodied in the Balanced Growth and Economic Planning Act of 1975 sponsored by Senators Hubert Humphrey and Jacob Javits (a Democrat and a Republican).

At times, the entire American economy is removed from the free-market economy altogether, and is placed under rigid government control in the same way as Germany and Italy were under the Nazi and Fascist economic systems. This happened for a time during the Nixon administration, when wage and price controls were applied across the board. Under this system, the appearances of private capitalism are preserved—private ownership of corporations, the dividends for shareholders, and so on—but it is all a sham. The government controls everything then, not the free market. And if the system remains in force for a prolonged period, the government ends up either owning or running everything permanently.

It is pointless to argue about labels, to dispute whether the United States is headed for a socialist or a fascist type of future. Government control is government control, whether it is exercised by a commissar or a gauleiter. And the constant expansion of government control means a constant shrinkage of the free-market economy, where competition and efficiency in the market place ensure that the best producers enjoy the greatest success. Under the controlled economy, the inefficient private monopoly and the featherbedded state corporation flourish mightily in raising prices and providing redundant jobs. The economy sinks into a morass of inefficiency, boondoggling and waste.

The future and the past

It is late in the onrush of economic forces, but the situation can still be corrected—provided Americans know what is at stake.

The growing role of government intervention in the free market and the constant increase of government transfer payments to non-productive sectors of society will tip the economy over in the end if present trends continue. But that is a long, gradual process. The most urgent present danger is that the constant weakening of the dollar through inflation will weaken the United States. The neverending printing of new dollar bills undermines the American economy. The inflation thus caused destroys the social fabric. The social turmoil resulting from this can end up by collapsing the American political system.

Fiat currency—money created unceasingly without any kind of backing in gold or silver or any other tangible value—can eventually destroy all confidence in the American economic, social, and political system.

It has all happened before in American history. In that dreadful winter of 1777-78 at Valley Forge, General Washington's army nearly starved to death in Pennsylvania and the American Republic was almost stillborn. And yet, while the freedom fighters were starving, the British forces at Philadelphia only 18 miles away were comfortably quartered, well-fed, and their officers were enjoying a brilliant social and theatrical season.

Why? Because the British were paying the Pennsylvania farmers free-market prices with good, hard silver coin. The American army was paying with Continental notes—a paper currency so debased that "not worth a Continental" became a commonplace. The Continental Congress had authorized the printing of the first notes in 1775 and by 1777 had issued so many of them that commodity prices were nearly five times higher than before the Revolutionary War. But this was not all. The Revolutionary authorities in Pennsylvania, seeking to control the surging inflation, decided to try a period of price control, limited to domestic commodities essential for the use of the army.

Many farmers refused to sell their goods to Washington's army at the controlled prices. Few of them would take paper continental money anyway. Some sold their farm produce to the British for gold and silver. The Pennsylvania farmers two hundred years ago were no doubt as patriotic as the average American citizen is today. But one has to face economic realities. A farmer with a family to feed and care for through a harsh winter cannot hand over an entire year's crop for worthless paper.

As Washington himself said when that terrible winter was over: "Men may talk of patriotism. They may draw a few examples from ancient history of great achievements performed by its influence. But whoever builds upon them as a sufficient basis for conducting a long and bloody war will find themselves deceived in the end. We must take the passions of men as nature has given them. I do not mean to exclude altogether the idea of patriotism. I know it exists, and I know it has done much in the present contest. But I will venture to assert that a great and lasting war cannot be supported on this principle alone. It must be aided by a prospect of interest, or some reward."

Two hundred years later, with the government facing a $70 billion budget deficit, the American currency is once again becoming as suspect as the worthless Continental.

Now, as then, the Republic has enemies. Its major adversary, the Soviet Union, is the heir to the world's only remaining 19th-Century colonial power, the Czarist Empire, conqueror of all Central Asia. This is an expansionary, proselytizing power, self-righteous in the conviction that it is the ultimate realization of irresistible historical forces as defined by Karl Marx. At the slightest sign of weakness it moves in to extend its power—in Berlin, in Cuba, in Angola, as it did earlier in the Baltic republics, in Eastern Europe, and Mongolia.

If inflation and depression should debilitate the American economy—and with it the entire Western economy—to the extent that military resistance to Soviet expansion becomes doubtful, the leaders in the Kremlin might make a fatal miscalculation. This seems to be the most urgent present danger of war.

12

The more things change . . .

This book is written as the United States approaches the completion of another century of life. If it is not exactly the worst of times, neither is it precisely the best. In the last few years the nation has been hit by runaway inflation, the highest unemployment rate in many decades, the worst recession in forty years, and political scandals in Washington. It has also lost its first war. The Women's Liberation Movement is raising a storm, among other assorted internal problems, and many people are convinced that the country is going to hell in a handbasket.

Are we talking about 1976?

Not necessarily. It might just as well be a rerun of 1876. One shocking scandal after another has tormented the administration of President Ulysses S. Grant, the hero of a Civil War that brought no sweet taste of victory to anyone. After the Civil War inflation has come the depression of the early 1870s. The President's advisers, a tricky, money-grubbing bunch headed by Vice-President Schuyler Colfax, have been run through the courts and come out on the wrong side of the law. There is bribery, fraud, stock manipulation, flim-flammery in the United

States Customs, even a whisky scandal that sent President Grant's good friend General John McDonald to jail.

And as the male-chauvinist government is falling apart, Victoria Claffin Woodhull has had the Women's Lib effrontery to run for President as the candidate of the Equal Rights Party. New York Representative Shirley Chisholm did no better in her bid for the presidency a hundred years later.

In 1875 there was even a former President around who had been subjected to the ordeal of an impeachment vote in the Senate. He has just made a triumphal return to Washington as Senator Andrew Johnson, where his Senate seat is decked with flowers, and former colleagues who seven years ago voted for his impeachment as the unworthy successor to Abraham Lincoln come eagerly forward to shake his hand.

Well, perhaps this historical rerun is not precisely faithful in every detail—at the time of this writing, at least, Richard Nixon sits unre-elected in San Clemente—but it is close enough. When you hear orators making speeches nowadays of patriotic gloom, bemoaning the lost Spirit of 1776 that thrust this nation on its path to greatness, just ask them: Where was that spirit in the inflation, recession, and political morass of 1876?

The United States survived the first hundred years. It has survived the second hundred years and done a few things besides, such as winning a couple of world wars and reaching the moon. It will be around for a while still, provided there are no nuclear wars. Perhaps even then.

The author hopes this book will help you to survive, too.

Index